THE BAVLI AND ITS SOURCES

Number 85
THE BAVLI AND ITS SOURCES
The Question of Tradition
in the Case of Tractate Sukkah

by
Jacob Neusner

THE BAVLI AND ITS SOURCES
The Question of Tradition
in the Case of Tractate Sukkah

by
Jacob Neusner

Scholars Press
Atlanta, Georgia

THE BAVLI AND ITS SOURCES
The Question of Tradition
in the Case of Tractate Sukkah

©1987
Brown University

Library of Congress Cataloging in Publication Data

Neusner, Jacob, 1932-
  The Bavli and its sources.

  (Brown Judaic studies ; no. 85)
  Includes index.
  1. Talmud. Sukkah--Criticism, Redaction.
  2. Talmud Yerushalmi. Sukkah--Criticism, Redaction.
  I. Title. II. Series.
  BM506.S93N48 1987 296.1'25066 87-4665
  ISBN 1-55540-117-1 (alk. paper)

Printed in the United States of America
on acid-free paper

Contents

For my friend and colleague

on the National Council on the Arts

JOSEPH EPSTEIN

Accomplished writer and scholar,
editor of
The American Scholar,
and
Professor of English at
Northwestern University

who understands the relationship between tradition and new beginnings,
values both,
and knows the difference between the one and the other.

This is my tribute to a person of taste, intellect,
and wit beyond compare,
and a token of appreciation for unearned friendship, unmerited regard,
which are the best kind.

Preface

A variety of writings containing statements attributed to sages, or rabbis, came to closure between the editing of the Mishnah, in ca. A.D. 200, and the formation of the Bavli, or Talmud of Babylonia, in ca. A.D. 600. These writings in the history of Judaism have formed not only a literary corpus, exhibiting traits in common, but – in the judgment of that same Judaism – also a theological and legal tradition formed out of prior sources, making a cogent and authoritative statement in common and forming a continuous set of writings. That tradition formed out of prior sources, moreover, is understood to derive from a continuous process of tradition, with sayings handed on from an earlier generation to a later on until a complete and final statement came to full expression in the Bavli. Hence the Bavli is supposed to stand in relationship to prior writings as a summary statement stands to the sources that are summarized. It is supposed to respond to a received program and to restate a vast corpus of already-circulating and traditional materials.

The issue of this monograph, for the case at hand is to ask whether in literary terms a tradition can live with, and within, a system. We deal in particular with the dual Torah of Judaism, which is is made up not of sources transformed into a single source, e.g., in the Talmud of Babylonia, but of an essentially independent construction and system, one that stands upon its own ground and takes its own position, framed in a balance and proportion of its own, and so issues its own distinctive statement. The Judaic system of the dual Torah – so we shall see – recognizes a corpus of authoritative writings, but that corpus does not form a tradition, a "tradition formed out of prior sources." The Bavli, we shall see, does not fall into the classification formed by books that take over from the predecessors' materials to be handed on continuators, materials that therefore are continuous with one another. The Bavli is not part of a traditional literature, each of the documents of which stand in close relationship with its neighbors, fore and after, each borrowing from its predecessor, handing on to its successor, a nourishing tradition.

To explain what this study proposes to accomplish in analyzing the cogency – connection and continuity – of the relationships of a later document to earlier writings, let me begin with an analogy drawn from the stars. All stars shine as suns of their respective systems. But each star, our sun for example, also gives light as part of a larger galaxy or congeries. And these themselves constitute components of still larger ones: the milky way for instance, and so, toward infinity, onward in the distant reaches of imagination to the entirety of matter.

Seen near at hand, our sun is not merely and only a star, but the only light in the firmament, so it appears by day. But at night when we see the skies, we realize that ours is not the only light, the sole sun, but a star like other stars. And, penetrating into deep space, we understand that the whole – our solar system, our galaxy – finds its place in an infinity of space and matter beyond all measure.

The dual Torah revealed by God to Moses, our rabbi, at Sinai, which we call Judaism, is that infinity. So it is with the documents of Judaism. Each gives light on its own. Each comprises part of its larger constellation. But all of them all together constitute the one whole Torah of Moses, our rabbi, or, in secular language, Judaism. How then do individual stars of the firmament of Judaism form a galaxy? I hope, specifically, to map the heavens – that is, the Torah, or Judaism – to chart how the particular documents of the Judaism of the dual Torah form that single, one whole Torah of Moses, our rabbi. I frame the matter in concrete and literary terms, these state the physics. But the issue encompasses the fundamental structure and system of Judaism: that galaxy of all the stars of Sinai, the astronomy, even the cosmology and ultimately the cosmogony.

But back to the engineering that turns physics into facts of hardware capable of escaping our gravity. Hard as it is to come to grips with the whole, seen all at once, so difficult it is to reckon with the textual commonalities that form of a community of texts the textual commmunity of Judaism. And who can chart – let alone navigate – the heavens imagined in the Judaism of the dual Torah! What force, what gravity, magnetism, mass of matter and anti-matter, holds the whole together? How to know how texts deemed to form a tradition formed out of prior sources transcend their respective boundaries and so reach outward to the farthest limits of the textual community. For by definition these are not indicated by the covers of a book or even the sides of a book shelf.

Having worked out [1] the description of texts, read one by one, in such works as my *Judaism: The Evidence of the Mishnah, The Integrity of Leviticus Rabbah,* and parallel studies, to [2] the analysis of those same texts seen in relationship to one another, that is, to comparison and contrast among a set of documents, hence to connection, as in *Judaism: The Classical Statement. The Evidence of the Bavli,* on the relationship of the Yerushalmi and the Bavli (part of which is reviewed in Chapter Two), *Comparative Midrash: The Plan and Program of Genesis Rabbah and Leviticus Rabbah* and *From Tradition to Imitation: The Plan and Program of Pesiqta deRab Kahana and Pesiqta Rabbati,* I here proceed to [3] the interpretation of texts under the aspect of continuity, that is to say, eternity. This exercise begins with literature, but points toward a sequel addressing the traditionality of an important idea, which in turn defines yet a third experiment of systemic description.

To point toward the question beyond: if we wish to understand how to describe as a whole the Judaism of the dual Torah, we find that we do not craft a question of a literary character. That negative proposition forms the underside of the positive thesis concerning the character and definition of the Bavli. That definition derives, for our purposes, from the Bavli's authorship's relationship to the extant literature that constituted an important component of its sources. To state matters that lie beyond these pages, the Bavli's system requires analysis in its own terms and context, and, so far as the Bavli has constituted the premier statement of Judaism, the document requires systemic description, analysis, and interpretation, pretty much on its own terms and in its own framework. The Bavli, not the literary canon of which it forms the centerpiece, forms the theological canon of Judaism. But I have some other notions of how to proceed with this protracted inquiry of mine.

Let me spell out the three dimensions of any ancient text of Judaism and then specify the dimension I propose to measure in this book. The relationships among the documents produced by the sages of Judaism may take three forms: complete dependence or total continuity one to the next (hence "traditional"), connection, that is, intersection in diverse manner and measure, and, finally, complete autonomy. That dimension of connection provokes considerable debate and presents a remarkably unclear perspective. For while the dimensions of autonomy and continuity take the measure of acknowledged traits – books on their own, books standing in imputed, therefore socially verified, relationships – the matter of connection hardly enjoys the same clear definition.

On the one side, intrinsic traits permit us to assess theories of connection. On the other, confusing theological and social judgments of continuities and literary and heuristic ones of connection, people present quite remarkable claims as to the relationships between and among documents, alleging, in fact, that the documents all have to be read as a single continuous document: the Torah. When we can describe the relationships between two documents or among three or more, we shall know what a given group of editors or authorities contributed on its own, and also how that authorship restated or reworked what it received from a prior group. Determining that relationship further guides us to principles of exegesis of documents, allegations and formulations of ideas and rules. If a document depends on some other, prior one, then what we find in the later writing is to be read in light of the earlier (but, of course, never vice versa). If there is no clear evidence of dependence, then the later document demands a reading in essentially its own terms. Determining the relationship of document to document forms the necessary second step. Finding out what changed and what remained the same in the unfolding of the system as a whole tells us the history of the system as its canonical writings contain that history. Seeing the documents as a continuous and final statement, we take the measure of that third dimension that takes its perspective from a distance and encompasses all of the documents: the system as a whole. It sees the documents as continuous not from one to the next but all in all, all together, all at once.

Let me specify my goal, even though in this book I take only one step toward it. What I ultimately want to know is what holds the whole together. How did a corpus of writing became a canon of theology and law? But in the present book, I deal not with the large issue of the Torah viewed whole and in its entirety, but of the lesser issue of traditionality as (allegedly) evidenced in the document identified as the traditional statement par excellence: a mere restatement of what its (prior) sources have already stated. For from the Talmud of the Land of Israel, Genesis Rabbah, and Leviticus Rabbah, through Pesiqta deRab Kahana, onward to The Fathers According to Rabbi Nathan and ultimately concluding in the Talmud of Babylonia, a rather cogent set of statements may be discovered to define the premises of one writing after another. Specifically, powerful interest in history and salvation, recurring emphasis on the correspondence between Israel's holy way of life and the salvation of Israel in history, the reading of Scripture as an account of the present and future – these will have struck the compositors of diverse documents as not fresh but traditional, meaning, ineluctable and necessary. These statements comprise one critical component of the Judaism of the dual Torah.

We already have a clear thesis on the historical unfolding of that Torah, and, consequently, the history of literary components of the system and the structure of their relationships seem to me fairly clear. Compositors of writings of the two centuries from the Mishnah to the first of the two Talmuds, specifically, will have found puzzling the theological premises of the literature put together from the fourth century forward. For the authors of the Mishnah, with its close companion in the Tosefta, the compilers of tractate Abot, the author-compilers of Sifra to Leviticus – none of these circles of authorship took so keen an interest in the issue of salvation or in the correspondence between the biblical narrative and contemporary history. I have already offered an account of where, when, how, and why so complete a shift from one consensus to another took place.

But I have yet to describe – let alone analyze and interpret – that fresh consensus that came to full expression after 400 not document by document, but as a cogent statement characteristic, as premise, of them all. The historical study of the unfolding of ideas in the canonical sequence of rabbinical writings, worked out in my *Foundations of Judaism* (Philadelphia, 1983-1985: Fortress), and the comparative study of midrash in the canon of the dual Torah addressed in a variety of writings (spelled out in the preface of my *From Tradition to Imitation: The Plan and Program of Pesiqta Rabbati and Pesiqta deRab Kahana* [Atlanta, 1987: Scholars Press for Brown Judaic Studies]) have brought us to the question that clearly transcends the comparative method in the study of documents. That question defines the research problem worked out in this book and points toward further studies. It is undertaken here, to begin with, and will yield through its own logical unfolding a sequence of further studies. So much for the context of the present work. The issues and methods of this book in particular are spelled out in Chapter One.

The foregoing prospectus points toward the larger context in which this monograph takes its place. This book forms the first in a planned three stage inquiry into literature, history of ideas, and structure, aimed at spelling out the cogency of the Judaism of the dual Torah, that is, written and oral, which in late antiquity came to its final and complete expression in the Bavli. What I want to describe is the system as a complete and whole composition, with its own points of emphasis and proportion, and, further, I hope to accomplish not only the description, but also the analysis and interpretation, of that same great Judaism. That is the Judaism of the dual Torah, oral and written, of Moses, our rabbi, that began in the revelation at Sinai. The work begins, as it must, with a problem of description, specifically, of literature as a medium for the delivery of a cogent statement that transcends any single book – that "tradition" of which I spoke just now – then proceeds to an analytical problem, the history of an idea that forms one central component of the encompassing intellectual system at hand, and, finally, moves onward to a still broader exercise of interpretation, which I shall describe in due course. I have in mind a kind of unfolding collage, in which each of the components bears its own integrity and autonomy, yet points toward a larger whole, of which it forms a part. The canvas is empty, except in my mind's eye.

Let me in conclusion point to what I conceive to be at stake in solving the problem of traditionality and spell out what is at stake in the problem of literary description with which this sizable exercise commences. Theologians of the tradition formed out of prior sources of Judaism correctly identify as the premise of all exegesis deep connections between one document and the next, so that all documents impose meanings upon each, and each demands a reading in the setting of the whole literature. The position at hand addresses the *entirety* of the writings of the ancient rabbis, all together, all at once, everywhere and all the time. Here I begin to investigate the continuities among all documents, thus a textual community. Issues of the continuity of documents form a first step toward the much larger description of the whole of canonical Judaism: the Judaism of the dual Torah. That is a Judaism that to begin with invokes its tradition formed out of prior sources to define itself: a Judaism of the dual Torah as against a Judaism that appeals to a different symbol altogether from a canonical one, e.g., the Judaic system of the Essenes of Qumran, with its teacher of righteousness as its critical symbolic expression.

Each document in the corpus of the rabbinic writings of late antiquity bears points in common with others. They form a tradition, and each document constitutes a partial statement of that complete tradition. But, as we now understand, we have first of all to know whether and how all – or at least some – of them constitute a tradition formed out of prior sources? There is a necessary but not sufficient answer to that question. The points in common include citing a common Scripture in an essentially uniform way (so it would seem) and more important, addressing a shared program of interest to the common Scriptures. But the more profound fact provides the sufficient response. No document of the Judaism under discussion, that which came to its original expression in the Mishnah, ca. A.D. 200, and reached its full statement, in late antiquity, in the Talmud of Babylonia, stands on its own. All documents reach us as the Torah, that is to say, through the medium and the consensus of the Judaic community of the dual Torah, and all of them join together because of their authority in that community, their standing as statements of the (dual) Torah.

I commenced by invoking the metaphor of the stars in the heavens. Let me close by a more mundane analogy, one of a library. A tradition in its cogent, canonical statement may be compared to a library building, made up of individual books, organized in groups within their appropriate classifications, on their appropriate shelves. Books all together form a library. But each title addresses its own program and makes its own points. Books produced by a cogent community constitute not merely a library but a tradition formed out of prior sources: a set of compositions each of which contributes to a statement that transcends its own pages. The books exhibit intrinsic traits that make of them all *a community of texts*. We should know on the basis of those characteristics that the texts form a community even if we knew nothing more than the texts themselves. But that does not make a tradition formed out of prior sources of them all, only of those components of the corpus that exhibit the requisite traits. A book enjoys its own autonomous standing, but it also situates itself in relationship to other books of the same classification. Each book bears its own statement and purpose, and each relates to others of the same classification. The community of texts therefore encompasses individuals who (singly or collectively) comprise (for the authorships: compose) books. What makes of all books, without regard to indicative traits, is more than that set of facts that indicate how a book does not stand in isolation. Specifically, in the Judaic system of the dual Torah, moreover, all parties concur as premise that the documents at hand form a tradition formed out of prior sources. In the language of Judaism, all of them find a place in – and as part of – the Torah. And that fact defines what to me is the next stage in the problem of the history of Judaism, which, as is clear, I take to be the traditionality of the system.

That is a fact we know on the basis of information deriving from sources other than the texts at hand, which, on their own, do not link each to all and all to every line of each. Extrinsic traits, that is imputed ones, make of the discrete writings a single and continuous, uniform statement: one whole Torah in the mythic language of Judaism. The community of Judaism imputes those traits, sees commonalities, uniformities, deep harmonies: one Torah of one God. In secular language, that community expresses its system – its world view, its way of life, its sense of itself as a society – by these choices, and finds its definition in them. Hence, in the nature of things, in literary terms, the community of

Judaism forms *a textual community*, and, in social and theological terms, the corpus of the writings of Judaism form, all together, the Torah, that is, the tradition formed out of prior sources. That cogent community that forms a tradition formed out of prior sources out of a selection of books therefore participates in the process of authorship, just as the books exist in at least two dimensions. What I want in the end to know is how the community has accomplished the task of identifying its tradition formed out of prior sources: why this, not that? And do we find that encompassing "this, not that" implicit everywhere, even though made explicit only here and there? That is to say, even while recognizing that traditionality is imputed and decided, I wonder whether people looked for one set of qualities, rather than some other, in determining the status of a piece of writing, e.g., presence or absence of a certain set of ideas, relationship to other statements on the same subject, reasons and points of rational decision: the rules of why this, not that, so far as these rules accommodate facts and judge them.

True, in the later stages, we shall deal with a question of society and theology. But we ask a literary question to begin with, and so, to find out the rules of traditionality that lead me into the center and heart of the system at hand, I turn first to a sample of the canonical literature, which I describe as exemplary of a canonical method of exegesis, then, in a later study, to a central idea, which I analyze as a substantial mode of linkage and union of the canonical system, and, in a third and I hope, final inquiry, I address the whole all together and all at once. At this point I cannot say how I shall do so, but I know – at least –what it is that I must do. I propose to take the measure of the dimension of continuity not between one book and the next but *among* all the books of the tradition formed out of prior sources. What that means is to ask how diverse treatments of a given topic are formed into a single statement, and, for that purpose, I take a Bavli tractate and its disposition of the topic assigned to it.

And yet, even while taking the measure of that dimension, I recognize that we weigh out social, not narrowly literary, extrinsic and adventitious, not intrinsic and cogent and logical qualities. This study through its limited case therefore addresses the whole, seen all together and all at once. For the case at hand it marks off the outer limits of the galaxy of writings – the walls of the library building – that all together form the tradition formed out of prior sources. Drawing upon the analogy of books in canonical relationship, we may say that the third dimension finds its perspective in the larger building that takes in all the books all together. It of course comprises the community that determines what falls within the tradition formed out of prior sources and what does not.

In Chapter Six of this book I systematically deal with some current debates on the character of rabbinic literature in general. I take this occasion to make my final statement on this matter. Future research carries me in a fresh direction.

I happily acknowledge the good advice, in planning and executing this monograph, of my friend and co-worker, William Scott Green; of my colleagues and companions, Ernest S. Frerichs, Wendell S. Dietrich, and Calvin Goldscheider; and of my students-teachers, Paul Virgil Flesher and Richard Eric Cohen. Discussions with the graduate students forced me to revise my entire category-system for this book, and protracted arguments with William Green reshaped the issue. I also discussed issues important here with Professor Robert Berchman, University of Virginia, who works on related questions in the Christian and philosophical literary heritage of late antiquity. Spending time with such as these makes the life of learning an on-going pleasure.

JACOB NEUSNER

The first candle of Hanukkah, 5747
December 26, 1986

Program in Judaic Studies
Brown University
Providence, Rhode Island 02912-1826 U.S.A.

Chapter One

Sources and the Question of Tradition

I

The Bavli as Tradition or System

This book asks, in a concrete and particular instance, whether a system of applied reason and sustained, rigorous rational inquiry can coexist with a process of tradition. I argue that it cannot. So far as a process of tradition takes over the formation of a cogent and sustained statement, considerations extraneous to rational inquiry, decided, not demonstrated facts – these take over and divert the inexorable processes of applied reason from their natural and logically necessary course. And the opposite is also the case. Where a cogent statement forms the object of discourse, syllogistic argument and the syntax of sustained thought dominate, obliterating the marks of a sedimentary order of formation in favor of the single and final, systematic one. So far as an authorship proposes to present an account of a system, it will pay slight attention to preserving the indicators of the origins of the detritus of historical tradition, of which, as a matter of fact, the systemic statement itself may well be composed.

The threads of the tapestry serve the artist's vision; the artist does not weave so that the threads show up one by one. The weavers of a tractate of the Bavli, as we shall see, make ample use of available yarn. But they weave their own tapestry of thought. And it is their vision and not the character of the threads in hand that dictate the proportions and message of the tapestry. In that same way, so far as processes of thought of a sustained and rigorous character yield writing that makes a single, cogent statement, tradition and system cannot form a compatible unit. I shall show in a small sample of a vast literature that where reason governs, it reigns supreme and alone, revising the received materials and, through its own powerful and rigorous logic, restating into a compelling statement the entirety of the prior heritage of information and thought.

I therefore contrast thought received as truth transmitted through a process of tradition against thought derived from active rationality by asking a simple question: does what is the most rigorously rational and compelling statement of applied reason known to me, the Talmud of Babylonia or Bavli, constitute a tradition and derive from a process of traditional formulation and transmission of an intellectual heritage, facts and thought alike? Or does that document make a statement of its own, cogent and defined within the requirements of an inner logic, proportion, and structure, imposing that essentially autonomous vision upon whatever materials its authorship has received from the past? We shall know the answer through a sequence of simple tests, which concern the framing of the program of inquiry and the character of the sustained discourse of the Bavli. Specifically, if I can show that in literary terms the Bavli is not traditional, formed out of the increment of received materials, the form of the reception of which governs, but – in the sense now implied – systemic, that is, again in literary terms orderly, systematic, laid out in a proportion and order dictated by the inner logic of a topic or generative problem and – and therefore – authoritative by reason of its own rigorous judgment of issues of rationality and compelling logic, then I can offer a reasonable hypothesis resting on facts of literature. Specifically I can contribute a considerable example to the debate on whether tradition may coexist with the practical and applied reason of utter, uncompromising logical rationality and compelling, autonomous order.

Since, quite clearly, I use tradition in a literary sense, as referring to a process by which writings of one kind and not another take shape, let me then define what I mean by tradition and place into the context of Judaism the issue I have framed, to begin with, in such general terms. For if any noun follows the adjective, "Rabbinic," it is not "Judaism" but "tradition." And by "tradition" people mean two contradictory things.

First, when people speak of "tradition," they refer to the formative history of a piece of writing, specifically, an incremental and linear process that step by step transmits out of the past an essential and unchanging fundament of truth *preserved in writing*, by stages, with what one generation has contributed covered by the increment of the next in a sedimentary process, producing a literature that, because of its traditional history as the outcome of a linear and stage by stage process, exercises authority over future generations and therefore is nurtured for the future. In that sense, tradition is supposed to describe a *process* or a chain of transmission of received materials, refined and corrected but handed on not only unimpaired, but essentially intact. The opening sentence of tractate Avot, "Moses received Torah from Sinai and handed it on to Joshua," bears the implication of such a literary process, though, self-evidently, the remainder of that chapter hardly illustrates the type of process alleged at the outset.

The second meaning of tradition bears not upon process but upon content and structure. People sometimes use the word tradition to mean a fixed and unchanging essence deriving from an indeterminate past, a truth bearing its own stimata of authority, e.g., from God at Sinai.

These two meanings of the same word coexist. But they are incompatible. For the first of the two places a document within an on-going, determinate historical process, the latter speaks of a single statement at the end of an indeterminate and undefined process, which can encompass revelation of a one-time sort. In this book I use only the first of the two meanings. When, therefore, I ask whether or not the Bavli is a traditional document, I want to know whether the present literary character of the Bavli suggsts to us that the document emerges from a sedimentary process of tradition in the sense just now specified: an incremental, linear development, step by step, of law and theology from one generation to the next, coming to expression in documents arrayed in sequence, first to last. The alternative is that the Bavli originates as a cogent and proportioned statement through a process we may compare – continuing our geological metaphor – to the way in which igneous rock takes shape: through a grand eruption, all at once, then coalescence and solidification essentially forthwith. Either the Bavli will emerge in a series of layers, or it will appear to have formed suddenly, in a work of supererogatory and imposed rationality, all at once, perfect in its ultimate logic and structure.

That inquiry frames not a theological but a literary question, and it is the one I propose to investigate here. When, in my conclusion, I maintain that the Bavli is not a traditional document, I issue a judgment as to its character viewed as literature in relationship to prior extant writings. Everyone of course must concur that, in a theological sense, the Bavli is a profoundly traditional document, laying forth in its authorship's terms and language the nature of the Judaic tradition, that is, Judaism, as that authorship wishes to read the tradition and have it read. But this second sense will not recur in the pages that follow.

In framing the issue of tradition versus system, I sidestep a current view of the literature of formative Judaism. That view, specified presently, ignores the documentary character of each of the writings, viewing them all as essentially one and uniform, lacking all documentary definition. In a variety of studies I have argued precisely the opposite. Before proceeding, let me allude to these prior works, which come to conclusion in this last statement of the matter as I see it after fifteen years of study.

I began in 1972 with the Mishnah and the Tosefta, at first seeing them as Mishnah-Tosefta, only later on understanding that they are essentially distinct statements, each with its tasks and purpose. My *History of the Mishnaic Law* (Leiden, 1974-1986) in forty-three volumes, and associated studies worked on that matter, yielding *Judaism: The Evidence of the Mishnah* (Chicago, 1981: University of Chicago Press). Subsequent studies of the Yerushalmi, The Fathers According to Rabbi Nathan, Genesis Rabbah, Leviticus Rabbah, Pesiqta deRab Kahana, Pesiqta Rabbati, and the Bavli, have shown me that each of these documents is subject to precise definition in its own terms, as to both rhetorical and logical plan and topical program. Three works provide a good picture of the basic argument and method worked out in a variety of monographs and books: *The Integrity of Leviticus Rabbah: The Problem of the Autonomy of a Rabbinic Document* (Chico, 1985: Scholars Press for Brown Judaic Studies), *Comparative Midrash: The Plan and Program of Genesis Rabbah and Leviticus Rabbah* (Atlanta, 1986: Scholars Press for Brown Judaic Studies), and *From Tradition to Imitation. The Plan and Program of Pesiqta deRab Kahana and Pesiqta Rabbati* (Atlanta, 1987: Scholars Press for Brown Judaic Studies). In two other works, I have applied the results to specific allegations concerning the character of that same literature deriving from Orthodox-Jewish literary critics, who see the whole as uniform and interchangeable, lacking all documentary specificity. The systematic reply to these approaches, which restate in literary terms the received theology of Judaism and its hermeneutic, is in these works: *Canon and Connection: Judaism and Intertextuality* (Lanham, 1987: University Press of America), which addresses the propositions on the character of the canonical writings of formative Judaism currently set forth by Shaye J. D. Cohen, Lawrence H. Schiffman, and Susan Handelman; and *Midrash and Literature: The Primacy of Documentary Discourse* (Atlanta, 1987: Scholars Press for Brown Judaic Studies), which addresses the characterization of Midrash-compilations deriving just now from James Kugel. In the concluding chapter of this book I go over some of the results of the former work. In all instances I lay forth sizable samples of the literature, and test the allegations of the Orthodox Jewish literary critics against that evidence. In my view the results prove somewhat one-sided, but, of course, the way forward lies through further dialogue on these interesting questions.

Now to the issue at hand. When I ask whether or not the documents of the Judaism of the dual Torah exhibit shared traits of logic, rhetoric, or topic that justify imputing to them not merely points of intersection or connection but continuities and commonalities, I do not ask an invented question. It is a position maintained by a sizable sector of those who revere the Torah and interpret it today. I shall show that, as a statement of the continuities of a traditional character, deriving from a long and incremental process of handing on materials from generation to generation and – more to the point – document to document – that position contradicts the evidence of the Bavli, which, we must remember, constitutes the single most authoritative canonical writing of Judaism. What I shall show in this book is a simple proposition.

The Judaism of the dual Torah knows not traditions to be recited and reviewed but merely sources,[1] to be honored always but to be used only when pertinent to a quite independent program of thought.

That is to say, to go over the first definition of tradition with which I commenced, the components of the Torah of that Judaism do not contribute equally and jointly to a single comprehensive statement, handed on from generation to generation *and from book to book,* all of them sources forming a tradition that constitutes the Torah. Each has a particular message and make a distinctive statement. Obviously, all fit together into a common statement, the Torah or Judaism. That fundamental theological conviction defines Judaism and cannot – and should not – give way before the mere testimony of literary evidence. But it is the fact that whatever traits join the whole of the rabbinic

---

[1]And I should imagine that, when work on the traditions used by the Bavli's authorship makes solid progress, we shall have good reason to say the same of the Bavli's authorship's approach to traditions as much as to sources.

corpus together into the single Torah of Moses our Rabbi, revealed by God to Moses at Sinai, they are not literary traits of tradition.

In literary terms, the various rabbinic documents commonly (and, from a theological perspective, quite correctly) are commonly represented as not merely autonomous and individual statements, or even connected here and there through shared passages, but in fact as continuous and and interrelated developments, one out of its predecessor, in a long line of canonical writings (to Sinai). The Talmud of Babylonia, or Bavli, takes pride of place – in this picture of "the rabbinic tradition" – as the final and complete statement of that incremental, linear tradition, and so is ubiquitously described as "*the* tradition," par excellence. In this concluding monograph I shall demonstrate that, vis-à-vis its sources, the Bavli represents an essentially autonomous, fresh, and original statement of its own. How so?

Its authorship does not take over, rework, and repeat what it has received out of prior writings but makes its own statement, on its own program, in its own terms, and for its own purposes.

Every test I can devise for describing the relationship between the authorship of the Bavli and the prior and extant writings of the movement of which that authorship forms the climax and conclusion yields a single result. The authorship at hand does not pursue anyone else's program, except only that of the Mishnah. It does not receive and refine writings concluded elsewhere. It takes over a substantial heritage and reworks the whole into its own sustained and internally cogent statement – and that forms not the outcome of a process of sedimentary tradition but the opposite: systematic statement of a cogent and logical order, made up in its authorship's rhetoric, attaining comprehensibility through the syntax of its authorship's logic, reviewing a received topical program in terms of the problematic and interests defined by its authorship's larger purposes and proposed message. The samples of the Bavli we shall review constitute either composites of sustained, essentially syllogistic discourse, in which case they form the whole and comprehensive statement of a system, or increments of exegetical accumulation, in which case they constitute restatements, with minor improvements, of a continuous tradition. In my view, the reader is going to review sustained, directed, purposive syllogistic discourse, not wandering and essentially agglutinative collections of observations on this and that, made we know not when, for a purpose we cannot say, to an audience we can scarcely imagine, so as to deliver a message that, all together and in the aggregate, we cannot begin to recapitulate. But it is for the reader to judge the evidence.

True, the authorship of the Bavli drew upon a sizable corpus of materials indeterminate character and substance, which we assuredly do classify as traditions handed on from their predecessors. Hence the authorship of the Bavli made use of both sources, completed documents, and also traditions, transmitted sayings and stories, ordinarily of modest proportions, not subjected to ultimate redaction. But the authorship of the Bavli did whatever it wished with these materials to carry out its own program and to make its own prevailing statement. These received materials, undeniably formulated and transmitted in a process of tradition, have been so reworked and revised by the penultimate and ultimate authorship that their original character does not define the syntax of argument and the processes of syllogistic discourse, except by way of supplying facts for someone else's case. Whether or not we can still discern traces of received statements, even in wordings that point to an origin other than with or authorship, is beside the point. Proof of my case does not derive from the failure or success of scholars to identify the passages of the Bavli that antedate the penultimate or ultimate work of composition.

To be sure, I regard as ultimately unsuccessful the convoluted effort by such scholars as David Weiss Halivni, in his *Sources and Traditions*,[2] to tell us not only the original form but also the later (by them utterly undocumented) literary history, of these unredacted sayings. Endless speculation on what may have been masks the simple fact that we do not know what was. But that is not much to the point anyhow. The point is what we have, not what we do not have, and we have the Bavli to tell us about the work of the penultimate and ultimate authorship of the Bavli. That suffices. The facts are what they are.

In its final, literary context defined by the documents or sources we can identify, the Bavli emerges as anything but the seal of "tradition" in the familiar sense. For it is not based on distinct and completed sources handed on from time immemorial, subserviently cited and glossed by its own authorship, and it does not focus upon the systematic representation of the materials of prior documents, faithfully copied and rehearsed and represented. We have, of course, to exclude the Mishnah, but this fundamental document is treated by the authorship of the Bavli in a wholly independent spirit, as Chapter Two demonstrates. The upshot is that the Bavli does not derive from a process of tradition in the first sense stated above, although, as a faithful and practicing Jew, I believe that the Bavli truly constitutes "tradition" in that second, theological sense to which I referred: a new statement of its own making and a fresh address to issues of its own choosing. But as I shall now show, the *literary* character of the process that created the Bavli is irrelevant to the demonstration of that *theological* proposition, which derives its proof from the entire history of Judaism from the Bavli onward. Viewed as literature, the Bavli is not a traditional document at all. It is not the result of an incremental and linear process; it does not review and restate what others have already said; its authorship does not regard itself as bound to the program and issues received from prior ages. The Bavli constitutes a systemic and not a traditional statement.

---

[2]Referred to in the present chapter.

II
The Literary Context of Judaic Tradition

The premise of this inquiry is simple. The Talmud of Babylonia, or Bavli, draws upon prior materials. The document in no way was not made up out of whole cloth by its penultimate and ultimate authorship, the generations that drew the whole together and placed it into the form in which it has come down from the seventh century to the present day. The Bavli's authorship both received out of the past a corpus of *sources*, and also stood in a line of *traditions* of sayings and stories, that is, fixed wordings of thought the formulation and transmission of which took place not in completed documents but in ad hoc and brief sentences or little narratives. These materials, deriving from an indeterminate past through a now-inaccessible process of literary history, constitute traditions in the sense defined in the preface: an incremental and linear process that step by step transmits out of the past an essential and unchanging fundament of truth and writing.

Traditions: some of these prior materials never reached redaction in a distinct document and come down as sherds and remnants within the Bavli itself. These are the ones that may be called traditions, in the sense of materials formulated and transmitted from one generation to the next, but not given a place in a document of their own.

Sources: others had themselves reached closure prior to the work on the Bavli and are readily identified as autonomous writings. Scripture, to take an obvious example, the Mishnah, tractate Abot (the Fathers), the Tosefta (so we commonly suppose), Sifra, Sifré to Numbers, Sifré to Deuteronomy, Genesis Rabbah, Leviticus Rabbah, the Fathers according to Rabbi Nathan, Pesiqta deRab Kahana, Pesiqta Rabbati, possibly Lamentations Rabbah, not to mention the Siddur and Mahzor (order of daily and holy day prayer, respectively), and various other writings had assuredly concluded their processes of formation before the Bavli's authorship accomplished their work. These we call *sources* – more or less completed writings.

This book addresses the problem of the Bavli's relationship to prior sources, so as to answer an important aspect of the question of how traditional – again, in the sense just now specified – the Bavli's authorship actually was. The relationship of the Bavli's authorship to extant but unredacted traditions presents a separate issue. While much effort has been invested in that issue, it rests on speculation, has produced no incontrovertible results, and may, for the moment, be set aside.[3] What we can investigate with considerable precision is the relationship between the authorship of the Bavli and the then-extant documents demonstrably accessible to, and occasionally utilized by, their predecessors and themselves.

Before proceeding, the reader will be helped by perspective upon the literature and its formation. The Bavli comes at the end of a set of writings produced by sages of Judaism from the Mishnah, about 200 to the Bavli itself, about 600 A.D. These writings rest on two base-documents, compilations of exegesis of Scripture called Midrash-collections, which refer to the Scriptures of ancient Israel (to Christianity, the Old Testament, to Judaism, the Written Torah), and the Tosefta, or supplements, and the two Talmuds, the one of the Land of Israel or the Yerushalmi, the other of Babylonia, which refer to the Mishnah (in Judaism, the first component of the Oral Torah ultimately encompassing all the literature at hand). All of the writings of Judaism in late antiquity copiously cite Scripture. More important, some of them serve (or are presented and organized) as commentaries on the former,the written Torah, others as amplifications of the latter, the Mishnah as the beginning of the transcription of the oral Torah. Since Judaism treats all of these writings as a single, seamless Torah, the one whole Torah revealed by God to Moses, our rabbi, at Mount Sinai, the received hermeneutic naturally does the same. All of the writings are read in light of all others, and words and phrases are treated as autonomous units of tradition, rather than as components of particular writings, e.g., paragraphs – units of discourse – and books – composite units of sustained and cogent thought.

My method, worked out in the shank of the book, is to survey a sample of the tractate at hand, nearly 50% of the whole. I want the reader to see very graphically precisely the extent and character of the utilization or neglect, by the authorship of the Bavli, of the antecedent documents. That is why I reprint an enormous selection of the whole. But I took a large sample, rather than the whole, for two reasons, first, because of the essential uniformity of the Talmudic literature, which allows even a modest sample to tell us the shape and structure

---

[3]The most current efforts to demonstrate what the authorship of the Bavli had for traditions (in the sense of the present discussion) and how it made use of those traditions derive from David W. Halivni and Shamma Friedman. The work of the former, in three volumes bearing the title, *Sources and Traditions* (Hebrew: *meqorot ummesorot*), is presented for the English reader in three systematic accounts by students of mine in books I have edited: *The Formation of the Babylonian Talmud. Studies on the Achievements of Late Nineteenth and Twentieth Century Historical and Literary-Critical Research* (Leiden, 1970: E. J. Brill), *The Modern Study of the Mishnah* (Leiden, 1973: E. J. Brill), and in William Scott Green, ed.,*Law as Literature. Semeia* XX (Chico, 1983: Scholars Press for Society of Biblical Literature); and my students have done the same for Friedman in that same *Semeia* volume. But it should be noted that Halivni and Friedman work in ways that will not have surprised the received exegetical tradition of the Bavli, and in no way have they asked questions that their predecessors in Talmud-exegesis will have found incomprehensible. The source-criticism of the Bavli's materials begins, after all, in the pages of the Bavli itself, as the reader will note in the sample presented in this book.

of the editorial conventions that apply throughout, and also simply because the sheer bulk of the entire tractate would demand more space than is necessary graphically to make the point I wish in my study to establish. I survey my sample to find out how the "tradition," namely, the Bavli, in the case of Bavli tractate Sukkah, relates to its "sources," namely, the prior literature on the same subject as is treated in our tractate. That survey is meant to yield a set of facts pertinent to the larger question I seek to investigate, the issue of continuities among documents, or, in terms of history of religions, the definition of the canon and – more to the point – the exegesis of exegesis.

That is why I conduct a survey of my sample as to its use of prior writings. I do this in two ways. First, in Chapter Two I compare the whole of the exegesis of Mishnah-tractate Sukkah Chapter One accomplished by the authorship of the Yerushalmi, Talmud of the Land of Israel, with the complete exegesis of that same chapter produced by their counterparts in the Bavli. I want to know whether the Bavli authorship has taken over and improved upon a received source, or whether they have made up what is essentially their own tradition, to be handed over to the future. Then, in Chapters Three, Four, and Five, I survey the relationship between the larger part of the entire Bavli tractate and the prior documentary statements, now extant, on the same subject, and in Chapter Six I spell out the consequences of the findings. I want to know where, when, why, and to what extent, a Bavli passage relates to a prior writing, an available source, and the very volume of Bavli discourse that – in terms of extant writings – represents an essentially new and unprecedented statement: not a reworking of sources but a new tradition altogether. I propose therefore to frame and test a hypothesis concerning the relationship between a document universally declared to be canonical, namely the Bavli, and the prior sources on which that document drew, and, in consequence, to form a still larger thesis on the literary character and definition of a canonical statement in the Judaism of the dual Torah.

To conclude: in contrasting tradition and system, I really want to know the answer to one question: is a document that is received as authoritative (in theological terms, "canonical") essentially a restatement of what has gone before, or is a such a writing fresh and original? If the answer is that the Bavli restates a consensus formed through ages, then our conception of the literary definition of the canon of Judaism will take one form. If the answer is that the Bavli's authorship makes an essentially new statement, then the issue of the continuities among documents will prove to stand quite independent of the traits of the writings accepted within the prior and available documents. Then, as I shall explain in Chapter Six, how we read the rabbinic writings and the status, as to traditionalism or innovation, we impute to them, will take on a quite new meaning.

III
Sources or Tradition: The Literary Criteria

The issue of this book, therefore, is whether or not, in the study of the Judaism of the dual Torah, oral and written, we may introduce the notion of tradition. Many maintain that the literary documents of Judaism constitute an on-going corpus or truth spun out in a continuous process and handed on from generation to generation. But is that the fact, and can we demonstrate it? To conduct an experiment on that question, I choose the authoritative, theologically-canonical statement of the Judaism of the dual Torah, the Talmud of Babylonia or the Bavli. The Bavli is everywhere represented as a traditional document. Its (ultimate) authorship is portrayed as mainly taking up materials from prior sources and reworking them into a systematic and canonical statement for generations to come. The Bavli, therefore, is portrayed as essentially traditional, that is, a document that heavily draws upon sources, enjoys standing and authority because of its representation of what is in those sources, and stands in an on-going traditional relationship with those sources. It follows that the Judaic system presented by the Bavli also falls into the classification of traditional. What in particular makes the Bavli traditional, it is argued, is its relationship to the prior writings of the system of which it constitutes the authoritative statement. Hence the Bavli comprises a statement of sources that form "the tradition," hence may be classified as a traditional document.

In Chapters Two, Three, Four, and Five I test that position by examining a sizable sample of a tractate and assessing its relationship to the extant compilations upon which its authorship drew. I ask precisely what elements of the Bavli, for the sample in hand, derive from such sources. My answer, worked out with its implications for the hermeneutics of the Bavli and of other Judaic writings in the same analogy, is that from the Bavli a tradition starts. But it is essentially a new tradition, not a restatement of sources handed on in, and as, tradition and now reworked for a further stage of transmission through tradition. In Chapter Six I relate to broader issues of hermeneutics the facts yielded by our sample.

The Bavli supposedly draws upon and reshapes available ideas and reworks them into a definitive statement, hence turns sources into a tradition. To test that claim I have devised a simple experiment.

If the authorship at hand resorts to prior writings and presents us with what is at its foundations a systematic and comprehensive summary and restatement of them, then the Bavli will take up an honorable position at the end of a long process of tradition.

But if we find that the authorship of the Bavli follows an essentially independent and fresh program of its own, then the Bavli will prove to have inaugurated a tradition but not to have received and transmited one. It will follow that, for the Judaism of the dual Torah, holy scripture, authoritative sources whether preserved orally or in writing, as such play no categorical role whatsoever.

The Bavli will then constitute an independent and fresh statement of its own authorship, not a restatement of what its authorship has received from prior generations, and assuredly not a statement of a cumulative and incremental tradition. The Bavli, rather, will come forth as a statement that in time to come, beyond its redaction, would *become* traditional, but for reasons not related to its own literary let alone theological and legal traits. That set of choices explains the interest and importance of determining the relationship between the Bavli and the extant sources of the Judaism of the dual Torah that reached closure prior to the Bavli.

To state the result that, in highly graphic form, the reader is about to survey: the Bavli is mostly the work of its own authorship, acting independently on its singular program of Mishnah-exegesis and amplification, alongside its distinctive program of Scripture-exegesis and amplification, both programs demonstrably unique to that authorship alone so far as extant sources and documents indicate for our sample. In the Bavli-sample at hand we look in vain for large tractates or even sizable units of discourse that refer to, or depend upon, the plan and program of prior documents. When, moreover, we shall survey how earlier authorships dealt with the same materials – [1] the Mishnah-chapter before us, and [2] an important set of verses of Scripture pertinent to the theme of the tractate – we come up with a single and uniform result.

What earlier authorships wished to investigate in the Mishnah, the points they wished to prove by reference to verses of Scripture important in our tractate – these have little or nothing in common with the points of special concern systematically worked out by the authorship of the Bavli. The Bavli's authorship at ca. 600 approaches Mishnah-exegesis with a program distinct from that of the Yerushalmi's authorship of ca. 400, and the Bavli's authorship reads a critical verse of Scripture within a set of considerations entirely separate from those of interest to the authorships of Leviticus Rabbah and Pesiqta deRab Kahana of ca. 450 and 500. Any notion that the Bavli's authorship has taken as its principal task the restatement of received ideas on the Mishnah-topics and Scripture-verses at hand derives no support to speak of from the sample we shall examine.

That finding, alas, will contradict familiar and much-cherished convictions concerning the character of the Bavli, and of Judaism, that is to say, the larger canonical corpus of which it forms a principal representative. Reaching the world of commonly held opinions in the the song, *Tradition,* that conviction leads us to expect the principal document of Judaism to say pretty much what had been said before, and, many would add, beginning at Sinai. That corpus is held to form a continuous statement, beginning in an earlier writing, standing behind, generating, and therefore continuing in a later one. Consequently, the corpus is called "traditional," in the sense that one document leads to the next, and all of the documents come to their climax and conclusion in the final one of late antiquity. To the documents of the Torah – oral and written – is imputed not only the status of tradition in the sense just now defined but also a relationship of continuity which we may call imputed canonicity, so that, we are told, we may freely cite a passage from one document alongside a counterpart from another, treating them as part of a single – hence, continuous statement, and, in theological terms, one might say, canonical one, though our issue is not to be confused with canonical research. And that claim for the Bavli and the literature prior to it of *traditionality* bears with it not merely theological, but literary implications about the nature of the documents and the correct way of reading them. Because of those implications as to literature we can test the claim at hand and ask whether it indeed so describes the documents as to find substantiation in literary facts.

It is, therefore, legitimate to ask whether the Torah – that is, the tradition formed out of prior sources of Judaism – constitutes a cumulative tradition. And it is correct to answer that question by assessing the traits of continuity that join document to document – so it is alleged – in a single textual community, one formed out of a long process of formulation and transmission in a continuous relationship of tradition, hence, in an exact sense, a traditional literature.

IV

Tradition and the Bavli in Particular

I wish now to broaden the framing of the issue at hand, which is, on what basis traditional status is imputed to the writings that antedate the Bavli and therefore also to the Bavli at the end. I wonder whether and how – on literary grounds alone – the principal documents of the Judaism of the dual Torah can be shown to exhibit continuities from one to the next. If they do, then, *on literary grounds alone*, we may claim that the writings contitute sources that all together form a tradition, a set of documents making a single unitary, continuous, and, therefore, also cogent, statement. If they do not, then we shall have to seek other than documentary evidence for the traditional status and character imputed to these same writings by the theology and law of formative Judaism.

Again to state with emphasis: *I therefore want to know whether and how – again, in concrete, literary terms – a document makes its part of such a traditional statement, speaking, for its particular subject, in behalf of the entirety of the antecedent writings of the Judaic system at hand and standing in a relationship of continuity – not merely connection – with other such writings.*

How, in other words, does the authorship of a corpus of writings that unfold on after another take up sources and turn them from traditions into a systematic and cogent statement. I ask the question in the case of a given topic. To answer the question, for obvious reasons I turn to the document universally assigned canonical and official status in Judaism from antiquity to the present day, the

Talmud of Babylonia. In the centuries beyond the closure of the Bavli in ca. A.D. 600, people would universally turn to the Bavli as the starting point for all inquiry into any given topic, and rightly so. Since the Bavli made the first and enduringly definitive statement, we impute to the Bavli canonical status. If, therefore, we wish to ask about how a variety of sources turned into a tradition, that is to say, about the status as statements of a continuous tradition of documents of the formative age of the Judaism of the dual Torah, we shall inquire into the standing of a Bavli-tractate as testimony on its subject within the larger continuous system of which it is reputed to form a principal part. What we want to know about that testimony therefore is how the Bavli relates to prior documents. The reason is that we want to know whether or not the Bavli constitutes a statement of a set of such antecedent sources, therefore a step in an unfolding tradition, so Judaism constitutes a traditional religion, the result of a long sedimentary process. As is clear, the alternative and complementary issue is whether or not the Bavli makes its own statement and hence inaugurates a "new tradition" altogether (in that theological sense of tradition I introduced in the preface). In this case the Judaism defined by the Bavli is not traditional and the result of a sedimentary process but the very opposite: fresh, inventive, responsive to age succeeding age.

I take up a Bavli tractate specifically because, on any given topic, a tractate of the Bavli presents the final and authoritative statement that would emerge from the formative period of the Judaism of the dual Torah. That statement constituted not only an authoritative, but also an encompassing and complete account. That is what I mean by the making of a traditional statement on a subject: transforming in particular the received materials – whatever lay at hand – into a not-merely cogent but fixed and authoritative statement. What I wish to find out is the canonical status of the Bavli, insofar as the authorship of the Bavli transformed its antecedents, its sources, into traditions: the way things had been, are and must continue to be, in any given aspect of the life and world view of Israel, the Jewish people, as the Bavli's authorship understood the composition of that Israel. Accordingly, I mean to investigate how a principal authorship in Judaism has taken up whatever sources it had in hand and transformed them into the tradition of Judaism: the canonical statement, on a given subject, that would endure.

V

The Literary Corpus and its Cogency

Let me set forth the issue of cogency as a principal criterion for *traditionality* as I here frame that issue in literary terms. Do we have a collection of books that happen to make, each its own particular statement? Or do the books form a cogent and whole statement all together? If the former, then "the tradition" – so to speak – *begins* with each book and its authorship. If the latter, then we may speak of sources which do accumulate, in a continuous process of transmission, aand which do comprise and constitute an incremental and linear tradition. That is, we may really claim to discover, describe, analyze and interpret "the (ancient, on-going, linear) tradition." That is why I identify as a principal criterion for traditionality the matter of cogency from book to book – attested not through mere collusion of conceptions but concrete intersection of specific formulations, the material and verbally demonstrable interplay of unfolding conceptions formulated in the same language. That criterion marks an important way to test the hypothesis of traditionality imputed to the writings of the rabbinic corpus. In this context, one may even invoke the notion of canon, in the sense of a theologically-recognized body of writings deemed (if only after the fact) to make a single, correct statement. But not canonicity but rather traditionality in the literary sense now fully spelled out, is the issue here.

Since all inquiry – however aimed at a theoretical result – begins with some one document and its material traits, I conduct a simple, empirical experiment. The specific research problem of this book – to come down to earth – is how the Bavli (the Talmud of Babylonia), as exemplified in one tractate, relates to its sources, by which I mean, materials it shares with other and (by definition) earlier-redacted documents. The question that defines the problem is how the Bavli has formed of available writings (redacted in documents now in hand) a single, cogent, and coherent statement presented by the Bavli's authorship as summary and authoritative: a canonical statement on a given subject. In what ways does a Bavli-tractate frame such a (theologically-canonical) statement out of what (as attested in extant writings) its authorship has in hand?

The result of pursuing these questions should yield the answer to yet another: can we discern within the Bavli's treatment of a subject documentary traits of *traditionality*, that is, laying down a summary, final and experienced judgment for all time? And can we see within the Bavli elements of a program to turn sources into a single tradition, on a given topic? When I can answer that program of questions, I can form a hypothesis, resting on literary facts, concerning the literary and doctrinal traditionality of a sample item within the rabbinic corpus of late antiquity.

That is to say, I can frame a theory on – to state with emphasis – *how the Judaism of the dual Torah speaking through the Bavli in conclusion constituted of its received materials a whole and proportioned system – way of life, world- view, addressed to a defined Israel – and turned into a systemic statement, that is,* a statement of the tradition *handed down in and formed out of prior sources, a variety of available writings on any given subject.*

VI

How Documents Relate

The question before us arises from the fact that that Judaic system – the Judaism of the dual Torah, as authoritatively stated by the Bavli – encompassed also extant and prior documents, making of the these diverse writings now more than a mere collection of books, but *a tradition formed out of prior sources,* that is (from the system's perspective) a single, whole, homogeneous, cogent and (therefore) authoritative statement. So a still more wide-ranging theoretical statement is in order. The matter may be expressed in a simple way. I discern three dimensions by which any document of that Judaism may be measured: autonomy, connection, continuity. As to *autonomy*: a book in the tradition formed out of prior sources at hand stands by itself, within its own covers. But, as to *connection*, that same book also relates to other books of the same tradition formed out of prior sources through specific connections, indicated by intrinsic traits of rhetoric, topic, and logic or by shared materials, common to a number of documents. And, as to *continuity*, it also forms part of an undifferentiated tradition formed out of prior sources, that is, the Torah, or (a) Judaism, through the dimension of complete continuity. Hence among those three dimensions, autonomy, connection, continuity, we now address the third. It follows that the Judaism of the dual Torah transformed a variety of writings from a literary *corpus* into a systemic theological-legal *tradition formed out of prior sources.* The problem of this book therefore is to take the first step toward the description of that Judaism. We begin by turning to the authoritative literature and asking where and how that literature exhibits internal traits of traditionality, I mean, coherence to a broad, systemic composition.

The three dimensions by which we take the measure of a document, autonomy, connection, and continuity, have now to be briefly described. Documents – cogent compositions made up of a number of complete units of thought – by definition exist on their own. That is to say, by invoking as part of our definition the trait of cogency of individual units as well as of the entire composite, we complete a definition of what a document is and is not. A document is a cogent composite of cogent statements. But, also by definition, none of these statements is read all by itself. A document forms an artifact of a social culture, and that in diverse dimensions. Cogency depends on shared rhetoric, logic of intelligible discourse, topic and program – all of these traits of mind, of culture. Someone writes a document, someone buys it, an entire society sustains the labor of literature. Hence we place any document into its culture and society. That social context of documents forms a necessary, but not sufficient, condition of the traditionality of a set of documents. What suffices, beyond the social setting, is the consensus of the group upon a given documentary statement, and to discover the basis of that consensus is to uncover what holds the social group together, its inner agreement on matters the group can scarcely articulate: points of self-evidence, matters of implicit certainty.

We move still further afield as we introduce social consider into literary analysis. But it is a fact that each document exists both in a textual, literary context, and also in a social dimension of culture and even of politics. As to the former, documents may form a community whose limits are delineated by shared conventions of thought and expression. Those exhibiting distinctive, even definitive traits, fall within the community, those that do not, remain without. These direct the author to one mode of topic, logic, and rhetoric, and not to some other. So much for intrinsic and literary traits. As to the extrinsic ones, readers – that is, the members of the faith, who constitute in this context the textual community, which chooses and therefore recognizes canonical writings and rejects others, therefore knowing at least implicitly why this, not that – bring to documents diverse instruments of intelligibility, knowledge of the grammar of not only language but also thought. These social endowments prove decisive. For they explain why people can read one document and not some other. One relationship therefore derives from a literary culture, which forms the authorship of a document, and the other relationship from a social culture. The literary bond links document to document, but it is only the essentially social bond that links reader to document – and also document (through the authorship, individual or collective) to reader. The one relationship is exhibited through intrinsic traits of language and style, logic, rhetoric, and topic, and the other through extrinsic traits of curiosity, acceptance and authority. While documents find their place in their own literary world and also in a larger social one, the two aspects have to remain distinct, the one textual, the other contextual. Moving from the literary characteristics and contents to the social context draws us upward into that structure and system, that Judaism, to which the tradition formed out of prior sources testifies, and which has – by the way – formed, among many other systemic components, the tradition formed out of prior sources too.

It follows that relationships between and among documents also matter for two distinct reasons. The *intrinsic* relationships, which are formal, guide us to traits of intelligibility, teaching us through our encounter with one document how to read some other of its type or class. If we know how to read a document of one type, we may venture to read another of the same type, but not – without instruction – one of some other type altogether. The *extrinsic* relationships, which derive from context and are relative to community, direct us to how to understand a document as an artifact of culture and society. Traits not of documents but of doctrines affecting a broad range of documents come into play. The document, whatever its contents, therefore becomes an instrument of social culture, e.g., theology and politics, a community's public policy. A community then expresses itself through its choice of documents, the community's tradition formed out of prior sources forming a principal mode of such self-definition. So, as I said, through intrinsic traits a document places itself within a larger community of texts. Extrinsic traits, imputed to a document by not its authorship but its audience, selects the document as canonical and make of the document a mode of social definition. The community through its mode of defining itself by its canonical choices forms a textual community – as community expressed through the books it reads and values. These theoretical considerations place into its large context the inquiry before us. But there is one quite practical outcome, treated in Chapter Six, to be introduced at the very outset, the matter of hermeneutics. How are we supposed to read and interpret, by a set of general rules, any particular rabbinic writing? What rules of intellectual syntax tell us the order, proportion, sense, of sentences?

One principal issue worked out in establishing a community of texts is hermeneutical, the chief outcome of defining a textual community, social and cultural. The former teaches us how to read the texts on their own. The latter tells us how to interpret texts in context. When we define and classify the relationships between texts, we learn how to read the components – words, cogent thoughts formed of phrases, sentences, paragraphs –of those texts in the broader context defined by shared conventions of intellect: rhetoric, logic, topic. More concretely, hermeneutical principles tell me how, in light of like documents I have seen many times, to approach a document I have never before seen at all. Hermeneutics teaches me the grammar and syntax of thought. In Chapter Six, as I said, I shall spell out the hermeneutical implications of the study at hand.

But here at the outset the issue is not hermeneutical. At issue is not the reading and interpretation of texts but their social utility, their status as cultural indicators. When I know the choices a community has made for its tradition formed out of prior sources and can explain and interpret the traditionality – the exegesis of exegesis that defines the tradition formed out of prior sources expressed by the question, why this, not that? – I can find my way deep into the shared viewpoint of that community, moving from the contents of the texts to the contexts in which those texts bear meaning. And that brings us back to the basic matter: a text exists in diverse contexts, on its own, among other texts, and as part of a much larger social tradition formed out of prior sources, e.g., a library or a court of appeal for authoritative judgments such as proof-texts supply. A text testifies to more than its contents, but also to relationships extrinsic to it, and in situating a text in relationship to its larger context – including the literary context – we gain entry into that textual community, that canonical world, that in describing the Judaism of the dual Torah as a whole, we must enter. It is important now to help us sort out the most basic matters for discussion. Now to return to the Bavli in particular and the final details of the empirical experiment conducted in Chapters Two through Five.

VII
The Bavli and the Issue of This Book

In light of these theoretical questions of the expression of an incremental tradition and orderly as against the cogent systemic statement of a position, the concrete problem of this book proves obvious. What I want to know is how the Bavli has formed of the received and available writings (attested by documents now in hand) a single, cogent, authoritative and sufficient – hence, by the way, canonical – statement on a given subject. In what ways does a Bavli-tractate frame an authoritative statement out of what its authorship had in hand? Let me spell out the information I seek and how I propose to find it.

On any given topic a tractate of the Bavli presents the final and authoritative statement that emerged from the formative period of the Judaism of the dual Torah. That judgment of Judaism from the formation of the Bavli to the present day justifies our asking the Bavli to tell us whether or not the Bavli's statement is traditional or essentially constructed fresh. If the Bavli's statement constituted not only the authoritative, but also encompassing and complete account, then we deal with a traditional statement and, it follows, Judaism as the Bavli defines the system is a traditional religion. If the Bavli's statement appears to be made up by its own authorship in terms of its own interedsts and program, then the Judaism of the Bavli emerges as not a traditional religion but a systemically constructed and created one, the work of a generation capable of speaking far beyond its time through a system framed to begin with for an occasion. If, therefore, we wish to ask about the traditionality of a document of the formative age of the Judaism of the dual Torah, we shall inquire into the relationship of a Bavli-tractate to its already-available and autonomous, distinct sources. Obviously, the layers of discourse that took shape within which the Bavli itself attest to a process of formation too. No one maintains that the Bavli was made up, as we now have it, all at once; everyone recognizes that the Bavli refers to prior materials, beginning, after all, with the two documents upon which all else rests, the Mishnah and Scripture, the oral and written Torahs.

But the Bavli as we know it represents the work of its penultimate and ultimate framers and redactors; no evidence now suggests that a long, slow process of sedimentary formation – to appeal for an analogy now to geology – accounts for the state and condition of the Bavli as we know it. Rather, a labor of agglutination and conglomeration of pretty-much finished materials – sayings and stories, complete units of discourse – has yielded the Bavli that we know. That labor then testifies to the character and conscience of the laborers: tradents of received materials, lovingly preserved, engaged minds reworking this, that, and the other thing into an essentially fresh and fundamentally cogent creation. The reader will immediately see that the Bavli is made up of clearly-identifiable components, units of discourse with a beginning, middle, and end. The reader will furthermore observe that these units of discourse have been put together in accord with a plan we may discern. A process of editing already composed materials has given us the document. An equally well-crafted and carefully planned set of literary-rhetorical and logical-syllogistic conventions has dictated the principles of rhretoric and logic that govern the composition of the several constituents. As between sedimentary – hence traditional – or agglutinative and conglomerative – hence inventive and creative – processes, we make our choice on the basis of evidence. But what evidence will tell us how to choose?

Let me now specify the kinds of factual information that will permit me to frame a reply to that question. If I want to know criteria for authority and sufficiency, I have to ask about the relationship between a document and prior treatments of the topic of said document. For one critical criterion of continuity – of forming a tradition out of available sources – is the capacity to take in, hold together, and rework the entirety of a prior corpus of information, writing, on a given subject. The literary test of traditionality is whether or not the canonical statement has drawn together and reworked in a cogent way whatever lay to hand in prior writings. If the test proves affirmative, then we may propose as one substantial and necessary criterion for traditionality a particular relationship to the entirety of prior writing. If it proves negative, then the entire literary dimension of the problem of traditionality turns out to weigh the wind, measure what has no weight. A different approach to the criteria by which the entirety of the literature of Judaism forms a single canonical statement will require invention and exploration. So to the issue at hand.

That is why my particular concern is the Bavli's relationship to prior treatments of a given subject, with special interest in how the authorship of the Bavli has made use of what it had in hand, and how in its sorting out of available materials it has defined the task of making a full and authoritative statement. In assessing the stance of the Bavli, in making its final statement, vis-à-vis prior writings on a given topic, I can uncover the rules that guide an authorship in its work of summary and systematization: of systemic statement of the whole, all together and all at once, on a given subject. I can conceive of no better way of uncovering how people make a statement we now realize was canonical from the beginning, than situation those people in the setting of what had gone before – and had not attained the canonical status that the Bavli's authorship achieved for their document. So far as traditionality constitutes a literary question concerning rules of how one writes a canonical document, giving the signals to the community that one's writing constitutes a final, authoritative statement, through inductive inquiry into relationships I should be able to answer that question and describe those rules: why this not that. That interest requires me to collect answers to questions deriving from these comparative inquiries:

1. *The topical program* of prior writings on the subject as compared to the topical program of the Bavli on the same subject, with attention to questions such as these: does the Bavli follow the response to the Mishnah characteristic of the authorship of the Tosefta? the Sifra (or Sifré to Numbers or Sifré to Deuteronomy, where relevant) Does the Bavli follow the response to relevant passages of Scripture that have caught the attention of compilers of Midrash-exegeses in Genesis Rabbah, Leviticus Rabbah, Pesiqta deRab Kahana, and other documents generally thought to have come to closure prior to the Bavli?

2. *The Bavli's use or neglect of the available treatments ("sources") in the prior literature:* if the Bavli does make use of available materials, does it impose its own issues upon those materials or does it reproduce those materials as they occur elsewhere? Has the authorship of the Bavli carried forward issues

important in prior writings, or has it simply announced and effected its own program of inquiry into the topic at hand?

3. *The traits of the Bavli's statement, that is, derivative and summary at the end, or essentially fresh and imputed retrospectively?* In consequence of the detailed examination of the Bavli's authorship's use of and response to available sources, how may we characterize the statement of the Bavl as a whole in comparison to prior statements? And, since that statement is canonical by the definition of the entire history of Judaism, we ask about the upshot: the shape and character of a canonical statement on a given subject. At the end of Chapters Three, Four, and Five, I answer these questions for the several samples reviewed there. But the reader will know the answer before reading what I say. For I have used different type faces to indicate what is unique to the Bavli and what is shared by the Bavli with prior writings. Regular type is what is unique; italics, for the Mishnah, and bold-face type, for the Tosefta and other documents, are used. The acres of regular type present a landscape distinctive to the territory before us. The Bavli is a special place, with its own flora and fauna, a kind of Australia of Judaism.

Readers familiar with probability-theory and statistics will find no difficulty with my sample for the Bavli as a whole. The document, as everyone knows, is rhetorically and logically uniform; the important differences from tractate to tractate are only in topic. Since the propensity to draw upon available materials – given the vast range available, encompassing, after all, complete exegeses of the important books of scriptural law as well as the entire Mishnah – can serve any tractate equally, my requirement for a tractate for a sample was simple. I needed on which covers a topic treated in Scripture, to make sure that an available scriptural exegetical compilation would serve as a testimony to extent compositions.

I took Sukkah, because it is on a topic important in both Leviticus and Deuteronomy. I could reasonably expect constituent elements of Sifra, Sifré to Deuteronomy, and Leviticus Rabbah, to contribute to my tractate's topic. The Yerushalmi moreover presents for the same Mishnah-tractate a systematic exegesis. Tosefta of course is available. Hence by definition I had a sample-tractate that could yield important points of intersection with prior documents. The proportions of shared materials would therefore produce significant results, in a way in which a Bavli-tractate on a topic unimportant to Scripture – Arakhin, for instance – might not. I needed a tractate the authorship of which would be expected systematically and in an orderly way to draw heavily upon the extant documents. I wanted one that would be sufficiently large to allow for a sizable sample, but not so large as to require a still more tedious review of the obvious than – as it turned out – Bavli-tractate Sukkah has yielded. For I suspected at the outset what has turned out to be the case. To state matters in terms of the simple typography of this book, nearly everything is in plain type. Or, to put matters in more elegant terms, my sample yields a very one-sided result indeed: Bavli is Bavli, not a replay of Yerushalmi, not a reprise of Sifra, where pertinent, or Sifré to Deuteronomy, where relevant, not a rerun of Tosefta to Sukkah, not a restatement of the issues and results of any prior document – let alone of all of them together. The Bavli uses bits and pieces of this and that. But its statement is anything but traditional, in the sense already defined. It is *systemic*.

My sample covers the better part of Bavli Sukkah. In Chapter Two I survey the whole of Chapter One of both Yerushalmi and Bavli Sukkah. This is done in order to answer a particular question about the relationship between those two documents. Then in Chapters Two, Three, and Four I present half of Chapter One and all of Chapters Two and Four. I should estimate that, in total volume, I cover approximately 40-45% of the whole. The pages are specified at the beginnings of the surveys of the several chapters of Bavli. To survey the entirety of the medium-sized tractate at hand – 56 folios – would have made this book unmanageably long, relative to the simple question I am asking. But I did wish to present to the reader graphic and striking evidence for the thesis at hand, concerning the essentially autonomous standing of the Bavli for our case. I originally conceived of presenting a much larger sample, but the results of the first two surveys, given in Chapters Two, then Three, Four, and Five, seemed so one-sided that a smaller sample seemed to me to suffice. I need hardly add that my original conception was that I should survey, also, Arakhin, Sanhedrin, Berakhot, and Sotah, which I have retranslated in part for the purposes of experiments such as this one. But I could not only not ask the reader to turn so many pages of plain type; I also could not ask myself to prove four more times what seems to me so obvious. If others will undertake similar experiments, I shall be the first to express thanks for their sharing this tedious work; and if their results prove different from mine, I shall insist on priority in expressing thanks as I reconsider the thesis offered here.

In all instances I give the opening discourse of the Bavli on Mishnah-tractate Sukkah, because that is characteristically the point at which the authorship of the Bavli presents the scriptural foundations for the Mishnah's statements. Since in hand are exegetical studies of Scriptural books which systematically pursue that same issue, it seemed to me that at that point we should most likely come across points of intersection and common interest between the Bavli and some prior writing. I believe the sample is sufficient, in any event, to establish or to call into question the probability of the thesis at hand. On the basis of the results of this rather sizable sample, I should expect to reach reasonably sound conclusions on the issue at hand.

Before proceeding to the shank of the inquiry, however, one preliminary question demands attention: what about the Yerushalmi? Why focus solely on the relationship between the Bavli and its sources and ignore the issue as it affects the counterpart-document? To these questions we turn in the next chapter.

Chapter Two

The Special Case of the Yerushalmi

I

A Null Hypothesis

Since the Talmud of Babylonia constitutes the second of the two Talmuds devoted to Mishnah-exegesis, separated from the first by about two centuries, the Bavli by definition stands connected to two prior documents, the Mishnah and the Yerushalmi. But – also by definition – it stands autonomous of the entirety of the rabbinic canon. Why so? Because it can be, and usually is, studied entirely on its own, delivering its own message in its own terms. And – again by definition   the Bavli forms part of, and stands continuous with, "the one whole Torah of Moses, our rabbi." Accordingly, proponents of the document claim in its behalf a critical place within the canon of Judaism. So the Bavli forms part of a larger continuity of texts, all of them making their contribution to Judaism. Among the three dimensions by which we describe and analyze any document, in this case, the Bavli – autonomy, connection, continuity – however, it is the issue of connection that for the moment seizes and retains our attention – in this case, connection to the Yerushalmi.

To state the issue simply, if the Bavli carries forward the exegetical program of the Yerushalmi, repeating, refining, restating that received plan of Mishnah-commentary, then the Bavli stands in a traditional relationship to its predecessor, the Yerushalmi. A single, unbroken chain of tradition reaches into the Bavli.

If, on the other hand, the authorship of the Bavli can be shown to have made its own decisions, worked out its own program, and so made a statement in its own behalf upon an entire, received heritage, the Bavli will emerge not as traditional in intent and execution but as systemic and singular. The document will stand not at the end of a long line of tradition, but at the outset of a fresh program entirely – and that despite the undeniable fact that the Bavli makes ample use of prior documents, particular Scripture and the Mishnah, as well as, in much less measure to be sure, the Tosefta. But use of what is in hand does not signify traditional intent and program, any more than a composer's working within the received canon of harmony or an artist's utilizing a familiar palette attests to traditionalism.

Since the Bavli forms the second of the two Talmuds that undertake the systematic exegesis of Mishnah-tractates and the restatement, in encompassing terms, of the Torah's message on their respective topics, the Bavli's relationship to its predecessor provides indicative data. If we wish to assess the Bavli's use of prior sources, therefore, we ask first of all about the relationship of the Bavli to the Yerushalmi. With the issue clear, let me make the criteria concrete.

If we can demonstrate a systematic exercise of refinement, completion, summary, we may assign to the Bavli a position at the end of a sustained and continuous process of thought – tradition in the exact sense. It will stand to reason that, for the case at hand, the power of the Bavli to make what we stipulate to be the canonical statement on its topic derives from its character as a summary and conclusion. The Bavli will fall into the classification of a traditional document, one that encompasses a long past of thought and development of doctrine and law, topic by topic, problem by problem.

If, on the other hand, the authorship of the Bavli has defined an essentially fresh and therefore original program of Mishnah-exegesis, we shall have to see the Bavli as an original statement of an essentially fresh system. We shall then close off the possibility that a corpus of writings yields as its canonical statement a conclusion that encompasses and harmonizes the whole of an antecedent body of writings, joining each of its extant elements into a single cogent statement. The Bavli will then turn out to have made a statement not of tradition, deriving from prior sources, but of a system of its own, based upon a wholly autonomous act of intellect and reflection. In that sense the choice – as best as I can phrase it in two words – is tradition or system.

II

The Yerushalmi in Particular

Why the Bavli took priority over the Yerushalmi, as it ultimately did, I cannot say. That is not a compelling issue for our study of internal evidence, and for all we know, the happenstance of politics or instituional history may settle the question. True, in my *Judaism: The Classical Statement. The Evidence of the Bavli* (Chicago, 1986: University of Chicago Press) I systematically compared the Yerushalmi and the Bavli and showed one important reason that the Bavli and not the Yerushalmi served as the medium for the complete and final statement of late antiquity. It was that the authorship of the Bavli for the construction of its large-scale redactional structures resorted to both the oral and also the written Torah, that is, to the Mishnah and also to Scripture. By contrast, the authorship of the Yerushalmi ordinarily appealed for its principal redactional structures to the former but only rarely to the latter. But that reason, discovered out of an inductive inquiry into internal evidence concerning redactional policy and program, while necessary, scarcely proves sufficient in the present setting. So it is the qualities of the Bavli that guide us to the literary definition of traditionality – so far as there can be a literary definition at all. And, it must follow, the relationship of the authorship of the

Bavli to the Yerushalmi's treatment of a given aspect of the topic at hand will therefore constitute only the decisive aspect of our inquiry.

Let me now specify the operative question and the criteria for answering it:

Does the Bavli carry forward the exegetical program of the Yerushalmi?

Or does the authorship of the Bavli invent its own, altogether singular and distinctive topical-exegetical program for the same chapter of the Mishnah?

A comparison of the two documents will allow us to settle at the outset a number of important questions. These concern the relationships of connection between the Bavli and prior writings. For what we shall now see is that the Bavli is autonomous, singular, distinctive. Its authorship delivers its message in a way that is its own and works out an exegetical program, on precisely the same chapter of the Mishnah, that is particular to itself, not dictated by the prior Talmud's treatment of the same materials. It therefore is in substantial measure distinct from the other Talmud. The Bavli is far more than a secondary development of the Yerushalmi.

We need hardly dwell on the simple fact that both the Yerushalmi and the Bavli organize their materials as comments on Mishnah sentences or paragraphs. A further important but equally obvious fact is that the two compositions differ from all other documents of the rabbinic canon both in their focus – the Mishnah – and in their mode of discourse. That is to say, Mishnah exegesis and expansion find their place, in the entire corpus of rabbinic writings of late antiquity, solely in the two Talmuds. What is shared between the two Talmuds and the remainder of the canon deals with Scripture exegesis, on the one side, and deeds and sayings of sages, on the other. To give one simple example, while Leviticus Rabbah contains exegeses of Scripture found also in one or another of the two Talmuds, there is not a single passage of the Mishnah subjected, in Leviticus Rabbah, to modes of analysis commonplace in the two Talmuds, even though on rare occasion a Mishnah sentence or paragraph may find its way into Leviticus Rabbah. So the two Talmuds stand together as well as take up a position apart from the remainder of the canon. These two facts make the definitive points in common sufficiently clear so we may address the more difficult issue of whether and how the two Talmuds differ from one another, meaning, whether, where, and how the authorship of the Bavli has accepted the program of its predecessors and so given us the seal of tradition, and when that authorship has gone its own way and so given us its own systemic statement. That is what is now at stake.

III

The Alternative Theses

To unpack and explore that issue, we shall entertain a series of propositions and examine evidence marshalled to test those propositions. We begin from the simplest point and move to the more complex and subtle ones. I can imagine no more obvious and self-evident point of entry than this: the two Talmuds not only treat the Mishnah paragraphs in the same order, they also say much the same thing about them. We take up the simplest proposition.

A. The two Talmuds say pretty much the same thing in the same words. The Bavli, coming later, depends upon and merely amplifies or augments the Yerushalmi.

or:

B. The two Talmuds treat the Mishnah paragraph in distinct and distinctive ways. They use different language to make their own points. Where they raise the same issue, it derives from the shared text, the Mishnah, and its logic. Both Talmuds respond to the Mishnah; the Bavli does not depend overall on a conventional program supplied by the Yerushalmi.

The sample at hand will decisively settle matters in favor of B. In what follows, I compare and contrast the exegetical program of the Yerushalmi, given in the right-hand column, against that of the Bavli, given in the left. My précis of each unit of discourse deals only with the issue at hand: what did the exegetes of the Mishnah paragraph wish to ask? Unless there is a clear reproduction of the same discussion in both Talmuds, I do not present the actual texts. The system of division and signification worked out in my translation of Yerushalmi as well as Bavli Sukkah is followed throughout. It has the merit of consistent principles of division, so we are comparing passages that, in a single, consistent way, are identified as whole and complete. Where passages are congruent I indicate in the Bavli column by cf. and the Yerushalmi unit. Where they intersect, I indicate with an equal sign (=). I present the Mishnah-passages in italics.

IV

Yerushalmi and Bavli on Mishnah-Tractate Sukkah 1:1A-F

1:1A-F

A. *A sukkah that is taller than twenty cubits is invalid.*
B. *R. Judah declares it valid.*
C. *And one which is not ten handbreadths high,*
D. *one which does not have three walls,*
E. *or one, the light of which is greater than the shade of which,*

F.   *is invalid.*

Yerushalmi

I. Basis for Judah's dispute with rabbis: analogy to the Temple's dimensions. M. Er. 1:1.

II. Why sages regard a sukkah that is too tall as invalid.

III. Rab: A larger sukkah is valid even if it is very tall.

IV. Hoshaiah: If one builds an intervening floor, so diminishing the distance from roof to floor in part of a sukkah, what is the status of the space unaffected by the intervening floor?

V. If one lowered the sukkah roof by hanging garlands, does that lower the roof to less than the acceptable height?

VI. How do we know that air space ten handbreadths above the ground constitutes a domain distinct from the ground? M. Shab. 1:1.

VII. Rabbi, Simeon, Judah: Sukkah must be given dimension in length, breadth, and must have four walls. Dispute.

VIII. Hiyya-Yohanan: Sukkah is valid if it has two walls of normal size and a third of negligible dimensions.

IX. A braided wall as a partition.

X. M. Kil. 4:4.

XI. Tips of laths that protrude from sukkah roofing are treated as part of the sukkah.

XII. Citation and discourse on M. 1:1E-F: If light is half and half, it is valid/invalid.

Bavli

I. Relationship of M. Suk. 1:1 to M. Er. 1:1:   what differentiates sukkah from erub law. = Y. I.

II. Scriptural basis for position of sages at M. 1:1A. [cf. Y. I.]

III. If sukkah roofing touches walls of sukkah, the sukkah may be higher than twenty cubits.

IV. Dispute of Judah/sages + precedent supplied by T. Suk. 1:1A-E = Y. III.

V. Sukkah must hold person's head and greater part of his body. Discourse: M. Suk. 2:7.

VI. Who stands behind view that house not 4 x 4 cubits is not regarded as a house. = Y. II.

VII. Diminishing the height of a sukkah by raising the floor. [cf. Y. IV.]

VIII. Diminishing the height of a sukkah by lowering the roof with hangings. = Y. V.

IX. Putting sukkah roofing on posts.

X. M. 1:1C: Scriptural basis for rule that sukkah less than ten handbreadths in height is invalid.

XI. Continues X.

XII. Continues X.

XIII. Sukkah has to have three walls, with the third of negligible [cf. Y. VIII] dimensions. = Y. VII-VIII.

XIV. Where does builder set the little wall?

XV. Continues foregoing.

XVI. M. 1:1E-F: definition of valid roofing = Y. XII.

XVII. Sukkah must be permanent, not temporary, in character. Various authorities who take that view.

XVIII. Continues XVII.

XIX. Two sukkah, one inside the other.

XX. Sukkah built for gentiles, women, cattle, Samaritans is valid, if the roofing is valid.

Before proceeding to the comparison of the two Talmud's treatment of the same passage, let us briefly review how, overall, each one has composed its materials.

Yerushalmi to M. Suk. 1:1A-F. The Yerushalmi provides a substantial discussion for each of the Mishnah's topical clauses in sequence, furthermore bringing together parallel rulings in other tractates to enrich the context for discussion. It would be difficult to point to a more satisfactory inquiry, on the part of either Talmud, into the Mishnah's principles and problems. Unit I takes up the noteworthy parallel between M. 1:1A and M. Er. 1:1A. The main point in both cases is the scriptural basis for the dimensions specified by the law. The effort to differentiate is equally necessary. Hence the difference between one sort of symbolic gateway and another, or between one wall built for a given purpose and another wall built for some other purpose, has to be specified. Unit II undertakes a complementary discourse of differentiation. It is now between a sukkah and a house. The two are comparable, since a person is supposed to dwell in a sukkah during the festival. Unit III, continuous with the foregoing, further takes up the specified measurement and explains it. Unit IV raises a difficult question, dealing with the theory, already adumbrated, that we extend the line of a wall or a roof or a cornice in such a way as to imagine that the line comes down to the ground or protrudes upward. At unit IV we seem to have a sukkah roofing at an angle, extending from the middle of a sukkah outwards, above the limit of twenty cubits. Unit V asks about lowering the sukkah roofing by suspending decorations from it or raising the sukkah floor by putting straw or pebbles on it. Both produce the effect of bringing the sukkah within the required dimensions of its height. Unit VI does not belong at all; it is primary at Y. Shab. 1:1. I assume it was deemed to supplement M. 1:1C. Unit VII takes up the matter of the required walls for the sukkah, M. 1:1D. Once again the scriptural basis for the rule is indicated. Unit VIII carries forward this same topic, now clarifying the theoretical problems in the same matter. At unit IX we deal with an odd kind of partition, a braid partition. This discussion is primary to Y. Er. 1:9 and is inserted here because of IX and X. The inclusion of unit X is inexplicable, except as it may form a continuous discourse with unit IX. It is primary at Y. Er. 1:8. Units XI and XII are placed where they are as discussions of M. 1:1E. But only unit XII takes up the exegesis of the Mishnah's language.

Bavli to M. Suk. 1:1A-F. The protracted Bavli passage serving M. 1:1A-F not only works its way through the Mishnah paragraph but systematically expands the law applicable to that paragraph by seeking out pertinent principles in parallel or contrasting cases of law. When a unit of discourse abandons the theme or principle connected to the Mishnah paragraph, it is to take up a secondary matter introduced by a unit of discourse that has focused on that theme or principle. Unit I begins with an analysis of the word choice at hand. At the same time it introduces an important point, M. Er. 1:1, namely, the comparison between the sukkah and a contraption erected also on a temporary basis and for symbolic purposes. Such a contraption is a symbolic gateway that transforms an alley entry into a gateway for a courtyard and so alters the status of the alley and the courtyards that open on to it, turning them into a single domain. As one domain, they are open for carrying on the Sabbath, at which time people may not carry objects from one domain (e.g., private) to another (e.g., public). That comparison is repeatedly invoked. Units II and III then move from language to scriptural sources for the law. Unit IV then stands in the same relationship to unit III, and so too unit V. Unit VI reverts to an issue of unit V. Thus the entire discussion, II-VI, flows out of the exegetical requirements of the opening lines of the Mishnah paragraph. But the designated unit-divisions seem to mark discussions that could have stood originally by themselves. Unit VII then reverts to the original topic, the requisite height of the sukkah (= Y. IV-V). It deals with a fresh problem, namely, artificially diminishing or increasing the height of the sukkah by alterations to the inside of the hut. One may raise the floor to diminish the height or lower the floor to increase it. Unit VIII pursues the same interest. It further introduces principles distinct from the Mishnah's rules but imposed upon the interpretation of those rules or the amplification of pertinent cases. This important exercise in secondary expansion of a rather simple rule through the introduction of fresh and rather engaging principles – "curved wall," fictional extension of walls upward or downward and the like – then proceeds in its own terms. Unit IX is continuous in its thematic interest with unit VIII. Unit X reverts to the Mishnah paragraph, now M. 1:1C, and asks the question usually raised at the outset about the scriptural authority behind the Mishnah's rule. This leads us into a sizable digression on scriptural exegesis, with special interest in establishing the analogy between utensils in the temple and dimensions pertinent to the sukkah. The underlying conception, that what the Israelite does on cultic occasions in the home responds to what is done in the cult in the temple, is familiar. Units XI and XII pursue the same line of thought. Then unit XIII reverts once more to the Mishnah's rule, M. 1:1D. Now we take up the issue of the walls of the sukkah. These must be three, in the rabbis' view, and four in Simeon's. Each party concedes that one of the requisite walls may be merely symbolic. The biblical source for the required number of walls forms the first object of inquiry. Unit XIV then takes up the symbolic wall. Unit XV reverts to a statement on Tannaite authority given in unit XIII. Subject to close study is a somewhat complicated notion. There are diverse kinds of sukkah buildings. One, we know, is a sukkah erected to carry out the religious duty of the festival. But a person may build a sukkah to extend the enclosed and private area of his home. If he places such a sukkah by the door, the area in which it is permitted to carry objects – private domain – covers not only the space of the house but also the space of the sukkah. That sukkah, erected in connection with Sabbath observance, is compared to the sukkah erected for purposes of keeping the festival. The issue is appropriate here, since the matter concerns the character of the walls of the sukkah built for Sabbath observance. Unit XVI then returns to the Mishnah paragraph. Unit XVIII moves back from the Mishnah's statements and deals with the general principle, taken by some parties, that the sukkah must bear the qualities of a permanent dwelling. That issue intersects with our Mishnah paragraph in connection with Judah's and Simeon's views on the requirement that there be a roof of a certain height and four walls. But the construction as a whole stands independent of the Mishnah paragraph and clearly was put together in its own terms. XVIII takes up XVII.M. Units XIX and XX evidently are miscellaneous – the only such units of discourse in the entire massive construction. I cannot point to a more thorough or satisfying sequence of Babylonian Talmudic units of discourse in which the Mishnah's statements are amplified than the amplifications themselves worked out on their own. The whole is thorough, beautifully articulated, and cogent until the very end.

Since, intersecting in topic and problematic, the Bavli goes over the ground of the Yerushalmi at several points, pursuing essentially the same problem, we have to ask about possible borrowing by the Bavli from the Yerushalmi, not of theses or conventions of interpretation but of whole constructions. To show the points of word-for-word correspondence such as they are, let us now consider side by side one suggestive item, Y. III = B. IV.

Y. 1:1

III.

A. [As to the invalidity of a sukkah more than twenty cubits high,] R. Ba in the name of Rab: "That applies to a sukkah that will hold only the head and the greater part of the body of a person and also his table.

B. "But if it held more than that, it is valid [even at such a height]."

C. [Giving a different reason and qualification,] R. Jacob bar Aha in the name of R. Josiah: "That applies [further] when the walls do not go all the way up with it [to the top, the roofing] but if the walls go all the way up with it to the roofing, it is valid."

D. [Proving that C's reason, not A-B's, is valid, we cite the following:]

E. Lo, the following Tannaite teaching differs [in T.'s version]: Said R. Judah, "MSH B: The sukkah of Helene was twenty cubits tall, and sages went in an out, when visiting her, and not one of them said a thing."

F. They said to him, "It was because she is a woman, and a woman is not liable to keep the commandment of sitting in a sukkah."

G. He said to them, "Now did she not have seven sons who are disciples of sages, and all of them were dwelling in that same sukkah!" [T. Suk. 1:1].

H. Do you then have the possibility of claiming that the sukkah of Helene could not hold more than the head and the greater part of the body and the table of a person? [Surely, someone of her wealth would not build so niggardly a sukkah.]

I. Consequently, the operative reason is that the sides of the sukkah do not go all the way up [to the sukkah roofing at the top, leaving a space].

J. It stands to reason, then, that what R. Josiah has said is so.

K. [And the Tannaite teaching] does not differ [from sages' view], for it is the way of the rich to leave a small bit of the wall out beneath the sukkah roofing itself, so that cooling air may pass through.

B. 1:1

IV.

A. [The specification of the cited authorities, II.A, C, E, on the minimum requirements of the sukkah, now comes under discussion in its own terms.] The following objection was raised:

B. A sukkah which is taller than twenty cubits is invalid.

C. R. Judah declares it valid [M. 1:1A-B], even up to forty or fifty cubits.

D. Said R. Judah, "MSH B: The sukkah of Helene in Lud was twenty cubits tall, and sages went in and out, when visiting her, and not one of them said a thing."

E. They said to him, "It was because she is a woman, and a woman is not liable to keep the commandment of sitting in a sukkah."

F. He said to them, "Now did she not have seven sons [who are disciples of sages, and all of them were dwelling in that same sukkah]" [T. Suk. 1:1A-E].

G. "And furthermore, everything she ever did was done in accord with the instruction of sages."

H. Now what need do I have for this additional reason: "Furthermore, everything she ever did was done in accord with the instructions of sages"?

I. This is the sense of what he said to them: "Now, if you say that the sons were minors, and minors are exempt from the religious duty of dwelling in the sukkah, since she had seven sons, it is not possible that among them was not a single one who no longer needed his mother's tending [and so would be required to dwell on his own in the sukkah]."

J. "And if, further, you should maintain that a minor who no longer needs his mother's tending is subject to the law only on the authority of rabbis, and that woman paid no attention to rules that rested only on the authority of the rabbis, come and note the following: 'And furthermore, everything she ever did was done in accord with the instructions of sages.'"

K. [We now revert to the issue with which we began, namely, the comparison of the story at hand to the reasons adduced by the authorities at unit III:] Now with reverence to the one who said, the dispute applies to a case in which the walls of the sukkah do not touch the sukkah roofing, would a queen dwell in a sukkah, the walls of which do not touch the sukkah roofing?

L. [3A] [Indeed so! The reason is that] the space makes possible good ventilation.

M. But in the view of the one who has said that the dispute pertains to a small sukkah, would a queen ever dwell in a small sukkah?

N. Said Rabbah bar R. Ada, "At issue in the dispute is solely a case of a sukkah which is made with many small cubbies."

O. But would a queen take up residence in a sukkah that was subdivided into many small cubbies?

P. Said R. Ashi, "At issue is only [a large sukkah which had] such recesses.

Q. "Rabbis take the view that the queen's sons were dwelling in a sukkah of absolutely valid traits, while she dwelled in the recesses on account of modesty [i.e., not showing her face among the men], and it was on that account that rabbis said nothing to her [about her dwelling in what was, in fact, an invalid part of the sukkah].

R. "And R. Judah maintains the position that her sons were dwelling along with her [in the cubbyholes of the sukkah], and even so, the rabbis did not criticize what she was doing [which proves that the small cubbies of the sukkah were valid]."

The issue of Y. III.A and B. IV.A is the same. Tosefta's precedent, marked in bold face, is used differently in each Talmud. In the Bavli it makes a point relevant to B. IV.A, the height of the sukkah. It is entirely relevant to the purpose for which it is adduced. The sukkah of the queen was high, so sustaining Judah's view. The secondary issue, IV.K, links the precedent to unit III. The whole is integrated and well composed. By contrast, the Yerushalmi's use of the precedent is odd. The passage is explicit as to the large size of the hut, so Y.III.H is somewhat jarring. It really contradicts Y. III.G. Y. III.I then revises matters to force the precedent to serve Y. III.C. We cannot imagine that Bavli's author has depended on Yerushalmi's composition. He has used the precedent for his own inquiry and in his own way. Where, therefore, Yerushalmi and Bavli share materials, the Bavli's use of those materials – if this case is suggestive – will not depend upon the Yerushalmi's. Both refer back to the Mishnah and to the Tosefta, responding to the former in terms (here) of the exegetical program precipitated by the contents available in the latter.

The first exercise of comparison now requires extension. We shall therefore review the programs of each of the two Talmuds for Mishnah-tractate Sukkah chapter 1.

V

Yerushalmi and Bavli on Mishnah-Tractate Sukkah 1:1G-N

1:1G-N

G. *[9A] A superannuated sukkah –*

H. *The House of Shammai declare it invalid.*

I. *And the House of Hillel declare it valid.*

J. *And what exactly is a superannuated sukkah?*

K. *And which one made thirty days [or more] before the festival [of Sukkot].*

L. *But if one made it for the sake of the festival,*

M. *even at the beginning of the year,*

N. *it is valid.*

Yerushalmi

    I.   A qualification of the position of the Hillelites.

   II.   The dispute of the houses pertains also to Passover.

  III.   T. 1:4A-B.

  IV.   What blessing is recited over a sukkah when it is made?

Bavli

    I.   Scripture's support for the view of the House of Shammai.

   II.   How can the Hillelites accept as valid a sukkah not constructed for the purpose of observing the festival?

Yerushalmi to M. Suk. 1:2. Unit I glosses M. 1:2A-C. Unit II presents a dispute in a different matter but about the same principle. Unit III supplements M. with T. Unit IV indicates the blessing to be said in connection with making and using the sukkah.

Bavli to M. Suk. 1:1G-N [=Y.M.1:2]. Unit I clarifies the source of the law, and unit II introduces a separate, but related, consideration. The exegesis of the Mishnah's rule in relationship to scriptural proof text is thorough.

VI

Yerushalmi and Bavli on Mishnah-tractate Sukkah 1:2

1:2

    A.   *[9B] He who makes his sukkah under a tree is as if he made it in [his] house.*

    B.   *A sukkah on top of a sukkah –*

    C.   *the one on top is valid.*

    D.   *And the one on the bottom is invalid.*

    E.   *R. Judah says, "If there are no residents in the top one, the bottom one is valid."*

Yerushalmi

    I.   Clarification of M. 1:2B-D: How much space defines the separation of the two roofs, so that the upper one is deemed distinct and valid?

   II.   Clarification of M. 1:2E.

Bavli

    I.   Clarification of M. 1:2A re character of the tree's foliage.

   II.   Scriptural basis of M. 1:2B.

  III.   Augmentation of M. 1:2B-D.

  IV.   Clarification of M. 1:2B-D: how much space [= Y. I].

Yerushalmi to M. Suk. 1:2. The point is that the roof of the sukkah must be exposed to the firmament and not made up, A, in large part by the boughs of the tree. D follows the same principle, now with reference to a sukkah covered by another. Judah's view is that, without residents, the upper sukkah does not constitute a dwelling, thus excluding A's consideration. Unit I clarifies M.

1:2B's notion of two sukkah roofs near one another by raising a problem independent of M. Unit II amplifies Judah's meaning, M. 1:3E.

Bavli to M. Suk. 1:2. The point is that the roof of the sukkah must be exposed to the firmament and not covered, I.A, in large part by the boughs of the tree. D follows the same principle, now with reference to a sukkah covered by another. Judah's view is that, without residents, the upper sukkah does not constitute a dwelling, thus excluding A's consideration. Unit I then clarifies M. 1:2A. But the real interest is the notion that if invalid and valid forms of sukkah roofing are intertwined, with a greater portion of valid, the whole is valid. That principle, not demanded by the Mishnah's rule, clarifies that rule. Unit II proceeds to the scriptural basis for M. 1:2B. Unit III focuses upon that same rule, making a point that the Talmud's anonymous voice itself calls self-evident. Unit IV clarifies a secondary question – the relationship of the two sukkah constructions, upper and lower – but in so doing also invokes M. 1:2E. Since Y. I and B. IV go over exactly the same question, we shall once more compare the two units of discourse side by side to see how, if at all, they relate:

Yerushalmi

I.

A. In the case of two sukkah roofs, one on top of the other, in which the upper roofing was such that the light was greater than the shade [and hence invalid], while the lower one was such that the light was not greater than the shade on its own, but, together with the other roof, the shade was greater than the light –

B. What is the maximum of space that may be between the two roofs so that they should be deemed joined together [into a single sukkah roofing, hence a valid one for the sukkah beneath]?

C. There were two Amoras. One said, "Ten cubits," and the other said, "Four."

D. The one who maintained that ten cubits distance are permissible objected to the one who said that only four are permissible, "If it is because of the principle of forming a tent [that you want the two so close together], we find that a tent may be no more than a handbreadth [in its principal dimensions, hence also height]. [So you permit too broad a space between the two roofs.]"

Bavli

IV.

A. And how much space would there be between one sukkah and the other so that the lower sukkah would be invalid [as a sukkah beneath a sukkah]?

B. Said R. Huna, "A handbreadth. [If the space between the upper-sukkah roofing and the lower-sukkah roofing is less than a handbreadth, the two sets of roofing are regarded as one. [Then we do not have a case of one sukkah beneath another sukkah at all.]"

C. [Huna continues,] "For so we find that the handbreadth is the standard measure in connection with cases of overshadowing of corpse uncleanness, for we have learned in the Mishnah: A handbreadth of space by a handbreadth at the height of a handbreadth brings uncleanness [should it be left open in a partition between corpse matter in one otherwise closed room and another such room] or interposes against the passage of the same uncleanness [if such a space is closed off], but a space less than a handbreadth in height neither brings uncleanness [if open] nor interposes [if closed] [M. Oh. 3:7]. [The operative measure is a handbreadth. If the roof is higher than that distance, it is deemed a separate roof, and if it is lower, it is deemed part of the contained space]."

D.   R. Hisda and Rabbah bar R. Huna say, "Four [handbreadths], for we do not find a contained space taken into account if it is less than four handbreadths."

E.   And Samuel said, "Ten."

F.   What is the reason for the view of Samuel? The requisite measure for rendering the sukkah valid [ten handbreadths above the ground] also operates to render it invalid.

G.   Just as the requisite measure of height is ten handbreadths, so the distance that will invalidate likewise is ten handbreadths.

H.   [Arguing to the contrary conclusion on the basis of the same principle as F:] We have learned in the Mishnah: R. Judah says, "If there are no residents in the top one, the bottom one is valid" [M. 1:2E].

I.   What is the sense of "If there are no residents...valid"?

J.   If it is in concrete terms, that is, if the issue is that there really are no occupants, is this the governing criterion? [It is a random fact.]

K.   But rather is not the sense of there being no residents to mean, any [upper] sukkah which is not suitable for a dwelling [would leave the lower sukkah valid]?

L.   What would be an example of such a case? One which was not ten handbreadths in height.

M.   Would this then bear the implication that, in the view of the first [anonymous] authority [vis-à-vis Judah], even one which is not suitable for dwelling [would leave the lower sukkah] invalid? [This would then refute Samuel's position, above].

N.   When R. Dimi came, he said, "In the West they say, If the lower [sukkah's roof] cannot hold the weight of the pillows and blankets of the upper one, the lower one is valid. [The upper sukkah then is not sufficiently strong. Its floor, the roof of the lower sukkah, cannot carry the weight.]"

O.   Does this then bear the implication that the first of the two authorities takes the view that even if the [lower sukkah] is not suitable to bear [the weight of the upper, the lower one] is invalid?

P.   At issue between [Judah and the first authority] is the case of a [lower] sukkah, the floor-roof of which can bear the weight of the upper sukkah only with difficulty.

There is no reason to belabor the obvious. Once more, when the two Talmuds wish to deal with the same issue, the overlap is in conception; but there is no point of verbal contact, let alone of intersection. Each Talmud undertakes its own analysis in its own way. Each Talmud bases its discussion on the common source (the Mishnah, sometimes also the Tosefta), but each one builds its discussion on the basis of points made by its selection of authorities and pursues matters in terms of its own established conventions of rhetoric.

VII

Yerushalmi and Bavli on Mishnah-Tractate Sukkah 1:3

1:3

A. *[If] one spread a sheet on top of [a sukkah] on account of the hot sun,*

B. *or underneath [the cover of boughs] on account of droppings [of the branches or leaves of the bough cover],*

C. *or [if] one spread [a sheet] over a four-poster bed [in a sukkah],*

D. *it is invalid [for dwelling or sleeping and so for fulfilling one's obligation to dwell in the sukkah].*

E. *But one spreads it over the frame of a two-poster bed.*

Yerushalmi

I. One may not spread rugs over a sukkah roof, but may spread them on the sides.

II. M. 1:3B clarified.

III. M. 1:3E clarified.

Bavli

I. Clarification of M. 1:3B.

II. Continuation of foregoing: what is put up to decorate a sukkah does not diminish the height of the sukkah.

III. Decorations for a sukkah that extend above the roof.

IV. Clarification of M. 1:3C re canopied bed.

V. Sleeping in a canopied bed.

VI. Sleeping in a canopied bed in a sukkah, framed in accord with M. 2:1B.

The Yerushalmi's perfunctory discussion clarifies sentences in the Mishnah paragraph. The Bavli begins with analysis of the implications of the Mishnah's language, unit I attending to M. 1:3B. Unit II is inserted because it deals with decorations in a sukkah, important in the discussion of unit I. Unit III carries forward the same point of interest. Unit IV then reverts to the Mishnah, now to M. 1:3C, E, the contrast between two types of beds, explained just now. This leads to the secondary discussion at units V and VI. So the Bavli forms around the principal clauses of the Mishnah and then extends its discussion to secondary matters generated by its original inquiry. Obviously, the Bavli's framers have given a far more elaborate treatment to the Mishnah.

VIII
Yerushalmi and Bavli on Mishnah-Tractate Sukkah 1:4

1:4

A. *[If] one trained a vine, gourd, or ivy over it and then spread sukkah roofing on [one of these], it is invalid.*
B. *But if the sukkah roofing exceeded them,*
C. *or if one cut them [the vines] down,*
D. *it is valid.*
E. *This is the general rule:*
F. *Whatever is susceptible to uncleanness and does not grow from the ground – they do not make sukkah roofing with it.*
G. *And whatever is not susceptible to uncleanness, but does grow from the ground [and has been cut off] – they do make sukkah roofing with it.*

Yerushalmi

I.   Clarification of M. 1:4C.
II. Illustration of M. 1:4F-G.
III. Exegetical foundations for M. 1:4E-G about the status, as to cleanness, of what may be used for sukkah roofing.

Bavli

I.   Clarification of M. 1:4C-D.
II. Expansion on foregoing, with attention to M. 1:4A.
III. Exegetical foundations for M. 1:4F-G.
IV. Continuation of foregoing.
V.   Continuation of foregoing.

Yerushalmi to M. 1:4. Unit I complements the rule of M. 1:4A-D. Units II and III take up M. 1:4F-G, what may be used in sukkah roofing. Unit II provides some facts, and unit III, exegetical foundations for M.'s principle.

Bavli to M. 1:4. The Bavli's elaborate discussion, units I-II, accomplishes two things. First, it raises the question of the procedure to be followed in connection with M. 1:4C. Second, it introduces the underlying principle at issue whether the mere act of cutting down the vines also serves to render them suitable for the specific purpose of use as sukkah roofing, or whether some distinct act of designation, thus preparation, is required. The former view is worked out in unit I. Unit II then produces a striking analogy in which a quite different case – making strings into show fringes – is shown to invoke upon the same principle, namely, whether a mere act of destruction – cutting the vines, severing the string – suffices, or whether a clear-cut deed of deliberate and positive validation also is required. It is clear that the issue of show fringes need not involve the matter of the vines for sukkah roofing, but unit II makes a strong argument that the two cases must be worked out in tandem. Units III-V then present the familiar exercise of locating scriptural proof for a Mishnaic proposition.

Because Y. III and B. IV-VI not only go over the same problem, namely, discovering exegetical foundations for the Mishnah's rule, but also resort to the same antecedent materials in constructing their discussions, we have yet again to compare the two compositions side by side.

Yerushalmi

III.

A. Said R. Yohanan, "It is written, 'You shall keep the feast of booths seven days, when you make your ingathering from your threshing floor and your wine press' (Deut. 16:13).

B. "From the refuse of your threshing floor and your wine press you may make sukkah roofing for yourself."

C. R. Simeon b. Laqish said, "'But a mist went up from the earth and watered the whole face of the ground' (Gen. 2:6). [The analogy of the covering of the sukkah is to mist, which arises from the ground and is not susceptible to receive uncleanness.]"

D. Said R. Tanhuma, "This one is consistent with opinions held elsewhere, and that one is consistent with opinions held elsewhere.

E. "R. Yohanan has said, 'The clouds came from above,' and so he derives the rule from the reference to 'your ingathering.'

F. "R. Simeon b. Laqish said, 'Clouds come from below,' so he derives the rule from clouds [of mist]."

G. Said R. Abin, "This party is consistent with opinions held elsewhere, and that one is consistent with opinions held elsewhere.

H. "R. Yohanan compares the matter to one who sends his fellow a jug of wine, giving him the jug as well as the wine. [Along these same lines God gives the clouds along with the rain from heaven.]

I. "R. Simeon b. Laqish compares the matter to a priest, who said to his fellow, 'Send over your basket and take some grain for yourself.' [Clouds come from below, and God puts rain in them in heaven.]"

Bavli

III.

A. This is the general rule: Whatever is susceptible to uncleanness, etc. [M. 1:4F-G]:

B. What is the scriptural basis for this rule?

C. Said R. Simeon b. Laqish, "Scripture has stated, 'And a mist went up from the earth' (Gen. 2:6).

D. "Just as mist is something which is not susceptible to uncleanness and grows from the ground, so a sukkah must be made of some thing which does not receive uncleanness and grows from the ground."

E. That explanation is suitable to the person who holds that the sukkah in which Israel dwelled in the wilderness was clouds of glory.

F. But in the view of him who holds that the sukkah was the genuine article which the Israelites actually made for themselves [and not an analogy to clouds of glory], what sort of proof may one bring?

G. The problem at hand accords with that which has been taught on Tannaite authority:

H. "'For I made the children of Israel dwell in sukkot' (Lev. 23:43), meaning in clouds of glory," the words of R. Eliezer.

I. R. Aqiba says, "They were actually sukkot that people made for themselves."

J. Now [as just noted] the stated proof poses no problems to the view of R. Eliezer, but as to the position of R. Aqiba, what is there to say?

IV.

A. When R. Dimi came, [he said that] R. Yohanan said, "Scripture has stated, 'The festal offering of Sukkot you shall prepare' (Deut. 16:13).

B. "The sukkah thus is compared to the festal offering [brought as an animal sacrifice on the festival day].

C. "Just as the festal offering is something that does not receive uncleanness [animals fed from what grows from the ground are, in Yohanan's view, as if they too grow from the ground] and also grows from the ground [as just now explained], so the sukkah must be made of something that does not receive uncleanness and grows from the ground."

D. [12A] But what if you wish to propose a further analogy, just as the festal offering is of an animate being, so the sukkah must be made of an animate being?

V.

A. When Rabin came, he said that R. Yohanan said, "Scripture has stated, 'After you have gathered in from your threshing floor and from your winepress...' (Deut. 16:13). Scripture speaks of what is left on the threshing floor and the dregs of the winepress. [These grow from the ground and are not susceptible to uncleanness, so too the sukkah roofing, of which the verse at hand speaks, must conform to the same traits.]"

B. And may I say that Scripture speaks of the threshing floor itself and the winepress itself? [Perhaps somehow the sukkah must be composed of these objects?]

C. Said R. Zira, "Here it is written, 'Winepress,' and it is hardly possible to make use of a winepress for sukkah roofing!"

D. To this explanation R. Jeremiah objected, "And might I speculate that what is required is use of congealed wine which comes from Senir, like fig cakes? [Perhaps the sense of Scripture is that that is what must be used for sukkah roofing!]"

E. Said R. Zira, "We had a valid proposition in hand, but R. Jeremiah came along and threw an ax at it [and smashed it]!"

F. R. Ashi said, "'From your threshing floor' and not the threshing floor itself, 'from your winepress' and not the winepress itself [is to be the source of materials used for sukkah roofing]."

G. R. Hisda said, "Proof for the desired proposition derives from here: 'Go forth to the mountain and collect olive branches, branches of wild olive, myrtle branches, palm branches, and branches of thick trees' (Neh. 8:15). [All of these are not susceptible to uncleanness and grow from the ground, and, in context, are specified for use as sukkah roofing.]"

H. Myrtle branches fall into the category of branches of thick trees [of Lev. 23:40]. [Why specify the same species twice?]

I. Said R. Hisda, "The wild myrtle is for the sukkah roofing, and the branches of thick trees for the lulab."

The composition of the Yerushalmi is in two simple parts: first, the citation of Yohanan and Simeon b. Laqish; second, Tanhuma's and Abin's point that the two parties' explanations are coherent with things each says in another context. The contrast presented by the Bavli is stunning. Now we have an extended composition on Simeon b. Laqish's statement, given verbatim as it appears in the Yerushalmi. The Bavli's discussion, fully worked out in unit III, is totally its own. The interest of the framer is not in setting Yohanan up in a dispute with Simeon b. Laqish. Rather, he has chosen fully to analyze Simeon's proof and then to introduce an available composition on Tannaite authority, III.G-J. Yohanan is introduced on his own at unit IV. The proof is the same; but while the Yerushalmi suffices with a virtually unarticulated citation of proof texts, the Bavli beautifully articulates what is at issue and then tests matters. In the presentation of Yohanan's proof, the Bavli's framer gives us two complete versions – one at unit IV, the other at unit V.

For our purposes one question now must be settled. Does the Bavli's compositor draw upon the Yerushalmi's version? The answer is decisively negative. The Bavli's author draws upon a shared tradition, known also to the Yerushalmi's writer, that associates Simeon b. Laqish with Gen. 2:6, Yohanan with Deut. 16:13, and both with the present Mishnah paragraph. If the author of the Bavli version had had access to the Yerushalmi's treatment of the matter, he would not have been much impressed, for the point of interest of the Yerushalmi's expansion – the consistency of the two authorities with positions held elsewhere – simply bears no relevance to Bavli's point of entry.

It remains to observe that the two Talmuds come into contact not only through shared access to the Mishnah and to the Tosefta as well as some materials of earlier Amoraic authorities. The two Talmuds meet also in what appears to be a common exegetical program on questions or principles that bear upon a given Mishnah paragraph. But that common program derives over and over again from the contents of the Mishnah paragraph at hand, that is, the principles of law implied by a given rule. It may emerge from the overall task that, linking the Mishnah to Scripture, formed the center of the hermeneutic labor of everyone who received the Mishnah and proposed to deal with it.

IX

Yerushalmi and Bavli on Mishnah-Tractate Sukkah 1:5

1:5

A. *Bundles of straw, wood, or brush –*
B. *they do not make a sukkah roofing with them.*
C. *But any of them that one untied is valid.*
D. *And all of them are valid [as is] for use for the sides [of the sukkah].*

Yerushalmi

 I. Yohanan's explanation of M. 1:5A-B.
 II. What is attached to sheaves for sukkah roofing is not part of the sheaves.
 III. Scriptural basis for M. 1:5D.

Bavli

 I. Yohanan's explanation, as in Y.
 II. Judah-Rab: Sukkah roofing made with arrow shafts.
 III. Sukkah roofing with flax.
 IV. Sukkah roofing with licorice wood and wormwood.
 V. Sukkah roofing with palm tree, with reeds, etc.
 VI. Sukkah roofing with bundles.
 VII. A case.
 VIII. Interposition.
 IX. Grain cut for sukkah roofing.
 X. Continuation of foregoing.
 XI. Continuation of foregoing.

Yerushalmi to M. Suk. 1:5. Used when bound up, the bundles look not like roofing but like a storage area. The bundles in any case may serve as sides or side posts. Unit I supplies a rule for M. Unit II points out that used for one purpose, a sheaf will not be susceptible to uncleanness; used for another, it will be. Accordingly, we invoke the principle that protrusions of pieces of food affect the food to which they are attached when the sheaf is planned for use as food, but not when the sheaf is used for another purpose. This is relevant, in a general way, to M. 1:5A. Unit III provides a scriptural basis for M. 1:5D.

Bavli to M. Suk. 1:5. Unit I provides a discussion for M. 1:5A-B, a rather complex composition. Unit II proceeds to make its own point about other sorts of materials used, or not used, for sukkah roofing. Unit III pursues the same interest, which works its way through units IV and V. Unit VI takes up the secondary theme of what does, and does not, constitute a bundle, clarifying M. 1:5A only in a very general way. Unit VII makes the same sort of contribution. Unit VIII is included because of the appearance, in its catalog, of use for materials for sukkah roofing. Unit IX, with its appended supplements at X and XI, raises an interesting question about the status of the stalks of pieces of fruit as regards uncleanness. The basic principle is that if we regard them as useful, they also are susceptible; but if they are held to be useless, they are insusceptible. This is worked out with exceptional sophistication throughout, and I see no problems in following either the arguments or the relevance of the cases adduced in evidence. Units IX-XI ignore the Mishnah paragraph.

A verbatim comparison now is called for since it will reinforce an important, indeed critical, point. Where the Bavli's authors had access to materials used in the Yerushalmi, they followed their own exegetical program. They in no way limited themselves to whatever program the Yerushalmi may have defined. Quite to the contrary, where the Bavli's framers take over not only the same Mishnah paragraph but also the same antecedent unarticulated lemma (in what follows, Yohanan's explanation), the Bavli's authors do precisely what they want, adhering to a set of conventions distinctive to their own document. That fact cannot be more stunningly illustrated than it is in what follows.

Yerushalmi

I.

A. [As to M. 1:5A-B,] R. Hiyya in the name of R. Yohanan: "It is because [the sukkah] will look like a storage house."

B. R. Jacob bar Abayye, R. Sheshet in the name of R. Hiyya the Elder: "A bundle is made up of no fewer than twenty-five sticks [of wood].

Bavli

I.

A. Said R. Jacob, "I heard from R. Yohanan two [explanations], one for the rule at hand and the other for the rule that follows:

B. "He who hollowed out a space in a haystack to make a sukkah therein – it is no sukkah [M. 1:8D-E].

C. "[The reason for] one [of the rulings] is on account of a [precautionary] decree [on account of the possibility of a person's using a sukkah as a] storehouse.

D. "[The reason for] the other [of the rulings] is on account of the exegesis, '"You shall make" (Deut. 16:13) – and not make use of what is ready-made.'

E. "Now I do not know which of the two rulings [of the Mishnah at hand] is on account of the consideration of not using the sukkah as a storehouse, and which one of them is on account of the exegesis, '"You shall make" – and not from what is ready-made.'"

F. Said R. Jeremiah, "Let us see [how we may work matters out on the basis of a further ruling in Yohanan's name].

G. "For R. Hiyya bar Abba said R. Yohanan said, 'On what account did they rule: Bundles of straw, wood, or brush – they do not make a sukkah roofing with them [M. 1:5A-B]?

H. "'[It is because] there are times that a person will come in from the field in the evening, with his bundle [of produce] on his back, and he might just push it up and leave it on top of his sukkah, so as to allow the produce to dry. Then he will reconsider the matter and determine to make use of [the bundles] for sukkah roofing. Yet the Torah has said, "You will make" (Deut. 16:13) – and not from what is ready-made.'

I. "Now since the rule at hand is on account of a precautionary decree [lest the farmer use the sukkah] as a storehouse [in the scenario just now described, it must follow that] the other ruling [about hollowing out a haystake and turning it into a sukkah] is on account of the exegesis of 'You shall make' – and not what is ready-made."

J. And R. Jacob? [What left him in doubt as to Yohanan's explanations for the two rulings, since, after all, the teaching cited by Hiyya bar Abba was available?]

K. In point of fact, he had not heard the tradition [in Yohanan's name] made available by R. Hiyya bar Abba.

L. Said R. Ashi, "[Can we really say that the operative consideration in the ruling about] bundles of straw, wood, or brush is only on account of the precautionary decree [against using the sukkah as a] storehouse, but there is no consideration at all of the exegesis, '"You shall make for yourself" – and not from what is ready-made'?

M. "And [as to the ruling concerning] hollowing out a space in a haystack, [may we say that the operative consideration is only] on account of the exegesis, '"You shall make for yourself" – and not from what is ready-made,' while the criterion based on the precautionary decree [against using the sukkah as a] storehouse is not operative? [Surely each of the two rulings is susceptible to both of the available explanations!]"

N. [Then how can we explain the position of] R. Yohanan, [who invokes only a single consideration for each case]?

O. [Yohanan] may say to you, "In the present case, in which it is taught in the Mishnah, They do not make a sukkah roofing with them [M. 1:5B], [that prohibition applies] to begin with, [12B], in which case they do not make the sukkah roofing on account of a precautionary decree against [using the sukkah for a] storehouse.

P. "But as to the rule as the Torah would have it, it would be a valid procedure. [Rabbi's decree against it, making the law more strict than the Torah requires, is in fact applicable only to begin with. But if one has actually done so, then after the fact the procedure is acceptable.]

Q. "And in that other case [hollowing out a hole in a haystack for use as a sukkah], in which case the Mishnah is phrased, It is no sukkah [at all] then, even after the fact, on the authority of the law of the Torah, it also does not constitute a valid sukkah."

X

Yerushalmi and Bavli on Mishnah-Tractate Sukkah 1:6

1:6

A. *"They make sukkah roofing with boards," the words of R. Judah.*

B. *And R. Meir prohibits doing so.*

C. *[If] one put on top of it a board which is four handbreadths broad, it is valid,*

D. *so long as one not sleep underneath [that particular board].*

Yerushalmi

I. Clarification of the subject of dispute at M. 1:6A, the character of the boards.

II. Same for M. 1:6C-D.

Bavli

I. Clarification of character of the boards under dispute at M. 1:6A-B, in light of M. 1:6C-D.

II. If one turned the boards on their sides.

The Yerushalmi's contribution is to supply comments on the several clauses of the Mishnah paragraph. Bavli's unit I presents a beautifully articulated dispute between Rab and Samuel, making points along the lines of those of the Yerushalmi but in a vastly expanded range of inquiry. Unit II goes on to a secondary issue. Comparing the Yerushalmi's to the Bavli's treatment of the passage at hand produces results entirely the same as the foregoing comparisons.

XI

Yerushalmi and Bavli on Mishnah-Tractate Sukkah 1:7

1:7

 A. *[15A] A timber roofing which had no plastering –*

 B. *R. Judah says, "The House of Shammai say, 'One loosens it and removes one [board] between each two.'*

 C. *"And the House of Hillel say, 'One either loosens it or removes one [board] from between each two.'"*

 D. *R. Meir says, "One removes one from between each two, and does not loosen [the others at all]."*

Yerushalmi

 I. Brief clarification of M. 1:7D.

Bavli

 I. Exegetical basis for the position of the two houses. Analysis of the positions of Judah and Meir.

XII

Yerushalmi and Bavli on Mishnah-Tractate Sukkah 1:8

1:8

 A. *One who makes a roof for his sukkah out of spits or with the side pieces of a bed –*

 B. *if there is a space between them equivalent to their own breadth,*

 C. *[the sukkah] is valid.*

 D. *One who hollowed out a space in a haystack to make a sukkah therein –*

 E. *it is no sukkah.*

Yerushalmi

 I. Clarification of M. 1:8B.

 II. Reason for the rule of M. 1:9D-E.

Bavli

 I. Does M. 1:8A-C refute the view of Huna, b. R. Joshua, re valid partition?

 II. Does M. 1:8A support the view of Ammi bar Tibiomi.

 III. Continues II.

 IV. Clarification of M. 1:8D.

The Yerushalmi's treatment is brief and routine. As to the Bavli, unit I brings the present passage into confrontation with its exact opposite, concerning the fence erected for creating a distinct domain. The same principle applies in both cases, namely, the fictive filling in of small gaps in a fence, roofing, or partition. If we do not fill in such a gap in one case, we ought not to think the principle applies in the other. On that basis the issue is worked out, and, as usual, the correct solution is to propose a distinction between the one case and the other. Unit II carries on the same exercise of bringing law in one topic to bear upon law in some other, and this is done by invoking the shared principle applicable to both. Unit III then reverts to the explication of the law as it applies to the sukkah in particular. Unit IV then completes the analysis of the Mishnah passage specifying limitations to the invalidity of the arrangement specified in the Mishnah; this further explains the underlying principle.

XIII
Yerushalmi and Bavli on Mishnah-Tractate Sukkah 1:9A-G

1:9A-G

A. *One who suspends the sides from above to below –*
B. *if the [the partitions] are three [or more] handbreadths above the ground,*
C. *[the sukkah] is invalid.*
D. *[If one builds the sides] from the ground upward,*
E. *if [they are] ten handbreadths above the ground,*
F. *[the sukkah] is valid.*
G. *R. Yose says, "Just as [the required height] from below to above [when the wall is built up from the ground] is ten handbreadths, "so [the required height] from above to below [when the wall is suspended from above toward the ground] is ten handbreadths [even though the bottom is not within three handbreadths of the ground]. [The operative criterion is the height of the partitions.]"*

Yerushalmi

I. Clarification of Yose's view, M. 1:9G.

Bavli

I. The relationship of this Mishnah paragraph to M. Er. 8:6.
II. Illustration and application of the law at hand.
III. Same as above.

Y. shows that three cited authorities concur that we draw an imaginary wall downward from above, which closes off the area beneath. B. goes over that same principle but in much different context and richer elaboration, and B. then proceeds to spell out the application of the law at hand. A comparison of the whole of Y. to the whole of B. would show that, while the principle at hand is the same – as it should be, since it is dictated by the Mishnah paragraph – the composition that follows in each Talmud is wholly distinct from the one in the other.

XIV

Yerushalmi and Bavli on Mishnah-Tractate Sukkah 1:9H-1:10

1:9H-1:10

   H.   *[17A] [If] one sets the sukkah roofing three handbreadths from the walls [of the sukkah], [the sukkah] is invalid.*

M. 1:9

   A.   *A house, [the roof of] which was damaged, and on [the gaps in the roof of which] one put sukkah roofing –*

   B.   *if the distance from the wall to the sukkah roofing is four cubits, it is invalid [as a sukkah].*

   C.   *And so too, [is the rule for] a courtyard which is surrounded by a peristyle.*

   D.   *A large sukkah, [the roofing of which] they surrounded with some sort of material with which they do not make sukkah roofing –*

   E.   *if there was a space of four cubits below it,*

   F.   *it is invalid [as a sukkah].*

M. 1:10

Yerushalmi

   I.   Clarification of M. 1:10B.

   II.   If one slept under inadequately roofed-over space, does one carry out his obligation to dwell in the sukkah?

   III.   Reversion to unit I, now with reference to M. 1:10D-F.

Bavli

   I.   Why was it necessary to give all three rulings, M. 1:9H, M. 1:10A-C, M. 1:10D-F? Each ruling had to be made explicit.

   II.   Amplification of M. 1:9H, M. 1:10A-B.

   III.   Different version of foregoing.

   IV.   If one diminished open space in sukkah roofing, the sukkah is validated. Reference to M. Oh. 10:1, 2.

   V.   M. 1:10A clarified.

   VI.   If one put sukkah roofing over a peristyle.

   VII.   Different version of foregoing.

   VIII.   Same issue as foregoing.

   IX.   A lath that protrudes from a sukkah.

Yerushalmi to M. 1:9H-1:10. Unit I draws upon the Mishnah paragraph to support a statement by Hiyya. Unit II clarifies the status of an invalid part of the roofing of an otherwise valid sukkah. Unit III reverts to the proposition of unit I.

Bavli to M. 1:9H-1:10. The sizable passage of Bavli at hand pursues its own interests and intersects with the Mishnah paragraph mainly to invoke that paragraph for illustrative purposes. Unit I starts with a familiar exercise of proving that the Mishnah does not repeat itself, the only word-for-word exegesis. Unit II asks an independent question, namely, the comparison between two sorts of invalid space in sukkah roofing – one, a gap, the other, a filling of invalid materials. Each is supposedly subject to a distinct minimum measure for invalidating the sukkah roofing. Unit III provides a second version of the same dispute, and this, as we see, provides a mirror image of the discussion at M. 1:6. It seems to me the person who has made up these protracted discussions had a rather sophisticated and comprehensive notion of how he wished to pursue the issue at hand. To the Mishnah paragraph, the entire discussion is tangential. Its principle is important in its own right. Unit IV is continuous with the foregoing. At unit V we revert to the Mishnah paragraph, now to M. 1:10A. This passage has been constructed around its own framework – Ishmael's sayings in his father's name – and not around our Mishnah passage. Unit VI raises a theoretical question but is inserted because it relates to M. 1:10C. But the issue is the theory of the law, not the amplification of the case of the peristyle. Unit VII is continuous with the foregoing. Unit VIII provides an illustration of the same matter. Unit IX does not seem to contribute in any way to the amplification of the rule of the Mishnah paragraph. As a composition it hangs together on its own.

XV

Yerushalmi and Bavli on Mishnah-Tractate Sukkah 1:11A-D

1:11A-D

A. *One who makes his sukkah in the shape of a cone or who leaned it up against a wall –*

B. *R. Eliezer declares it invalid,*

C. *because it has no roof.*

D. *And sages declare it valid.*

Yerushalmi

I. Citation and amplification of T. Suk. 1:10B-D.

Bavli

I. Same as in Yerushalmi.

II. Continuation of foregoing.

At the risk of taxing the reader's patience, I present a comparison of Y. unit I and B. units I-II. Here, once more, we see that, even when both Talmuds wish to make use of the same materials and say much the same thing, Bavli has no inclination to follow matters in the way that the Yerushalmi has done.

Yerushalmi

I.

A. R. Eliezer concedes [in regard to M. 1:12A-C] that if its roof is a handbreadth in size,

B. or if it was a handbreadth above the ground,

C. it is valid [T. Suk. 1:10B-D].

D. It has been taught: One who makes his sukkah like a house in the forest of Lebanon [so that the tree trunks serve as the walls, and the sukkah roofing is spread above] – it is valid.

E. For whom is such a ruling required?

F. Is it not required to clarify the position of R. Eliezer? [To him the issue is whether or not there is a clearly discernible roof, M. 1:12C, not whether the walls have been erected for the purpose of the sukkah.]

Bavli

I.

A. It has been taught on Tannaite authority:

B. R. Eliezer concedes that if one raised [the sukkah] a handbreadth above the ground or moved it a handbreadth away from the wall [as the case may be], it is a valid sukkah. [Now we have a roof, constituted either by the raised sukkah or by the space between the sukkah and the wall, with the open air space deemed fictively filled in, as we recall] [T. Suk. 1:10B-D].

C. What is the reason behind rabbis' ruling?

D. The inclining wall of the tent is deemed to fall into the category of a tent.

II.

A. Abayye came upon R. Joseph, who was sleeping in a sukkah in a bridal bed [with curtains that sloped down from a point, not forming a roof]. He said to him, "In accord with whose opinion do you do so? [You clearly regard it as all right to sleep in a sukkah in a covered bed. Presumably this is because you do not regard the canopy as intervening and forming a roof between the bed and the sukkah roofing.] Is this in accord with R. Eliezer [who does not regard a sloping roof as a roof at all]? Have you then abandoned the [majority] view of rabbis and acted in accord with R. Eliezer [a minority]?"

B. He said to him, "There is a baraita [a Tannaite teaching alternative to the version now in the Mishnah] that has matters reversed: 'R. Eliezer declares [the arrangement] valid, and sages declare it invalid.'"

C. He said to him, "Do you then abandon the version of the Mishnah and act in accord with the alternative version of a baraita [of lesser reliability]?

D. He said to him, "The version of the Mishnah in any case stands for the viewpoint only of an individual, for it has been taught on Tannaite authority:

E. "He who makes his sukkah in the shape of a cone or who leaned it up against a wall –

F. "R. Nathan says, 'R. Eliezer declares it invalid, because it has no roof, and sages declare it valid.'"

The Yerushalmi's interest in the passage of the Tosefta is in comparing two teachings, Tosefta's with the one that clarifies Eliezer's position. The whole then serves to explain what is at issue at M. 1:12C. The Bavli's interest is expressed at I.C-D, rabbis' position. Unit II then works out the implications of the matter. At issue for the Bavli are versions of the positions of Eliezer and sages, on the one side, and the decided law, on the other. The exegetical focus, then, is practical rather than theoretical. But for our purposes the main point is not to characterize the one Talmud as against the other. Rather, we want to see whether, when the two Talmuds deal with the same Mishnah paragraph, they say pretty much the same thing. They do not.

XVI

Yerushalmi and Bavli on Mishnah-Tractate Sukkah 1:11E-J

1:11E-J

E. *A large reed mat,*

F. *[if] one made it for lying, it is susceptible to uncleanness, and [so] they do not make sukkah roofing out of it.*

G. *[If one made it] for sukkah roofing, they make sukkah roofing out of it, and it is not susceptible to uncleanness.*

H. *R. Eliezer says, "All the same are a small one and a large one:*

I. *"[if] one made it for lying, it is susceptible to uncleanness, and they do not make sukkah roofing out of it.*

J. *"[If one made it for] sukkah roofing, they do make sukkah roofing out of it, and it is not susceptible to uncleanness."*

Yerushalmi

I. Clarification of M. 1:11E-G. What sort of mats are under discussion.

Bavli

I. Contrast of M. 1:11F and M. 1:11G.

II. T. 1:10E-L.

III. Types of mats and susceptibility to uncleanness.

The Yerushalmi's treatment of the matter is informative, not speculative. As to Bavli, unit I subjects the formulation of the Mishnah to a close reading, which allows reference to secondary considerations. Unit II is cited not only to complement the Mishnah but also to set the stage for unit III, which alludes directly to II.I. Unit III amplifies the matter of mats, such as at M. 1:11E. At the same time the issues of M. 1:11E-J – the consideration for what is susceptible to uncleanness – are worked out. So the entire construction is devoted to the exegesis of the Mishnah-paragraph.

XVII

The Autonomy of the Bavli's Program of Exegesis of the Mishnah

The Bavli and the Yerushalmi assuredly stand autonomous from one another. The authorship of the Bavli in its own way works out a singular and independent program of exegesis and amplification of the Mishnah. Word-for-word correspondences are few and, on the whole, peripheral. Where materials are shared, moreover, they derive from either the Mishnah or the Tosefta or some antecedent convention of exegesis.[1] But in all instances of shared language or conventional hermeneutics the framers of the Bavli worked things out on their own. They in no way accepted the Yerushalmi as a model for how they said things let alone for the bulk of what they said. What is shared, moreover, derives principally from the Mishnah. It comes, secondarily, from some sort of conventional program (partly encapsulated, also, in the Tosefta). The Tosefta has not dictated to the Bavli's authorship a topical or logical program, it has merely contributed occasional passages for systematic analysis, much as the Mishnah has contributed a much larger volume of passages for systematic analysis. In any event the Bavli's authors developed inherited intellectual conventions in a strikingly independent way. That fact leads us to see the Bavli's authorship's composition as an essentially autonomous statement, standing on its own, borrowing from prior compilations pretty much what suited its purpose – that alone.

On the other hand, the Bavli and the Yerushalmi most certainly do form a cogent part of a larger, continuous statement, that of "the one whole Torah of Moses, our rabbi" or, in modern theological language, a canon, that is, Judaism. That premise of all study of the canon of formative Judaism stands firm. Nothing we have reviewed leads us to doubt its validity for those documents. The particular aspect of continuity at hand, however, requires specification. How is the Bavli continuous with the Yerushalmi? *The Bavli meets the Yerushalmi in the Mishnah.* The two also come together, in markedly diminished measure, in the Tosefta and, still less, in some shared phrases deriving from post-Mishnaic authorities (e.g., those of the third-century masters Yohanan and Simeon b. Laqish). So in one specific way the two documents not only intersect but prove at one with one another and therefore continuous.

In somewhat more general ways, too, they wish to do much the same thing, which is to subject the Mishnah to a process of explanation and amplification.

---

[1] We shall see the same phenomenon when in Chapter Five we ask how the Bavli intersects with Sifra, Leviticus Rabbah, and Pesiqta deRab Kahana. What we shall see is that all three present in common a treatment of Lev. 23:40, but that the Bavli's authorship in connection with that same verse has an utterly distinct set of questions, out of all relationship with the authorships of Sifra and of Leviticus Rabbah = Pesiqta deRab Kahana. The points in common, which are verbally identical in all the four documents, are minor and peripheral to the foci of each document's authorship. So where we do find intersections, we also uncover evidence of the essential autonomy of the several authorships.

While the authors of the Bavli developed their own principles of hermeneutics, composition, and redaction, still, the upshot of their work, the Bavli as a whole, in the heavenly academy cannot have baffled their predecessors, who had earlier created the Yerushalmi. Apart from disagreements on tertiary details, the later of the two sets of authorities found themselves entirely at home in the conceptions, rhetoric, and documents created by their antecedent counterparts. That seems self-evident proof of the continuity of the Bavli with the Yerushalmi. If the two then turn out to be autonomous as well as continuous with one another, the real problem of nuance and differentiation is presented by matters of connection. These have forthwith to be divided into two parts: first, the connection of one document to the other; second, the connection of both documents to other components of the larger rabbinic canon. Here, once more, we find ourselves making self-evident observations.

To deal with the second question in summary fashion, the two documents are not only connected to one another but also stand essentially autonomous of the rest of the rabbinic canon, except (by definition) for the Mishnah and the Tosefta, which they serve. How so? In various passages, as we have noticed, we find shared materials in the two Talmuds and a common program of logic and rhetoric. What is shared between them, however, rarely also finds a place in other components of the canon of ancient Judaism. That is to say, while the two Talmuds constantly quote and explain the Mishnah, no other rabbinic document takes so sustained an interest in the Mishnah, or, indeed, much interest at all. So in the rabbinic canon the Talmuds occupy a place entirely their own, secondary to and continuous with the Mishnah-Tosefta. That place turns out to be set apart from the remainder of the canon. Counterparts to the Talmuds' treatment of the Mishnah rarely appear in any other rabbinic composition. The exception to the rule will be Sifra and, to a lesser degree, the two Sifrés. These in places do go over the same matters in much the same way as do the two Talmuds. But the exception proves null when we realize that, where Sifra and the two Sifrés share sizable statements with the two Talmuds (severally or together), it is ordinarily a common interest in the scriptural foundations of a Mishnaic law or, to a markedly diminished degree, one of the Tosefta. So that is hardly an exception since both Talmuds and the exegetical compilations on Leviticus, Numbers, and Deuteronomy meet in a common interest in the Mishnah and Tosefta. Why – to conclude with the obvious – do the two Talmuds stand essentially apart from the remainder of the canon? The two Talmuds form around the Mishnah, while most of the rest of the canon takes shape around books of the Hebrew Scriptures.

The other question – the connection of Bavli to Yerushalmi – brings us back to our main point, the issue of the traditionality of the Bavli, and therefore is the more important of the two. Let me unpack the question at hand. What we want to know concerns the Bavli in particular. The first and most fundamental question is this: Does the Bavli bear a message of its own? Or does the document essentially rest upon, and continue, the work of the Yerushalmi? If the Yerushalmi dictates the program and policy – the hermeneutic and rhetoric – of the Bavli, then we cannot speak of the Bavli as a document on its own. Its logic, its mode of inquiry, its rhetoric, its mode of thought – all these will turn out to belong to its precursors. What would define the Bavli then would be its authors ability to do better or to say at greater length what others had already done and said. In that case the Bavli would have to take its place as a secondary and subordinate component of that sector of the canon of Judaism defined, for all time, by the concerns and the circumstances of the framers of the Yerushalmi. In terms of the choices before us, the Bavli would emerge as traditional and not an essentially fresh systemic construction.

The contrary proposition is that while the Bavli shares with the Yerushalmi a common program and purpose, its authors carry out that program in their own way. By this thesis they should appear to define that purpose in response to interests shaped in their distinct context and framework. Then we may claim that the Bavli presents its own message, a systemic statement of an original character, much as in reshaping and reconstituting received conventions, the composer or the artist accomplishes something fundamentally original. Stated simply, this other proposition will maintain that the authorship of the Bavli accomplishes its own goals. True, its logic, its inquiry, its mode of thought may run parallel to those of the Yerushalmi. But that is only because they derive from sources common to both documents. In terms of this second hypothesis, the Bavli flows not from the Yerushalmi but from the Mishnah. That is the source, also, of the Yerushalmi and hence the cause of the parallel course of both documents. According to this second proposition, the Bavli is not secondary. It is not subordinate to the Yerushalmi in that larger sector of the canon of Judaism defined by the Mishnah.

As between these two propositions, the materials we have examined decisively settle the question in favor of the second. At point after point, we found the two documents connected not only *to* the common source but mainly or solely *through* that source. Where they go over the same problems, it is because the shared source presented these problems to the authors of both documents. In our comparison of the two documents, we found that the rhetoric and literary program of the Bavli owed remarkably little to those of its predecessor. The comparisons of actual texts yielded decisive evidence for several propositions.

First, there is remarkably little verbatim correspondence. The Bavli's authors scarcely ever made use of extensive constructions and only rarely of brief formulations also found in the Yerushalmi. So far as our modest sample suggests, they never did so when it came to detailed expository arguments and analyses. Where there is verbatim sharing, it is a Mishnah paragraph or Tosefta passage that is held in common, on the one side, or a prior, severely abbreviated lemma of an earlier Amoraic authority, on the other. Where the two sets of authors deal with such a shared lemma, however, each group does exactly what it wishes, imputing words to the prior authority (as if the said authority had actually spoken those words) simply not known to the other group.

Second and more important, what the framers of the Bavli wished to do with a saying of an earlier Amoraic authority in no way responded to the policy or program of the Yerushalmi's authors. Quite to the contrary, where both sets of authors shared sayings of Yohanan and Simeon b. Laqish, we noted that each set went its own way. In no aspect did the Yerushalmi's interest in these shared sayings affect the Bavli's treatment of them. The point in common was that prior authorities explained the same passage of the Mishnah. From that simple starting point, the Bavli's authors went in a direction not imagined by the Yerushalmi's. The power and intellectual force of the Bavli's authors in that context vastly overshadowed the capacities of the Yerushalmi's.

What the systematic analysis of a single chapter tells us, therefore, may be stated very briefly. The Yerushalmi and the Bavli are alike in their devotion to the exegesis and amplification of the Mishnah. Viewed as literary constructions, they share, in addition, a basic exegetical program, which flows from the Mishnah and in fundamental ways is defined by the inner logic and cogency of the Mishnah. In relationship to the Yerushalmi, therefore the Bavli's framers pursued their own interests in their own way. They reveal independence of mind and originality of taste. It must follow that the Bavli is sufficiently unlike the Yerushalmi to be judged as an autonomous document, disconnected from and unlike its predecessor in all the ways that matter.

True, in general the Bavli falls into the same classification as does the Yerushalmi. But in detail, it presents its own message in its own way. The genus is the same, the species not. The opening hypothesis has yielded a negative result. When confronting the exegesis of the Mishnah, which is its indicative trait and definitive task, the authorship of the Bavli does not continue and complete the work of antecedents. Quite to the contrary, that authorship made its statement essentially independent of its counterpart and earlier document.

That fact now defines the next stage of our inquiry: the composition of the Bavli in its own terms, in relationship to the other antecedent documents. For at issue is not the general relationship, now established, between the Bavli and the prior systematic exegesis of the same document to which the Bavli is devoted. It is the very specific ties between the Bavli and the *entirety* of the prior writings on the same subject. In this specific inquiry into treatments among diverse authorships of a single topical program, we shall uncover a variety of facts upon the basis of which to reach solid conclusions for the case at hand. The next three chapters tell the story.

Chapter Three

The Bavli and its Sources in the Case
of Tractate Sukkah Chapter One

I

Traditions of, or Ad Hoc Decisions on, Mishnah-Exegesis

Tradition is supposed to describe a process or a chain of transmission of received materials, refined and corrected but handed on not only unimpaired, but essentially intact. A traditional exegesis of the Mishnah will therefore cite a passage and gloss it, then another and gloss that. Secondary consideration of issues of principle, speculation on larger principles – these will not serve as primary vehicles of exegesis. A systemic reading of the Mishnah-paragraph, by contrast, will bring to bear upon the Mishnah a sustained and cogent program. The Mishnah will dictate topic, but the generative problematic of discourse will derive from the system that prevails and – merely by the way – attends, also, to the Mishnah-paragraph at hand. That choice will guide us in our reading of the first of the three sustained verbatim samples of our tractate, one which shows us how the authorship of the Bavli reads a given Mishnah-paragraph.

I have introduced brief observations on the first ten pericopae, to show the reader why I maintain we deal with well-composed, sustained and cogent propositions, syllogistic discourse with a beginning, middle, and end, following a clear program of inquiry. That program has told the authorship before us how not merely to put together diverse sayings, deriving from various times and persons, into a reasonably coherent statement. On the contrary, we have not a composite but a composition, with sayings all placed so as to serve the larger interests of argument or polemic of the single – and therefore, final – authorship. Beyond the observations on the opening units, I have not continued that mode of commentary, because there is no need to repeat a single, to me self-evident, point. Either we deal with the compositions of authorships capable of making diverse materials over into a single unfolding statement and argument, or we have in hand composites of discrete materials, ·patched together into a single continuous, but not really coherent and cogent, repertoire. I take the view that, in the aggregate, the Bavli's large scale discourse constitute not composites but compositions, and that in the Bavli we have not a scrapbook but a set of sizable statements of substantial integrity and cogency. But it is for the reader to decide through the scrutiny of the several units that follow, here and in Chapters Four and Five.

II

The Text: Bavli to Mishnah-Tractate Sukkah 1:1

I give the text in my own translation[1] and mark the text to indicate the presence of materials shared with prior documents (excluding the Yerushalmi, for reasons spelled out in Chapter Two). That is the sole purpose of this survey. The Mishnah-passage is given in italics. Then I use bold-face type to indicate that a passage occurs in an earlier compilation. I do not pay attention to the appearance of a passage in another tractate of the Bavli, in the theory that all of the Bavli's thirty-seven tractates came to their present state in more or less the same period of time. It would follow that the appearance of a passage in more than one tractate will tell us nothing about how the same general authorship has made use of materials produced in a prior period. My comments on each passage are limited to some redactional issues and addressed mainly to the question at hand. My sample of Chapter One covers Mishnah-tractate Sukkah 1:1 (2a-9a, inclusive).

I followed a simple procedure to assess the points of intersection with the documents redacted prior to the Bavli. First I surveyed the cross-references given in the Bavli itself. Where Bavli's editors referred to a Tosefta passage, I give that passage in bold face type, even though the wording is not exactly the same as that which we find in the Tosefta. Then, following A. Hyman, *Torah hakketubah vehammesurah,* I reviewed references in prior compilations of scriptural exegeses to all verses cited in the Bavli. I surveyed, in particular, Sifra, the two Sifrés, Fathers According to Rabbah Nathan, Genesis Rabbah, Leviticus Rabbah, Pesiqta deRab Kahana, Pesiqta Rabbati, and the other compilations closed by A.D. 600, in all instances accepting the view of the dating of documents as given by M. D. Heer in his authoritative table in *Encyclopaedia Judaica* s.v., *Midrash.* In this way I was able to determine the extent to which the authorship of the Bavli drew upon that available exegetical literature in their larger composition.

1:1 A-F

    A. *A sukkah which is taller than twenty cubits is invalid.*

    B. *R. Judah declares it valid.*

    C. *And one which is not ten handbreadths high,*

    D. *one which does not have three walls,*

    E. *or one, the light of which is greater than its shade,*

    F. *is invalid.*

---

[1]*The Talmud of Babylonia. An American Translation.* VI. *Tractate Sukkah* (Chico, 1984: Scholars Press for Brown Judaic Studies).

I.

    A. We have learned in the Mishnah at another passage: *The crossbeam above an alley-entry which is higher than twenty cubits [is invalid, and one therefore] should diminish it [making it lower]. R. Judah says, "It is not necessary to do so" [M. Er. 1:1A-B].*

    B. What differentiates the case of the sukkah, in which instance the rule is formulated in the language of unfitness [without remedy], from the case of the alley-way, in which instance the framer of the Mishnah has specified the remedy [for an improper arrangement]?

    C. Since [the religious requirement of building] a sukkah derives [from the authority] of the Torah, the framer of the passage uses the language, "unfit," while, since the arrangement creating an artificial alley-way derives from the authority of rabbis, the framer of the passage has taught the remedy [namely, diminishing the height of the crossbar].

    D. If you prefer, I shall propose a different solution:

    E. Even in matters deriving from the authority of the Torah one may well teach the required remedy. But in the case of the sukkah, with its numerous rules, the framer of the passage has simply framed matters in terms of unfitness. In the case of the alley-way, without numerous rules and regulations, the framer of the passage taught the remedy [for an improper arrangement].

The issue derives from the Mishnah-passage as it intersects with a counterpart rule elsewhere. No one suggests that the issue at hand derives from a prior tradition, even one of interpretation. The basic proposition at hand maintains that all components of the law join together to make a few utterly cogent and harmonious statements – a premise of exegesis particularly critical to a systemic hermeneutic, but not urgent, I should imagine, for a traditional one. But that proposal surely is subject to argument.

II.

    A. What is the scriptural source for the rule [that the sukkah may not be taller than twenty cubits]?

    B. Said Rabbah, "It is because [Scripture] has stated, 'So that your coming generations may know that I made the children of Israel dwell in sukkot' (Lev. 23:43).

    C. "[If the roof is] up to twenty cubits, someone will know that he is dwelling in a sukkah. If it is higher than twenty cubits, one will not know that he is dwelling in a sukkah, because [the roof] will be out of [the ordinary line of] sight."

    D. R. Zira said, "The proof derives from here: 'And there shall be a booth [sukkah] for a shadow in the daytime from the heat' (Is. 4:6).

    E. "[If the roof is] up to twenty cubits, someone will sit in the shadow of the [roof of the] sukkah. If it is higher than twenty cubits, one will not sit in the shadow of the [roof of the] sukkah [since the shadow will be cast by the walls entirely], but rather, in the shadow of the walls."

    F. Said to him Abayye, "But if someone made his sukkah in a glen between two hills [where there is no sun], would you maintain that in such a case it is not a valid sukkah? [Surely not!]"

G. He said to him, "In that case, if one removes the two mountains there
    will be shade deriving from the roof of the sukkah, but here, if you
    remove the walls of the sukkah, there will not be any shadow cast by the
    sukkah at all."

H. And Raba said, "The proof derives from here: 'You shall dwell in sukkot
    for seven days' (Lev. 23:42), is what the Torah has said. For all seven
    days, go out of your permanent dwelling and stay in a temporary
    dwelling.

I. "Now [if the roof is] twenty cubits high, someone will make the sukkah
    a merely temporary dwelling. If it is higher than that, someone will not
    make the sukkah a temporary dwelling but a permanent one." [Slotki, p.
    2, n. 13: Such a high structure requires firm foundations and walls, and
    these give it the characteristic of a permanent abode.]

J. Said to him Abayye, "But if so, if one has made the walls of his sukkah
    out of iron and then made a sukkah-roofing on them, would it be the case
    that this would not be a valid sukkah? [It certainly is a valid sukkah.]"

K. He said to him, "This is what I was saying to you: If the roof is up to
    twenty cubits in height, which is the sort of house that a person makes
    his temporary dwelling, if he makes it his permanent dwelling, he
    [nevertheless] carries out his obligation. But if the roof is higher than
    twenty cubits, which is the sort of house a man makes a permanent
    dwelling, if one makes it a temporary dwelling, he has not carried out his
    obligation."

L. [2B] [We now review the proofs of Rabbah, Zira, and Raba, and ask what
    is at fault that all parties do not concur on any one of the three proposed
    proof-texts.] All parties do not concur with the proof of Rabbah, for his
    proof-text depends upon the knowledge of the coming generations.

M. All parties do not concur with the proof-text of R. Zira, for the proof-
    text he cites refers to the days of the Messiah.

N. But R. Zira [would respond], "If so, the verse should make use of the
    language of a canopy: 'A canopy will serve for a shade in the daytime.'
    Why does the verse say, 'A sukkah shall serve for a shade in the
    daytime'? It serves to make two points [one concerning the proper
    height of a sukkah, the other concerning matters in the messianic age]."

O. Likewise as to the proof-text adduced by Raba, all parties do not concur,
    on account of the question raised by Abayye.

The syllogism that underlines the case is that the rules of the Mishnah
derive from Scripture. The power of the proof-text then is logically and
systematically to link a particular rule to a general, and scriptural, rule. Here too
the systemic focus is clear. For I maintain that the issue is not one of mere
authority, that is, tradition, but as is clear at L, something more: the cogency of
all proof-texts – once again, not a traditional but a systemic question. For a
traditional statement can suffice with whatever proof-text comes to hand and has
no need to sort out diverse possibilities. A systemic statement must link all the
data into a single cogent composition, as is surely accomplished here.

III.

A. [With reference to the proof-texts adduced in unit II we turn to the dispute
    at M. 1:1A-B]: In accord with what authority is the following statement:

R. Josiah said Raba said, "The dispute [of the Mishnah at M. 1:1A-B] treats a case in which the walls of the sukkah do not touch the sukkah-roof. But if the walls do touch the sukkah-roof, then even though the roof is higher than twenty cubits, the sukkah is valid."

B. In accord with whose view? It accords with Rabbah, who has said, "The reason is that the roof [if higher] will be out of sight. But since the walls touch the sukkah-roofing, the sukkah-roofing is not out of sight. [The eye will be led up the walls to the sukkah-roofing, which forms a single visual image with the walls.]"

C. In accord with whose view is the following statement that R. Huna made in the name of Rab: "The dispute concerns a case in which the roof is only four cubits by four cubits in area. But if it is larger than four cubits by four cubits in area, then even if the roofing is higher than twenty cubits, the sukkah is valid."

D. In accord with whom? It accords with the view of R. Zira, who has said, "It is because of the need to cast a proper shadow." Now since there is ample space in the sukkah-roofing, the shadow of the sukkah [will be suitable even though the roof is higher than twenty cubits].

E. In accord with which authority is the following statement which R. Hanan bar Rabbah made in the name of Rab: "The dispute concerns a case in which the sukkah can hold only someone's head, the greater part of his body, and his table, then even if the roof is taller than twenty cubits, the sukkah will be valid"?

F. In accord with whom? In accord with none of them [since even if the sukkah can hold more than one's head, etc., the stated reasons still pertain.]

G. Now R. Josiah surely differs from R. Huna and R. Hanan bar Rabbah, for they define a minimum measure for the extent [of the sukkah], while he does not do so.

H. But may we maintain that R. Huna and R. Hanan bar Rabbah differ as to what renders the sukkah valid?

I. The proposed theory will be as follows: one party maintains that what renders the sukkah valid is the four cubits of sukkah-roofing, and the other holds that what renders the sukkah valid is the capacity to contain the head, the greater part of the body, and the table [of a resident].

J. No, that theory is not valid. All parties concur that what renders a sukkah valid is the capacity to hold the head, the greater part of one's body, and the table. But in the present case, this is the point of difference:

K. One party holds that at issue in the Mishnah's dispute is a case of a sukkah which indeed holds one's head, the greater part of one's body, and his table. But if [a sukkah] holds more than one's head, the greater part of one's body, and his table, all parties concur that a sukkah with a roof above twenty cubits remains valid.

L. The other party [Judah, M. 1:1B] maintains the view that at issue in the Mishnah's dispute is a case of a sukkah from a size which suffices to hold one's head, the greater part of one's body, and his table, to a size of four cubits. But if the sukkah is larger than four cubits, all parties concur that the sukkah is valid.

What has been said above applies here without qualification.

IV.

A. [The specification of the cited authorities, III A, C, E, on the minimum requirements of the sukkah, now comes under discussion in its own terms.] The following objection was raised:

B. A sukkah which is taller than twenty cubits is invalid.

C. R. Judah declares it valid [M. 1:1A-B], even up to forty or fifty cubits.

D. Said R. Judah, "M'SH B: The sukkah of Helene in Lud was twenty cubits tall, and sages went in and out, when visiting her, and not one of them said a thing."

E. They said to him, "It was because she is a woman, and a woman is not liable to keep the commandment of sitting in a sukkah."

F. He said to them, "Now did she not have seven sons [who are disciples of sages, and all of them were dwelling in that same sukkah!"] [T. Suk. 1:1A-E].

G. "And furthermore, everything she ever did was done in accord with the instruction of sages."

H. Now what need do I have for this additional reason: "Furthermore, everything she ever did was done in accord with the instructions of sages"?

I. This is the sense of what he said to them: "Now, if you say that the sons were minors, and minors are exempt from the religious duty of dwelling in the sukkah, since she had seven sons, it is not possible that among them was not a single one who no longer needed his mother's tending [and so would be required to dwell on his own in the sukkah]."

J. "And if, further, you should maintain that a minor who no longer needs his mother's tending is subject to the law only on the authority of rabbis, and that woman paid no attention to rules that rested only on the authority of the rabbis, come and note the following: 'And furthermore, everything she ever did was done in accord with the instructions of sages'."

K. [We now revert to the issue with which we began, namely, the comparison of the story at hand to the reasons adduced by the authorities at unit III:] Now with references to one who said, the dispute applies to a case in which the walls of the sukkah do not touch the sukkah-roofing, would a queen dwell in a sukkah, the walls of which do not touch the sukkah-roofing?

L. [3A] [Indeed so! The reason is that] the space makes possible good ventilation.

M. But in the view of the one who has said that the dispute pertains to a small sukkah, would a queen ever dwell in a small sukkah?

N. Said Rabbah bar R. Ada, "At issue in the dispute is solely a case of a sukkah which is made with many small cubbies."

O. But would a queen take up residence in a sukkah that was subdivided into many small cubbies?

P. Said R. Ashi, "At issue is only [a large sukkah which had] such recesses.

Q. "Rabbis take the view that the queen's sons were dwelling in a sukkah of absolutely valid traits, while she dwelled in the recesses on account of modesty [i.e., not showing her face among the men], and it was on that account that rabbis said nothing to her [about her dwelling in what was, in fact, an invalid part of the sukkah].

R. "And R. Judah maintains the position that her sons were dwelling along with her [in the cubbyholes of the sukkah], and even so, the rabbis did not criticize what she was doing [which proves that the small cubbies of the sukkah were valid]."

The unfolding of this discourse shows us the larger traits of our document. The case is not introduced for the sake of preservation or even exemplification of the law. It is subjected to an analysis in terms of the larger program of the framer of the complete discussion. That is a mark of the systemic program, which draws into a single, sustained and on-going discourse the entirety of the received materials chosen for analysis.

V.

A. Said R. Samuel bar Isaac, "The law is that a valid sukkah must be able to contain a person's head, the greater part of his body, and his table."

B. Said R. Abba to him, "In accord with which party is this rule? Does it concur with the view of the house of Shammai *[at M. 2:7: He whose head and the greater part of whose body are in the sukkah, but whose table is in the house – the House of Shammai declare invalid. And the House of Hillel declare valid]."*

C. He said to him, "Then in accord with whose opinion [might one allege that this is decided]?"

D. There are those who report [the matter in the following terms:]

E. Said R. Abba, "And who says [that the law is as] you [have stated]?"

F. He said to him, "It is in accord with the House of Shammai, and do not move from that view."

G. R. Nahman bar Isaac objected [to the thesis of Abba, B]: "How [do we know that] the House of Shammai and the House of Hillel debate about a small sukkah, [so that the conclusion drawn at A, B would follow, in line with M. 2:7]? Perhaps the dispute concerns a large sukkah.

H. "It would then involve the case of one who sat at the entrance of the shadowed [part of the large sukkah], with his table in his house.

I. "The House of Shammai then maintain that we rule by decree [that such an arrangement is unacceptable], lest the person be drawn [into the house] after his table.

J. "The House of Hillel take the view that we make no such decree.

K. "From a close reading of the language of the Mishnah itself the same conclusion may be drawn, for it has been taught: *He whose head and the greater part of whose body are in the sukkah, but whose table is in the house – the House of Shammai declare invalid. And the House of Hillel declare valid [M. 2:7].*

L. "Now if matters were [as you say, that is, if the dispute involved a small sukkah, then the framer of the Mishnah should have used the language,] '... holds or does not hold... [one's head, the greater part of the body, etc.].'"

M. Now do they really not dispute concerning the validity of a small sukkah?

N. And has it not been taught on Tannaite authority: [A sukkah that holds one's head, the greater part of his body, and his table is valid. Rabbi says, "It is valid only if it is at least four cubits by four cubits."

O. And it has further been taught on Tannaite authority: Rabbi says, "Any sukkah that is not at least four cubits by four cubits is invalid."

P. And sages say, "Even if it holds only 'his head, and the greater part of his body, it is valid."

Q. Now note that there is no reference to one's table at all!

R. The cited [teachings on Tannaite authority] present inconsistencies among themselves, so would it not follow that one of them represents the view of the House of Shammai and the other the view of the House of Hillel? [At issue then is the validity of a small sukkah.]

S. Said Mar Zutra, "The Mishnah-paragraph before us also [supports the same view]. Take note that a close reading sustains it: *The House of Shammai declare invalid, and the House of Hillel declare valid.*

T. "Now if [at issue were a large sukkah, used in an improper manner, such as was proposed above,] then it should read, 'The House of Shammai say, "The user has not carried out his obligation,: and the House of Hillel say, "The user has carried out his obligation."' [At issue would be not the character of the sukkah but the use made of it by the owner.]"

U. But there is yet a problem, [since the language at hand is,] He whose head... [etc., as Nahman bar Isaac noted earlier, Gff.].

V. It must follow that there is a dispute on two matters, a dispute first about a small sukkah, second, about a large sukkah. The passage then presents a lacuna, and this is its proper wording:

W. He whose head and the greater part of whose body were in the sukkah, but whose table was in the house –

X. the House of Shammai say, "He has not carried out his obligation."

Y. And the House of Hillel say, "He has carried out his obligation."

Z. And he whose sukkah is able to contain only his head and the greater part of his body alone –

AA. the House of Shammai declare [the sukkah] invalid.

BB. And the House of Hillel declare it valid.

The issue of proof-texts finds its counterpart in the concern for the authorities behind a rule and the consistency of the positions held by those authoritives, respectively. The reason the framer of the discourse asks about authority is not to determine the correct decision of law. It is to ascertain whether and how diverse authorities sustain cogent and consistent positions – once more an inquiry into structure and system, not merely tradition.

VI.

A. [Reverting to the discussion of Rabbis' opinion, V N, above:] Who stands behind the following teaching, which our rabbis have taught on Tannaite authority:

B. A building that is not at least four cubits by four cubits [is not truly a "house," and so] is exempt from the requirement of placing a *mezuzah* and of building a parapet [Deut. 22:8], does not contract uncleanness through a *nega* [Lev. 14:34], is not permanently assigned to the ownership of a purchaser in line with the rules governing the transfer of real property in a walled city [Lev. 25:29]; on its account those who are in the battle line do not return from battle [if they have not used the house a requisite period of time, Deut. 20:5]; people do not provide an *erub*-meal for it [symbolically to create joint ownership among the houses in a given courtyard so as to permit carrying within the entire courtyard in the theory that the whole constitutes a single property] or a *shittuf*-meal for it [so as symbolically to create joint ownership among the courtyards of a single alley-way, for the same purpose as above]; people do not leave an erub-meal in such a house [so as to make it the locus of the symbolic joint meal]; [3B] they do not make of it an extension [outpost] between two towns [regarding such a building as a house equally location in two distinct towns, with the result that the two towns are regarded as one, so that people may walk on the Sabbath from one to the other]; and brothers or partners may not partition it [since it is too small].

C. [Since, in all of the cited matters, Scripture speaks of a house, and Rabbi has said that a sukkah is valid only if it is four cubits by four cubits,] may one say that the cited catalogue represents the views of Rabbi and not those of the rabbis [who would regard a building of smaller size as falling into the category of a house]?

D. You may say that the catalogue represents the views even of the rabbis.

E. They take the views stated there only with reference to a sukkah, which may serve as a random dwelling [not as a permanent house, and hence may be smaller than the normal proportions that would define a house]. But in respect to the definition of a house, which must be able to serve as a permanent dwelling, even rabbis would concur that if a building is four cubits by four cubits, it constitutes a suitable dwelling for people, and if not, it does not constitute a suitable dwelling for people.

F. [Proceeding to the analysis of the passage cited above, B, we move forward:] A master has said, "It is exempt from the requirement of placing a *mezuzah* and building a parapet, does not contract uncleanness through a *nega,* is not permanently assigned to the ownership of a purchaser in line with the rules governing the transfer of real property in a walled city; on its account those who are in the battle line do not return from battle."

G. What is the [scriptural] basis for that view?

H. The reason is that in all of these instances, Scripture makes reference to a house. [In no case among those listed is a building of such modest size regarded as a house.]

I. "People do not provide an *erub*-meal for it or a *shittuf*-meal for it; people do not leave an *erub*-meal in such a house."

J. What is the reason for that view?

K. It will not serve as [an ordinary] dwelling.

L. [But if that is the operative consideration, then, while] people may not place the *erub*-meal there for the purpose of joining houses into a single courtyard, a *shittuf*-meal might well be placed there [since it joins not houses but entire courtyards that open out into a single alley-way. The consideration of whether or not it is a house does not apply.]

M. What is the reason [for such a position]? It is that the building at hand is no worse than a courtyard in an alley-way [and falls into that same category]. For we have learned in a teaching on Tannaite authority: The erub-meals that serve courtyards are placed in a courtyard, and the shittuf-meals serving alleyways are located in alley-ways.

N. And we reflected on that teaching as follows: "Erub-meals serving courtyards are to be placed in a courtyard." And have we not learned in the Mishnah: He who places his erub in a gate-house, portico, or gallery – it is not a valid erub. And he who lives there [in the gate-house, portico, or gallery, and who does not share in the erub] does not prohibit [another from carrying objects in the courtyard] [M. Er. 8:4A-B]. [Hence these are not regarded as houses in the courtyard for the purposes of the erub-meal.]

O. Accordingly, I must interpret the cited statement [M] as follows: Erub-meals serving courtyards must be placed in a house located in the courtyard, and shittuf-meals serving alleyways must be located in a courtyard in that alley-way.

P. The matter at hand then [the house less than four cubits by four cubits] is no less [a case] than the courtyard in an alley-way [as proposed just now].

Q. "They do not make of it an extension between two towns": for it is not treated even as equivalent to a watchtower. Why not? Watchtowers [however modest] serve their purpose, but this serves no purpose.

R. "And brothers or partners may not partition it:" What is the reason? Because it is not in area four cubits by four cubits.

S. But if it were of such an area, would they be able to partition it?

T. And have we not learned in the Mishnah: People may not divide up a courtyard unless there will be four cubits for one resident and four for another [after the partition] [M. B.B. 1:6]?

U. Rather, read the matter simply as follows: The law of partition does not apply [to such a house] as it does to a courtyard.

V. For R. Huna has said, "A courtyard is [wholly] divided up in accord with its entry-ways."

W. And R. Hisda said, "One assigns four cubits to each entry way, and they partition the remainder equally."

X. The stated rules apply to a house, which one plans to keep standing. In such a case one assigns a courtyard [space to such a house]. But as to this building, which is going to be demolished, we do not assign it courtyard-space.

I need not repeat what has already been said; the reader may rapidly identify what I deem to be the systemic traits of this discourse.

VII.

A. [If a sukkah] was taller than twenty cubits and one attempted to diminish its height by placing on the ground blankets and pillows, that does not constitute a valid act of diminution [4A], and that is so even though the owner declared the objects to be abandoned [and null, of no value whatsoever] so far as all parties are concerned.

B. The reason is that his intention in the matter is null when measured against the prevailing view of all other people [who will nonetheless regard the blankets and pillows not as abandoned but as objects of value].

C. If he did so with straw and nullified [its value], this does indeed constitute an act of valid diminution, and all the more so if he did it with dirt and nullified [its value].

D. As to the use of straw which the man is not planning to remove later on, and as to dirt of indeterminate condition, there is a dispute between R. Yose and rabbis.

E. For we have learned in the Mishnah: *A house which one wholly filled with dirt or pebbles and which one abandoned is regarded as abandoned [M. Oh. 15:7].*

F. That is the case if one has abandoned the house. If one did not abandon the house, that is not the case.

G. And in this regard there is a Tannaite teaching:

H. R. Yose says, "Straw which one is not destined to remove, lo, it is in the category of ordinary dirt and is regarded as abandoned and dirt which one is destined to remove, lo, it is in the category of ordinary straw and is not regarded as abandoned [T. Oh. 15:5B] [= D].

VIII.

A. [If a sukkah] was higher than twenty cubits, but palm leaves were hanging down within the twenty cubits, if the shade that they cast is greater than the sunlight they let through, the sukkah is valid, and if not, it is invalid.

B. [If a sukkah] was ten handbreadths high, and palm leaves were hanging down into the space of ten handbreadths,

C. Abayye considered ruling that if the shade that they cast is greater than the sunlight they let through, the sukkah is valid, and if not, it is invalid.

D. [But] Raba said to him, "This really would be a disgraceful sort of dwelling, and no one would live in such a disgraceful dwelling [so the sukkah would be invalid to begin with]."

E. [If] it was higher than twenty cubits, but the owner built a ledge in it across the entire front of the middle [of the three] walls of the sukkah, and [the ledge] has sufficient space to constitute a valid sukkah, it is a valid sukkah.

F. [If the owner] built the ledge on the side wall, if from the edge of the ledge to the [opposite] wall of the sukkah is a space of four cubits [or more], the sukkah is invalid. If the space from the ledge to the wall is less than four cubits, it is a valid sukkah. [Slotki: It is valid because the roof above the area between the ledge and the opposite wall is regarded as a continuation of that wall which thus serves as a third wall for the ledge.]

G. What inference [does the framer of this case] wish to provide for us? Is it that we invoke the principle of the "curved wall"? [Slotki]?

H. But we have learned on Tannaite authority: As to a house which is lacking [the middle of its flat roof], and the owner put sukkah-roofing over that empty area, if from the wall to the sukkah-roofing is a distance of four cubits, the area is invalid [to serve as a sukkah].

I. Lo, if the distance is less than that, it is valid. [Accordingly, the principle yielded by the case at hand is not fresh, since it is readily derived from an available teaching.]

J. [No, it was necessary to make the principle explicit in the present case.] What might you have said? In that [available] case, it is valid because [each side] is suitable to serve as a wall [Slotki: it is not higher than the permitted maximum], but here, [where the sukkah is higher than twenty cubits] so that the wall is not suitable to serve as a wall for a sukkah, I might have held that it was not a suitable arrangement.

K. Thus the framer of the case informs us that that is not a consideration.

L. [If a sukkah] was taller than twenty cubits, and the owner built a ledge in the middle of the sukkah, if from the edge of the ledge to the wall is a space of four cubits in all directions, the area is invalid to serve as a sukkah. But if it is less than that space, it is valid.

M. What principle does the framer of the case wish to tell us? Is it that we invoke the principle of the "curved wall"? This is the same [case as the one just reviewed].

N. [No, it was necessary to specify the matter.] What might you have imagined? We invoke the principle of the "curved wall" in the case of a [wall in a] single direction, but we do not invoke that principle in all four directions.

O. Thus the framer informs us that that is not the case. [We invoke the principle for all four directions.]

P. [If a sukkah] was lower than ten handbreadths, and one made a hole in the ground of the sukkah so as to fill out the sukkah['s requisite space, from ground to roof] up to ten handbreadths, if from the edge of the hole to the wall there is a distance of three or more handbreadths, the sukkah is invalid. If the distance is less than this, [4B] it is valid.

Q. What differentiates the other case, in which you have maintained that the maximum distance may be four cubits, from the present case, in which the maximum acceptable difference is less than three handbreadths?

R. In the earlier case, in which there is a wall, a distance of as much as four cubits will suffice. Here, where the owner has to make a wall, if the distance from the hole to the wall is three handbreadths or less, it is acceptable, and if not, it is not acceptable.

S. If a sukkah was higher than twenty cubits, and the owner built in the sukkah a pillar ten handbreadths in height, with sufficient space [four cubits by four cubits] to constitute a valid sukkah,

T. Abayye considered invoking the principle that the partitions [formed for the sides of the pillar] are [imaginarily] projected upward [Slotki, p. 13, n. 1: As far as the ceiling, and that, since the sides are no less than ten handbreadths high and the distance between the top of the pillar and the roof is less than twenty cubits, the pillar constitutes a valid sukkah].

U. Raba, however, said to him, "To invoke that principle we require partitions that can be recognized, and that condition is not met here."

I should maintain that the discourse before us is sustained, smooth, and continuous, rather than a mélange of preserved sayings strung out in some sensible order. There is a beginning, middle, and end; we discern a purpose and an issue that joins the whole. These seem to me marks of deliberation and indications of a program of syllogistic proposition and rigorous argument. I cannot think of a better example of the power of such a program to dictate the composition and proportion of the whole, and I maintain that we do have a proportioned and well composed whole.

IX.

A. Our rabbis have taught on Tannaite authority:

B. If a person drove four posts into the ground and spread sukkah-roofing on them,

C. R. Jacob declares the arrangement a valid sukkah.

D. And sages declare it invalid.

E. Said R. Huna, "The dispute concerns an arrangement made at the edge of a roof. R. Jacob takes the view that we invoke the principle that the walls extend upward, and rabbis maintain that we do not invoke that rule.

F. "But if one erected such a contraption in the middle of the roof, all parties concur that the arrangement is invalid [since the sukkah has no walls]."

G. R. Nahman said, "If one erected the arrangement in the middle of the roof, there is a dispute."

H. The following question troubled [the later exegetes of the passage]: Is it true that there is a dispute in the case of such an arrangement built at the middle of the roof, but if it were located on the edge of the roof, all parties would concur that it is valid [in Nahman's view of the matter]? Or is it true that whether the arrangement is in this area [the middle of the roof] or in that [the edge of the roof] [in Nahman's view] there is a dispute?

I. The question stands unanswered.

J. The following objection was raised:

K. **If someone drove four poles into the ground and arranged sukkah-roofing on them,**

L. **R. Jacob declares [the contraption to be a] valid [sukkah].**

M. **And sages declare it invalid [cf. T. Suk. 1:12-13].**

N. Now lo, the ground is equivalent to the middle of the roof, and yet R. Jacob declares it valid.

O. That would constitute a refutation of the theory [F] of R. Huna [on what is at issue], would it not? It indeed constitutes a refutation.

P. Furthermore, there is a dispute as to such a contraption's being located at the middle of the roof, but if it is located at the edge of the roof, all parties concur that it is valid.

Q. Now may I propose that this too constitutes a refutation of R. Huna in both matters?

R. [No, not at all.] R. Huna may reply to you that the dispute pertains to such a contraption in the middle of the roof, and the same rule applies to one constructed at the edge of the roof.

S. And as to the fact that there is a dispute concerning such an arrangement in the middle of the roof, it serves to tell you just how far R. Jacob is prepared to go. For even if we deal with such an arrangement in the middle of the roof, [Jacob] even in such a case would declare it to be valid.

T. Our rabbis have taught on Tannaite authority:

U. If someone dug four [round] poles into the ground and put sukkah-roofing on them,

V. R. Jacob says, "[To determine whether we have valid walls,] we take a perspective such that, if one should cut the pole and plane it, what would result would be a beam with a handbreadth of space on one side and a handbreadth of space on the other. Then the poles are judged to form a rectangular corner piece [and so to constitute a double wall with each surface regarded as a wall unto itself], and if not, they are not required in that way." [If there are two walls, one in each direction, to be imputed to the pillar, we have an adequate sukkah.]

W. For R. Jacob says, "The measure for the assessment of a rectangular corner piece in the case of a sukkah is a handbreadth."

X. And sages say, "The appropriate measure is only if two [of the nearby walls] are fully articulated walls in accord with the law pertaining to them. In that case, then the third wall of the sukkah may be even so small as a handbreadth [in depth]. [So sages reject Jacob's view that we invoke the principle that the estimate, if met, would yield two valid walls for the sukkah, one on each side of the pillar. Sages insist on two fully valid walls, and here there is none.]

We may readily outline this discourse, with its beginning, middle, and end, and we may discern the points of unfolding logic and reason, the earlier coming first, the later coming last. These seem once more to point toward a plan that, from first to last, has told the composer of the whole where and how to place the received materials in the interest of producing a single and cogent statement.

X.

A. *And one [a sukkah] which is not ten handbreadths high [M. 1:1C]:*

B. How do we know [from Scripture] that that is the rule?

C. It has been stated [on Amoraic authority]:

D. Rab, R. Hanina, R. Yohanan, and R. Habiba repeated –

E. – in the whole of the Division of Appointed Times, in any case in which this set appears together, the name of R. Jonathan may be substituted for the name of R. Yohanan –

F. "The ark was nine handbreadths high, and the ark cover one more, thus, ten in all.

G. "And it is written, 'And there I will meet with you and I will speak with you from above the ark-cover' (Ex. 25:22)."

H. [5A] [And it has been taught on Tannaite authority:

I. "R. Yose says, 'The Presence of God never came down, and Moses and Elijah never went upward to the height, for it is said, "The heavens are the heavens of God, and the earth he has given to the children of men" (Ps. 115:16).'" [Slotki, p. 15, n. 4: Now since the Shechinah descended as low as the ark-cover it may be concluded that the boundary of the earth is at that level, viz., ten handbreadths from the ground. Consequently a wall whose height is less than ten handbreadths cannot be regarded as a valid wall.]

J. But did the Presence of God never come down to the earth? And has it not been written, "And the Lord came down upon Mount Sinai" (Ex. 19:20)?

K. It was only to the space above ten handbreadths over the mountain.

L. And is it not written, "And his feet shall stand in that day upon the Mount of Olives" (Zech. 14:4)?

M. It will still be above ten handbreadths [from the ground].

N. And did Moses and Elijah not go upward? And has it not been written, "And Moses went up to God" (Ex. 19:3)?

O. It was ten handbreadths below [the height].

P. And has it not been written, "And Elijah went up by a whirlwind into heaven" (2 Kgs. 2:11)?

Q. It was ten handbreadths below [the height].

R. And has it not been written, "He seizes hold of the face of his throne and he spreads his cloud upon him" (Job 26:9)? And in this connection R. Tanhum said, "This teaches that the All-Mighty spread over him some of the splendor of his Presence and his cloud."

S. This was nonetheless lower than ten handbreadths [from the height].

T. Nonetheless, it is written, "He seizes hold of the face of his throne"!

U. The throne was lowered down until it was ten handbreadths below the height, at which point he laid hold of it.

XI.

A. [Reverting to the main point, X G, above], now there is no difficulty in showing that the ark was nine handbreadths high, for it has been written, "And they shall make an ark of acacia wood, two cubits and a half shall be the length of it, and a cubit and a half the breadth of it, and a cubit and a half the height of it (Ex. 25:10) [and a cubit is six handbreadths, so a cubit and a half will be nine].

B. But how do we know that the ark-cover was a handbreadth in height?

C. It accords with what R. Hanina taught on Tannaite authority, "For all of the utensils that Moses made, the Torah defined the measure of their length, breadth, and height.

D. "In the case of the ark-cover, while the Torah specified its length and its breadth, it did not specify the dimensions of its height.

E. "Go and derive an analogy from the dimensions of the smallest of all of the utensils.

F. "For it has been said, 'And you shall make it a border of a handbreadth round about' (Ex. 25:25).

G. "Just as that is a handbreadth in height, so in the present case, the utensil is to be a handbreadth in height."

H. But should we not derive the measurement from the utensils themselves?

I. If you hold onto a great deal, you hold nothing, but if you hold onto a little, you will hold onto it. [Slotki, p. 16, n. 5: The lesser is included in the greater, but the greater is not included in the lesser. The selection of the lesser is therefore the safer course.]

J. Then let us derive the measurement from the dimensions of the plate [Ex. 28:36, still smaller than a handbreadth]!

K. For it has been taught on Tannaite authority:

L. The plate was like a gold plate, two fingerbreadths broad and stretching from ear to ear, and on it were inscribed two thin lines with a Y and H above, and "Holy" and an L below [yielding, from right to left, Holy to the Lord]."

M. And R. Eliezer b. R. Yose said, "I saw it in Rome, and on it was written, 'Holy to the Lord,' on a single line."

N. [It follows that the measurement of the plate is less than a handbreadth in height. Why not derive the measurement of the ark-cover from that analogy?] We form an analogy from one utensil to another, but we do not form an analogy from an ornament for a utensil.

O. And why not derive the measurement of the ark-cover from the analogy of the crown [of gold around the ark, Ex. 25:11]?

P. For in that connection a master has stated, "The crown was the smallest possible size."

Q. We establish an analogy between one utensil and another, but not between a utensil and an appurtenance to a utensil.

R. But the border also served as an appurtenance to a utensil.

S. The border was below [the top of] the table [Slotki, p. 17, n. 2: Joining its legs together and forming part of the structure].

T. That answer suffices for the one who maintains that the border was beneath the top of the table. But in the view of the one who maintains that the border was above it, what is there to say? For the object at hand served only as an appurtenance to a utensil.

U. Rather, we draw an analogy from an object to which the Torah has assigned a measure for another object to which the Torah has assigned a measure, but neither the plate or the crown should provide evidence, since in neither case did the Torah assign fixed measurements to them.

V. R. Huna said, "[We derive proof on the height of the ark-cover] from the verse that follows: 'Upon the face of the ark-cover on the east' (Lev. 16:14).

W. "And 'face' must be at least a handbreadth."

X. But might I propose that [the face] would be like the face [5B] of Bar Yokhani [a very large bird]?

Y. [No,] if you hold onto a great deal, you hold nothing, but if you hold onto a little, you will hold onto it [as at I, above].

Z. But I might propose that [the face] would be like that of a siparta [-bird] which is very small.

AA. Said R. Aha bar Jacob, "R. Huna [derives the lesson] from the use of the word 'face' in two passages, [applying by analogy the meaning imputed in one case to that appropriate in the other].

BB. "Here it is written, 'Upon the face of the ark cover' (Lev. 16:14).

CC. "And elsewhere it is written, 'From the face of Isaac his father' (Gen. 27:30). [A human face in the latter case is meant, hence a handbreadth in size, and the same dimension then applies in the former case]."

DD. But why not derive the lesson from the use of "face" with reference to the one above [God].

EE. For it is written, "As one sees the face of God, and you were pleased with me" (Gen. 33:10).

FF. [No,] if you hold onto a great deal, you hold onto nothing, but if you hold onto a little, you will hold onto it.

GG. Then how about deriving the besought dimension from the case of the cherub, for it is written, "Toward the face of the ark-cover shall the faces of the cherubim be" (Ex. 25:20)?

HH. Said R. Aha bar Jacob, "We have learned that the faces of cherubs are not less than a handbreadth."

II. R. Huna, for his part, also derived the same lesson from here.

JJ. And what is a cherub (KRWB)?

KK.   Said R. Abbahu, "Like a child [KRBY'), for so in Babylonia they call a child a 'rabei.'"

LL.   Said to him Abayye, "But [if you hold the face of a cherub was a handbreadth] how do you deal with that which is written, 'The first face was the face of the cherub, and the second face the face of a man' (Ez. 10:14)? So is the face of a cherub the same as the face of a man?"

MM. One face is large, the other small.

XII.

A.   And how [do you know] that the contained space [of the sukkah] not counting the covering is to be ten handbreadths? Perhaps that measurement encompasses the covering. [In that case, the sukkah from the roofing to the ground may be less than ten handbreadths, and only inclusive of the roofing from the top, must it be ten handbreadths in height.]

B.   The rule derives from the eternal house.

C.   For it is written, "And the house which King Solomon built for the Lord was threescore cubits long, twenty cubits broad, and thirty cubits high" (1 Kgs. 6:2).

D.   And it is written, "The height of the one cherub was ten cubits, and so was that of the other cherub" (2 Kgs. 6:26).

E.   And it has been taught on Tannaite authority:

F.   Just as we find in the eternal house that the cherubs were a third of the height of the house, so also in the case of the tabernacle [standing on the ark, inclusive of the ark and ark cover (Slotki, p. 18, n. 15)] they were a third of its height.

G.   Now how high was the tabernacle? It was ten cubits, for it is written, "Ten cubits shall be the length of a board" (Ex. 26:16).

H.   How much is that? Sixty handbreadths. If you take a third, what do you have? Twenty handbreadths. Then take off the ten for the ark and the ark-covering, and you are left with ten [the measure of the height of the sukkah].

I.   And it is written, "And the cherubim shall spread out their wings on high, covering the ark-cover with their wings" (Ex. 25:20).

J.   The All-Merciful thus regards [the wings] above ten handbreadths "roofing" [such as serves for a sukkah]. [Q.E.D.].

K.   How do we know that their wings rose above their heads? Perhaps they were at the same level with their heads [Slotki, p. 19, n. 1: In which case, the hollow space between the wings and the ark-cover was only ten handbreadths minus the thickness of the wings].

L.   Said R. Aha bar Jacob, "'Above' is what is written."

M.   And might I say that they were very high?

N.   Is it written, "Above and upward"? [The sense of the language would not support the notion that they were raised up very high.]

O.   [The proof just now given] affords no problems to the view of R. Meir, who has taken the position that all of the cubits were intermediate [normal] [with six handbreadths in a cubit, as stated above, X F].

P.   But in the view of R. Judah, who has said that the cubit-measure used in the building was six handbreadths, but that used for utensils was only five handbreadths, what is there to be said?

Q. How high were the ark and the ark-covering? Eight and a half, leaving eleven and a half handbreadths. [The ark was a cubit and a half, hence seven and a half handbreadths by Judah's measure, and the ark-cover one handbreadth. That will leave, between the ark-cover and the wings of the cherubim, eleven and a half handbreadths.]

R. Shall I then say that [in Judah's view] the sukkah is valid only if it is eleven and a half handbreadths in height? [Surely not!]

S. But R. Judah derived [the required measure, ten] on the basis of received law [transmitted orally, and not on the basis of exegesis of Scripture].

T. For R. Hiyya bar Ashi said Rab [said], "The [laws covering] measurements [of minimal quantities], of interpositions and partitions constitute law revealed to Moses at Sinai."

U. [But to the contrary] the laws governing minimal quantities derive from the Torah['s written rules, not from revelation orally transmitted], for it has been written, "A land of wheat and barley, vines, fig-trees, and pomegranates, a land of olive trees and honey" (Deut. 8:8).

V. And [in regard to the cited verse] R. Hanina said, "This entire verse is stated with reference to the provision of minimum measures [for various purposes, thus:]

W. "'Wheat' serves to make reference to a house afflicted with *nega*, as we have learned in the Mishnah:

X. *"He who entered a house afflicted with a nega, with his garments slung over his shoulder and his sandals and rings in his hands – he and they are unclean forthwith. [6A] If he was dressed in his garments with his sandals on his feet and his rings on his fingers, he is unclean forthwith. But they are clean until he will remain for a time sufficient to eat a piece of bread – a piece of bread of wheat and not a piece of bread of barley, reclining and eating it with condiment [M. Neg. 13:9].*

Y. "'Barley'; as we have learned in the Mishnah: *A barley-grain's bulk of a bone [of a corpse] imparts uncleanness if someone touches or carries it, but not if someone overshadows it' [M. Oh. 2:3].*

Z. "Vines:' That reference provides the measurement of a fourth-log of wine, constituted that minimum measure for which a Nazir becomes culpable [since he may not drink wine].

AA. "'Fig-trees': That reference provides the measurement of a minimum volume for which one becomes liable if he removes something on the Sabbath from one domain to another:

BB. "'Pomegranate': As we have learned in the Mishnah: *Any utensil [made of wood] belonging to a householder [becomes useless and therefore no longer susceptible to uncleanness] if in it there is a crack [or hole] the size of a pomegranate [so there is a hole that renders the utensil no longer a receptacle at all] [M. Kel. 17:1].*

CC. "'A land of olive-trees': A land all of whose minimal measures are the equivalent of the bulk of an olive."

DD. Do you really mean to say that all of the minimum measures are of the size of an olive? Lo, there are [to the contrary] those others that we already have catalogued!

EE. Rather, I should say, "...most of whose minimal measures are the equivalent of the bulk of an olive."

FF. "'Honey': This refers to the size of a large date. [On the Day of Atonement one who eats food the bulk of a large date becomes liable for violating the prohibition against eating, while if one eats food less than that bulk, he is not culpable]."

GG. [Reverting to the point at which we started, U], it follows that [the minimum measures] derive from the Torah [and not from laws revealed to Moses at Sinai and handed on orally]!

HH. Do you take the position that the stated measures are actually written down in the Torah? Rather, they are laws [handed on orally], and Scripture then provided general support [for the same measurements. But from Scripture one could not derive the measurements just now catalogued].

II. And the rules of interposition in fact derive from the Torah [vs. T], for it is written, "And he shall wash his body in water" (Lev. 14:9).

JJ. This indicates that there should be nothing to interpose between him and the water.

KK. [No, there is an aspect of the rules that derives from oral transmission], for, when the orally-transmitted law serves a purpose, it is as to the interposition of one's hair, in accord with the formulation of Rabbah bar bar Hana.

LL. For Rabbah bar bar Hana said, "A single knotted hair interposes [between the flesh and the water], while three do not interpose. As to the effect of two, I do not know the law."

MM. The interposition of one's hair also is a matter of law deriving from the Torah [and not from an orally-transmitted law].

NN. For it has been written, "And he shall wash [+ accusative particle] his body in water" (Lev. 14:9).

OO. [The use of the] accusative principle serves to indicate that at issue is what is attached to his body, that is, the hair.

PP. [Reverting to the original claim, then] when there is a matter of law [orally transmitted, in connection with interposition], it is in accord with that which R. Isaac said.

QQ. For R. Isaac said, "[6B] As matter of law deriving from the Torah, if most [of one's hair is covered with mud, each hair knotted singly (Slotki)], and the person pays attention to it, then the matted hair serves to interpose, but if he does not pay attention to it, then it does not interpose. And [sages] furthermore have made a decree concerning a case in which most of the hair is matted with mud but the person does not pay attention to it [indicating that in such a case, the hair interposes, even though the person pays it no mind], on account of a case in which most of the hair is matted with mud and the person does pay attention to it,

RR. "as well as concerning a case in which the small part [of one's hair is matted with mud] and the person does pay attention to it [in which case, the hair interposes, though it is not the bulk of the person's hair], on account of the case in which the bulk of the hair is matted with mud and the person pays attention to it."

SS. And why not let sages make a decree concerning a case in which the smaller part of one's hair is matted with mud, and the person does not pay attention to it, on account of the case in which the smaller part of one's hair is matted with mud and the person does pay attention to it?

TT. Or [let the decree be made on account of the rule governing the case in which] the greater part of one's hair is matted with mud, but one pays no attention to it?

UU. That very matter is subject to an [arbitrary] decree, and should we then go and impose yet another decree [applying a strict law to a matter which to begin with is subject to a decree [on our part? Such would be altogether too strict].

VV. "As to the laws of partitions [T]:" they are those to which we have already made reference [concerning the height of the sukkah].

WW. That view accords well with the position of R. Judah [S, who does not claim the measurements derive from Scripture], but as to the view of R. Meir, what is to be said?

XX. As to the point at which a law [transmitted orally] is needed, it concerns the principles of [the legal fictions involving] extension [Slotki, p. 22, n. 7: a partition that does not reach the ground or the ceiling may in certain conditions be deemed to touch the ground or the ceiling, respectively], junction [Slotki, p. 22, n. 8: small interstices, of less than three handbreadths, are disregarded, and the wall is deemed to be a solid whole], and the curved wall [Slotki, p. 22, n. 9: If a portion of the roof of a sukkah consists of materials that are legally unfit for the purpose, the sukkah may nevertheless be valid if that portion is adjacent to any of its walls and terminates within a distance of four cubits from that wall. That portion of the roof together with the wall it adjoins are regarded as one curved wall; and the space under the remainder of the roof consisting of suitable materials may be used as a proper sukkah].

XIII.

A. *One which does not have three walls [M. Suk. 1:1D]:*

B. Our rabbis have taught on Tannaite authority:

C. Two [of the walls must be] in accord with the law applying to them, but the third may be even a handbreadth.

D. And R. Simeon says, "Three must be in accord with the law applying to them, but the fourth may be even a handbreadth" [T. Suk. 1:13].

E. What is at issue between them?

F. Rabbis take the view that the traditional text [Slotki] is authoritative [without regard to the vowels placed with the consonants] while R. Simeon holds that the traditional mode of reading the text [inclusive of reference to the vowels] is authoritative.

G. The rabbis take the view that the traditional text is authoritative [without regard to the vowels], and sukkot two times [read without the vowel indicating the plural] while sukkot is written only once with the consonantal vowel indicating the plural, yielding four allusions in all [one, one, two]. You take off one needed for itself [teaching the fact that one must dwell in a sukkah], leaving three, that refer to the walls: two to be built in accord with the law applying to them, and the law transmitted orally comes along and reduces the requirement affecting the third wall, leaving it [suitable even if it is only] at a handbreadth.

H. R. Simeon holds that the traditional mode of reading the text is authoritative, and since the word sukkot is written three times, there are six available references in all.

I. You take off one verse of Scripture for itself [covering the fact that one has to make a sukkah], and you are left with four, three to be built in accord with the law governing them, and the law transmitted orally comes along and reduces the requirement affecting the third wall, leaving it at a handbreadth.

J. If you want, I shall explain the cited disputed [B-D] differently, conceding that all parties concur that the traditional mode of reading the text is authoritative.

K. Then in the present instance on what point do they differ?

L. One authority takes the view that the fact that the sukkah must be covered with sukkah-roofing requires a proof-text, and the other authority maintains that the fact that the sukkah must be covered with sukkah-roofing does not require a proof-text.

M. If you wish, I may concede that all parties concur that the traditional text is authoritative [and not the traditional mode of reading it].

N. Then in the present instance on what point do they differ?

O. One authority takes the view that when the law handed on orally comes along, it serves the purpose of lowering the requirements at hand, and the other authority holds that when the law transmitted orally comes along, it serves to add to what is required [Slotki, p. 23, n. 12: Scripture teaches us the necessity of three walls and tradition adds a fourth].

P. If you wish, I may concede that all parties concur that the law handed on orally serves to lower the requirements at hand, and, further, that the traditional text is authoritative.

Q. And in the present case, what is at issue between the contending parties?

R. At issue is whether or not one imposes an exegesis upon the first occurrence of a word [in a given series in which the same word is repeated, as in the case of the several uses of the work sukkot].

S. One authority takes the view that we impose a secondary exegetical meaning upon a word on the first occasion of its appearance [not as we read it above], and the other authority holds that we do not impose a secondary exegetical meaning upon a word on the first occasion of its appearance [just as we did not impose such a meaning above].

T. R. Mattenah said, "The scriptural basis for the view of R. Simeon derives from the following verse: 'And there shall be a sukkah for a shadow in the day time from the heat, and for a refuge for a cover from storm and from rain' (Is. 4:6). [This can be provided only by four walls]."

XIV.

A. Now as to the wall that may be only a handbreadth [of the three or of the four, as indicated just now], where does the builder set it?

B. Said Rab, "He sets it at right angles to one of the projecting walls [Slotki]."

C. R. Kahana and R. Asi said to Rab, [7A] "Let him set it in a slanting position [not at right angles]."

D. Rab remained silent.

E. It has been stated also upon Amoraic authority:

F. Said Samuel in the name of Levi, "One sets it at right angles to one of the projecting walls."

G. And so too is it taught in the house of study: One sets it at right angles to one of the projecting walls."

H. R. Simeon, and some say, R. Joshua b. Levi said, "One makes the projecting wall a handbreadth measured loosely and sets it up within three handbreadths of the wall, for whatever stands within three handbreadths of the wall is held to be joined to the wall." [Slotki, p. 24, n. 5: The total width now being four handbreadths and the prescribed minimum size of a sukkah wall being seven handbreadths, the wall constitutes the greater part of a valid sukkah wall.]

I. Said R. Judah, "A sukkah that is made like an open alley-way is suitable, and as to the wall a handbreadth in size, one may place it in any position that he wants.

J. R. Simeon, and some say, R. Joshua b. Levi said, "One makes a strip of four handbreadths and a bit more and sets it up within three handbreadths of the wall, for whatever stands within three handbreadths of the wall is held to be joined to the wall."

K. Now what differentiates the former case, in which you have held that what is sufficient is a handbreadth loosely measured, from the present case, in which you have said that what is required is a strip of four handbreadths [which would be considerably larger]?

L. In that other case, in which there are two walls that accord with the law governing the matter, it is sufficient to have a wall that is, in addition, merely a handful measured loosely. But here [where we have a sukkah in the shape of an alley-way [that is, open at the two ends], where there are not two clearly differentiated walls, if there is (in addition) a strip of four handbreadths, it is acceptable, and if not, it is not acceptable.

M. Said Raba, "Such an arrangement is acceptable only if it is in the form of a doorway." [Slotki, p. 25, n. 2: "It is not enough to attach one board of the width of four handbreadths to one of the walls (of the sukkah in the shape of an alley), but two posts each half a handbreadth in width must be attached to each opposite wall with a cross-beam joining them." This forms a recognizable house, not just an alley-way."]

N. There are those who say that Raba said, "And [a sukkah lacking a required wall] also is valid if it is in the shape of a doorway."

O. There is yet another version that has Raba say, "It must also have the shape of a doorway." [Slotki, p. 25, n. 5: One of the posts on which the cross-beam lies must be a full handbreadth wide.]

P. R. Ashi found R. Kahana making [a sukkah using a wall the size of] a handbreadth loosely measured, and making it in the shape of a doorway.

Q. He said to him, "Does not the master accord with the view of Raba, for Raba said, 'It also is valid if it is in the shape of a doorway'?"

R. He said to him, "I have taken a position in accord with a different version of what Raba said, for R. Raba said, 'It must also have the shape of a doorway.'"

XV.

A. "Two having the dimensions in accord with the law governing them" [= XIII B]:

B. Said Raba, "And so is the rule concerning [definition of a private domain for purposes of permitting carrying] on the Sabbath. [There must be three walls, two ordinary, one fictional. If such a sukkah is erected by the door of one's home, on the Sabbath he may carry from the sukkah to the house.]

C. "[Why so?] Since the [fictional] wall is regarded as a wall for the purposes of the sukkah, it serves also for the purposes of [establishing private domain for carrying on] the Sabbath."

D. Abayye objected [to the reasoning of C], "Do we invoke the argument [of analogy represented by the phrase beginning], 'since'?

E. "And has it not been taught on Tannaite authority: 'The rules covering a wall for the purpose of building a sukkah are equivalent to the walls covering [partitions to indicate a private domain for purposes of carrying on] the Sabbath [e.g., a sukkah attached to a door to permit carrying on the Sabbath], so long as between one reed [wall-marker] and the next is no space exceeding three handbreadths. But there is a further rule pertaining to [partitions for] the [sukkah built in connection with carrying on the] Sabbath that does not pertain to the sukkah, for [a domain constituted by a sukkah and so partitioned off for carrying on the Sabbath does not constitute a] permitted [domain] unless the standing part of the wall is greater than the breaches [in that same wall], a rule that does not apply to the sukkah [constructed solely in observance of the Festival].'

F. "Now is not the sense of the language, 'a further rule for sukkah in connection with the Sabbath' that we do not invoke [the argument of analogy beginning with the word] 'since'?"

G. [Raba replied], "No, the language indicating that 'a further rule applies to the Sabbath' refers to the Sabbath in general [and indicates that, overall, a valid wall is required, but not to] sukkah constructed to permit carrying on the Sabbath."

H. "If so, the framer of the passage should then have framed matters to indicate that the requirements governing a sukkah in general are more stringent than the requirements relating to the sukkah that is used [to permit carrying] on the Sabbath, for the sukkah in general requires [for the fictional, defective wall] a breadth of a handbreadth measured loosely, while the sukkah in regard to [carrying on] the Sabbath does not require such a measurement, but suffices with a mere side-post.

I. "For you [Raba] are the one who has maintained that if one has spread sukkah-roofing over an alley-way which is marked off by a side-post, it is a valid arrangement."

J. "It was not necessary at all to make such specification [concerning the imposition of a more strict rule]. [Why not?] If we invoke the argument beginning with the word 'since,' with the effect of applying the role governing the less strict case [the sukkah] to the more strict case [the Sabbath], we should surely invoke the same argument to apply the rule governing the more strict case to the less strict one [with the result that the side-post which is suitable to serve for purposes of the Sabbath is acceptable also with regard to the sukkah]."

K. [Reverting to the earlier] body [of discourse]: Said Raba, [7B], "If one has spread sukkah-roofing over an alley-way that is marked off by a side post, it is a valid [arrangement]."

L. And Raba said, "If one has placed sukkah-roofing on top of boards placed around wells, it is a valid arrangement." [A well which by definition constitutes private domain, located in a public domain, may not be used for its water, since one would have to transport the water on the Sabbath from the private domain of the well to public domain round about. To solve this problem, four corner-pieces will be placed around the well.

These indicate that the enclosed space is private domain, and the water may be taken and used within that space without violating the law against carrying from one domain to the other.]

M. And it was necessary [to make explicit the law about placing sukkah-roofing over an alley-way marked off by a side-post, the law on sukkah-roofing on the upright boards around a well, and the law that, since a wall the size of a handbreadth is acceptable for a sukkah, it also is acceptable as a valid wall to mark off private domain for carrying on the Sabbath].

N. For had we heard the rule only about the alleyways, we should have assumed that the reason is that there are two perfectly valid walls [so the arrangement is acceptable], but in regard to the corner-boards around a well, in which case there are not two valid walls at all, I might have said that such an arrangement was not acceptable.

O. If we had learned the rule governing the acceptability of sukkah-roofing placed over the corner-posts around a well, I might have assumed that the reason that such an arrangement is acceptable is that there are four walls, but if one spread sukkah-roofing over an alley-way, in which there are not four walls [even symbolically], I might have ruled that that would not be acceptable.

P. If we had heard the rule in these two cases, I might have supposed that where we invoke for the less strict case the rule pertaining to the more strict case, that poses no problems, but I might have supposed that we do not invoke the rule governing the less strict case for judging the more strict case.

Q. Accordingly, it was necessary to make explicit all three rules.

XVI.

A. *Or one, the light of which is greater than the shade of which, is invalid [M.1:1E-F]:*

B. Our rabbis have taught on Tannaite authority:

C. [When] the light [of the sukkah] is more than the shadow on account of [inadequate] sukkah-roofing, [the sukkah is invalid],

D. but not when the greater light is on account of the character of] the walls [which may not be opaque and so may permit light to fall into the hut].

E. R. Josiah says, "Also on account of the character of the walls."

F. Said R. Yemar bar Shelamayah in the name of Abayye, "What is the scriptural reason for the view of R. Josiah? It is because it is written, 'And you shall cover the ark with the veil' (Ex. 26:33).

G. "The veil constitutes a partition, and the All-Merciful has referred to it with the word used for sukkah-roofing.

H. "Therefore [the partition and not only the roof constitutes an aspect of the sukkah-roofing], and we require the partition to be similar to the sukkah-roofing [and opaque]."

I. And rabbis [who take the contrary view]?

J. They take the word, "You shall cover" [which uses the root of the word for sukkah-roofing] to mean that at the top the veil should bend so as to appear like roofing.

XVII.

A. Said Abayye, "Rabbi, R. Josiah, R. Judah, R. Simeon, Rabban Gamaliel, the House of Shammai, R. Eliezer, and 'others' all take the view that the sukkah must serve as a permanent [not only temporary] dwelling."

B. Rabbi: As it has been taught on Tannaite authority:

C. Rabbi says, "Any sukkah which is not of the area of four cubits by four cubits is invalid." [A space of less than that is insufficient for a dwelling for a human being.]

D. R. Josiah: As we have just now indicated [since he requires fully filled-in walls].

E. R. Judah: As we have learned in the Mishnah: *A sukkah which is taller than twenty cubits is invalid. R. Judah declares it valid [M. 1:1A-B] [since it can serve as a permanent dwelling].*

F. R. Simeon: As it has been taught on Tannaite authority:

G. **Two in accord with the law applying to them, and a third [wall] even a handbreadth. R. Simeon says, "Three walls in accord with the law applying to them, and the fourth even a handbreadth [since without three solid walls, the hut cannot be considered a permanent dwelling]."**

H. Rabban Gamaliel: As it has been taught on Tannaite authority:

I. He who makes his sukkah on top of a wagon or on top of on the deck of a ship – Rabban Gamaliel declares it invalid, and R. Aqiba declares it valid. [The former holds that on moving vehicles there cannot be a permanent residence.]

J. The House of Shammai: *As we have learned in the Mishnah: He whose head and the greater part of whose body are in the sukkah, but whose table is in the house – the House of Shammai declare the sukkah invalid, and the House of Hillel declare it valid [M. Suk. 2:7].*

K. R. Eliezer: As we have learned in the Mishnah: *He who makes his sukkah in the shape of a cone or who learned it up against a wall – R. Eliezer declares it invalid, because it has no roof, and sages declare it valid [M. Suk. 1:11A-D].*

L. "Others": As it has been taught on Tannaite authority:

M. Others say, "A sukkah make like a dovecote [round-shaped (Slotki)] is invalid, since it does not have corners."

XVIII.

A. Said R. Yohanan, "A sukkah that is shaped like a furnace [round shaped (=XVII M)], if in its circumference is enough space so that twenty-four men can sit around it, is valid, and if not, it is invalid."

B. In accord with whom does R. Yohanan rule?

C. He accords with the view of Rabbi, who has said, "Any sukkah that is not four cubits by four cubits is invalid [XVII C]."

D. But since a man occupies the space of a cubit, and since [in rabbinical mathematics, Pi = 3 so that] any circumference of three handbreadths has a diameter of a handbreadth, should it not be sufficient [if the sukkah in the shape of a circle] can seat only twelve [and not twenty-four]? [Why then A's measurement?]

E. [8A] The view [that Pi = 3] applies to a circle, but in the case of a square a greater perimeter is necessary.

F. But by how much is a square greater than a circle [inscribed therein]? It is greater by a quarter.

G. Then should it not be sufficient [if the sukkah in the shape of a circle] can seat only sixteen [and not twenty-four]?

H. That would be the case for a circle that is inscribed in a square, but in the case of a square inscribed in a circle, more would be required on account of the projection of the corners. [Slotki, p. 29, n. 11: The circumferences of the sukkah must therefore be large enough to contain a square of four cubits.]

I. But if the side of a square is a cubit, its diagonal is approximately one and two fifths cubits [Slotki]. Should not the circumference be seventeen cubits less a fifth? [Slotki, p. 29, n. 13: The diagonal of the square being equal to 4 + 4 x 2/5 = 5-3/5ths cubits, and Pi being approximately equivalent to three, a circumference of 3 x 5-3/5 cubits = 16 4/5 cubits ought to suffice.]

J. [Yohanan] did not give a precise figure.

K. While we may take the view that, where the difference is minor, one does not give a precise figure, do we say so [in the present case] when the difference is considerable?

L. Said Mar Qashisha, son of R. Hisda, to R. Ashi, "Do you maintain that a man occupies the space of an entire cubit? Three men can sit in the space of two cubits. How much is then [required for twenty four men]? Sixteen [would be enough]. So we require sixteen and four fifths, and [Yohanan] did not give an exact [but only an approximate] figure.

M. While we may take the view that one does not give an exact figure when it yields a strict ruling, do we maintain that one does not give an exact figure when it would yield a lenient ruling?

N. Said R. Assi to R. Ashi, "In point of fact a person occupies the space of a cubit. But R. Yohanan did not take account of the space occupied by persons at all." [Slotki, p. 30, n. 2: The men are considered as sitting around the circumference of the sukkah they themselves forming a circumference of twenty-four cubits, equivalent to the space occupied by twenty-four men, with a diameter of eight cubits. But the inner circumference formed by the sukkah is smaller, since its diameter is eight minus two, the space occupied lengthways by the legs of two men, one sitting at each end, is six cubits.] How many [cubits] would [the circumference of the sukkah] then require? Eighteen [Slotki, p. 30, n. 4: Since a diameter of six cubits has a circumference of eighteen cubits], though sixteen and four fifths cubits would be enough.

O. That is the sense of the statement that he did not give a precise figure, and here it is to impose a strict ruling [Slotki, p. 30, n. 5: instead of a circumference of 16-4/5, one of eighteen cubits is prescribed, while the difference in the diameter (6 – 5-3/5 = 2/5) is even less.]

P. Rabbis of Caesarea, and some say, the judges of Caesarea, say, "In the case of a circle inscribed in a square, the circumference is a quarter [less than the perimeter of the square], [8B] and in the case of a square inscribed in a circle, the circumference is a half [of the circumscribed square]. [Slotki, p. 30, n. 8: Thus if a circumference is twenty-four cubits, the figure given by R. Johanan, the circumscribed square has a perimeter of 24 + 24/3 = 32 cubits, while the inscribed square has a perimeter of approximately 32/2 = 16 cubits, the measurements prescribed by Rabbi.]

Q. But that is not the case, for lo, we notice that they are not that much [larger]. [It is not correct to claim that the perimeter of the circumscribed square is twice the perimeter of the inscribed square and that the circumference of the circle is therefore bigger than the latter by half of its perimeter (Slotki).]

XIX.

A. Said R. Levi in the name of R. Meir, "Two sukkot built for a potter, one inside the other [in the inner one, the potter works, in the outer, he shows his pots] —

B. "the inner one is not in the status of a sukkah and is liable to the requirement of having a mezuzah, while the outer one is in the status of a sukkah and is exempt from the requirement of having a mezuzah."

C. And why so? Let the outer one be regarded as the gatehouse for the inner one and be liable to the requirement of having a mezuzah?

D. It is on account of the impermanence [of both sukkot]. [The inner sukkah is fragile and of insufficient standing to be assigned a gatehouse.]

XX.

A. Our rabbis have taught on Tannaite authority:

B. A sukkah built for gentiles, women, cattle, and or Samaritans falls into the category of a sukkah on all accounts [and is] valid, so long as it has sukkah-roofing in accord with the law applying to it.

C. What is the sense of "in accord with the law applying to it"?

D. Said R. Hisda, "And the rule applies on condition that [the one who put on the sukkah-roofing] did so in order to create shade appropriate to a sukkah."

E. What is included by the language, "on all accounts"?

F. It is to encompass booths built for shepherds, watchmen, city guards, and keepers of orchards [given in mnemonic].

G. For our rabbis have taught on Tannaite authority:

H. A sukkah built for shepherds, a sukkah built for guards [for crops], a sukkah built for city guards, and a sukkah built for keepers of orchards on all accounts falls into the category of a sukkah [and is] valid, so long as it has sukkah-roofing in accord with the law applying to it [T. Suk. 1:4].

I. What is the sense of "in accord with the law applying to it"?

J. Said R. Hisda, "And the rule applies on condition that [the one who put on the sukkah-roofing] did so in order to create shade appropriate to a sukkah."

K. What is included by the language "on all accounts"?

L. It is to encompass booths built for gentiles, women, cattle, or Samaritans.

M. The Tannaite authority [who encompasses the listed items under the phrase, "on all accounts"] regards as having a stronger claim to acceptability the sukkahs built for gentiles, women, cattle, or Samaritans, because they are permanent in character, and he therefore repeated the language, "on all accounts" to encompass a sukkah built for

shepherds, watchmen, city guards, and keepers of orchards, none of
which sorts of sukkah is of a permanent character.

N. The Tannaite authority who phrased matters in terms of a sukkah built for
shepherds, watchmen, city guards, and keepers of orchards regards those
sorts of sukkah as having a stronger claim of acceptability because they
are built for categories that are obligated [to keep the religious
requirement of dwelling in a sukkah], and he therefore repeated the
language, "on all accounts" to encompass a sukkah built for gentiles,
women, cattle, or Samaritans, not categories obligated [to keep the
religious requirement of dwelling in a sukkah].

Let us first review the program of the Talmud-passage at hand, then return
to the particular questions that engage us. The protracted Talmud serving M.
1:1A-F not only works its way through the Mishnah-paragraph but
systematically expands the law applicable to that paragraph by seeking out
pertinent principles in parallel or contrasting cases of law. When a unit of
discourse abandons the theme or principle connected to the Mishnah-paragraph, it
is to take up a secondary matter introduced by a unit of discourse that has focused
on that theme or principle. Unit I begins with an analysis of the word-choice at
hand. At the same time it introduces an important point, namely, the
comparison between the sukkah and a contraption erected also on a temporary
basis and for symbolic purposes. That is a symbolic gateway, that transforms
an alley-entry into a gateway for a courtyard and so alters the status of the alley
and the courtyards that open on to it and turns them into a single domain. As
one domain, they are open for carrying on the Sabbath, at which time people
may not carry objects from one domain, e.g., private, to another, e.g., public.
That comparison is repeatedly invoked. Units II and III then move from
language to scriptural sources for the law. Unit IV then stands in the same
relationship to unit III, and so too unit V. Unit VI reverts to an issue of unit V.
So the entire discussion – II-VI – flows out of the exegetical requirements of the
opening lines of the Mishnah-paragraph. But the designated unit-divisions seem
to me to mark of discussions that can have stood originally by themselves. Unit
VII then reverts to the original topic, the requisite height of the sukkah. It deals
with a fresh problem, namely, artificially diminishing or increasing the height of
the sukkah by alterations to the inside of the hut. One may raise the floor to
diminish the height or lower the floor to increase it. Unit VIII pursues the same
interest. It further introduces principles distinct from the Mishnah's rules but
imposed upon the interpretation of those rules or the amplification of pertinent
cases. This important exercise in secondary expansion of a rather simple rule
through the introduction of fresh and rather engaging principles – "curved wall,"
fictional extension of walls upward of downward and the like – then proceeds in
its own terms. Unit IX is continuous in its thematic interest with unit VIII.
Unit X reverts to the Mishnah-paragraph, now M. 1:1C, and asks the question
usually raised at the outset about the scriptural authority behind the Mishnah's
rule. This leads us into a rather sizable digression on scriptural exegesis, with
special interest in establishing the analogy between utensils in the Temple and

dimensions pertinent to the sukkah. The underlying conception, that what the Israelite does on cultic occasions in the home responds to what is done in the cult in the Temple, is familiar. Units XI and XII pursue the same line of thought. Then unit XIII reverts once more to the Mishnahs rule, M. 1:1D. Now we take up the issue of the walls of the sukkah. These must be three, in rabbis' view, and four in Simeon's. Each party concedes that one of the requisite walls may be merely symbolic. The biblical source for the required number of walls forms the first object of inquiry. Unit XIV then takes up the symbolic wall. Unit XV reverts to a statement on Tannaite authority given in unit XIII. Subject to close study is a somewhat complicated notion. There are diverse kinds of sukkah-buildings. One, we know, is a sukkah erected to carry out the religious duty of the Festival. But a person may build a sukkah, also, to extend the enclosed and private area of his home. If he places such a sukkah by the door, the area in which it is permitted to carry objects – private domain – covers not only the space of the house but also the space of the sukkah. That sukkah, erected in connection with Sabbath-observance, is compared to the sukkah erected for purposes of keeping the Festival. The issue is appropriate here, since the matter concerns the character of the walls of the sukkah built for Sabbath-observance. Unit XVI then returns to the Mishnah-paragraph. Unit XVIII moves back from the Mishnah's statements and deals with the general principle, taken by some parties, that the sukkah must bear the qualities of a permanent dwelling. That issue intersects with our Mishnah paragraph in connection with Judah's and Simeon's views on the requirement that there be a roof of a certain height and four walls. But the construction as a whole stands independent of the Mishnah-paragraph and clearly was put together in its own terms. XVIII takes up XVII M. The mathematics at hand derive from Slotki's notes, as indicated. Units XIX and XX evidently are miscellaneous – the only such units of discourse in the entire massive construction. I cannot point to a more thorough or satisfying sequence of Talmudic units of discourse, in which the Mishnah's statements are amplified, then the amplifications themselves worked out on their own. The whole is thorough, beautifully articulated, and cogent until the very end.

1:1 G-N

G. *[9A] A superannuated sukkah –*

H. *The House of Shammai declare it invalid.*

I. *And the House of Hillel declare it valid.*

J. *And what exactly is a superannuated sukkah?*

K. *Any which one made thirty days [of more] before the Festival [of Sukkot].*

L. *But if one made it for the sake of the Festival,*

M. *even at the beginning of the year,*

N. *it is valid.*

I.

A. What is the scriptural basis for the position of the House of Shammai?

B. Scripture has said, "The festival of Sukkot, for seven days for the Lord" (Lev. 23:34).

C. [Since the statement thus indicates that sukkah must be "for the Lord,"] the sense is that we require the sukkah to be built solely for the sake of observance of the Festival.

D. And the House of Hillel?

E. They require that statement of Scripture [to stand behind the position of] R. Sheshet.

F. For R. Sheshet has said in the name of R. Aqiba, "How do we know that, as to the wood used for building a sukkah, it is forbidden [for use for any other purpose] all seven days of the festival?

G. "Scripture states, 'The festival of Sukkot, for seven days for the Lord' (Lev. 23:34). [This indicates that, for the entire period, what is devoted to observance of the festival must be used only for that purpose.]"

H. And it has been taught on Tannaite authority:

I. R. Judah b. Beterah says, "Just as the dedication to Heaven takes hold of the animal set aside for the festal offering [so that that animal may not be slaughtered for any other purpose but celebration of the festival], so the dedication to Heaven takes hold of whatever is used for the sukkah [with the same result].

J. "As it is said, 'The festival of Sukkot, for seven days for the Lord' (Lev. 23:34). The meaning is, 'Just as the animal set aside for the festal offering is to be only for the Lord, so whatever is used for the sukkah likewise is to be only for the Lord.'"

K. Now does not the House of Shammai also require the stated proof for the present proposition?

L. That indeed is the case.

M. But then what is the scriptural basis for the view of the House of Shammai?

N. Another verse of Scripture states, "You shall make the festival of Sukkot for seven days" (Deut. 16:13) – a sukkah that is made for the sake of the festival is what we require.

O. And the House of Hillel?

P. They require the force of that proof-text to indicate that one may construct a sukkah on the intermediate days of the festival of Sukkot.

Q. And the House of Shammai?

R. They take the view of R. Eliezer who has said, "People may not make a sukkah [to begin with] on the intermediate days of a festival of Sukkot."

II.

A. But does the House of Hillel [M. 1:1G, I] not concur with the view of R. Judah stated in the name of Rab?

B. For R. Judah said Rab said, "If one made show-fringes out of the hanging web or woof of a woven garment, or out of sewing threads, the fringes are not valid. If he made them out of tuft [attached for that purpose to a garment], the fringes are valid. [Attaching the tuft to the garment was for the purpose of making the show-fringes, while simply drawing out an available thread and twisting it would not constitute purposefully making show-fringes.]" [How, then, can the House of Hillel accept as valid a sukkah that is not constructed for the purpose of observing the festival, in line with the principle expressed in Rab's statement?]

C. "Now when I [Judah] repeated this statement before Samuel, he said to me, 'Also show-fringes made from tufts are invalid.'

D. "'For we require an act of weaving of the show-fringes that is done for its own sake [and in the present case, there is no such act].'"

E. Here too should we not require a sukkah that is made for its own sake [and not accept one constructed without the observance of the festival in mind]?

F. The case [of the fringes] is different, for Scripture has said, "You shall make twisted cords for yourself" (Deut. 22:12).

G. "For yourself" – to carry out your obligation.

H. But here too it is said, "The festival of Sukkot you shall make for yourself" (Deut. 16:13) –

I. [Thus:] "For yourself" – to carry out your obligation!

J. That verse [serves to prove a different proposition entirely, namely] to serve to exclude [the use of a sukkah] that has been stolen. [The sukkah one uses must be legally owned.]

K. But in the matter of show-fringes, surely the same usage then should serve the same purpose, namely, to exclude stolen show-fringes!

L. In that other context, a separate verse of Scripture is available, namely, "And you shall make for them" (Num. 15:38) – out of what belongs to them.

Unit I clarifies the source of the law, and unit II introduces a separate, but related consideration. The exegesis of the Mishnah's rule in relationship to scriptural proof-text is thorough.

III

The Result

These units have no counterparts and are made up to serve the interests of the present authorship alone: **1:1A-F:** I, II, III, V, VI, VII, VIII, X, XI, XII, XII, XIV, XVI, XVII, XVIII, XIX; **1:1 G-N:** I, II.

These units are built upon citation and exegesis of a passage of the Tosefta: **1:1A-F:** IV, (VII, mere citation), (IX, illustration of a principle, but the passage is not the center of discourse), XIII (continued at XV), (XVII, merely cited), XX; **1:1 G-N:** –.

Of the 22 units in all, I count 18 entirely automous ones, lacking any point of contact with a prior document. The other four take up passages that occur in the Tosefta, but none appears to intend a systematic inquiry into the Tosefta's materials parallel to the Talmud's systematic study of those in the Mishnah, paragraph by paragraph.

With respect to exegeses of Scripture, we wish to know whether or not available treatments of a biblical verse have guided the formation of any component of our Bavli-passage. Exegetical treatments bearing more than marginal relevance are as follows: Ex. 25:22: Not critical to our passage; in the same category: Ex. 19:20, Zech. 14:4, Ex. 19:3, 25:10-11, 26:16. 33, 1 Kgs. 6:2, 26, 2 Kgs. 2:11, Job 26:9, Ez. 10:14, etc.. These verses supply facts in an inquiry to which they are essentially tangential. No exegetical tradition in the passages in which they occur sets the issue at hand. Note in particular Lev. 23:34: No tradition other than Y. Suk. 2:7, which deals with "the fifteenth of the month" stated with reference to both Passover and Tabernacles; no point of contact with the present issue. The issue is unrelated. Lev. 23:42: Gen. R. 48:10: God paid Abraham's descendants back for his hospitality by having them dwell in booths for seven days. This also will be in the age to come. Pesiqta deRab Kahana 28/a: You shall eat in the sukkah for seven days, not eight days. No point of intersection with our passage at II.H. Y. Suk. 2:7: One is supposed to eat fourteen meals in a Sukkah, in line with Lev. 23:42. Lev. 23:43: Sifré Dt. 140: not relevant to the present passage; Pesiqta deRab Kahana Supplement 2:6 (Braude, pp. 471-2): not relevant. Deut. 16:13: Pesiqta deRab Kahana Supplement 2:6, 7, not relevant; neither passage deals with what is important here. The emphasis in both treatments of PRK deals with the world to come, God's relationship to Israel, the exile and return, and the like.

The upshot may be stated simply. I see no exegetical parallels, no point of intersection between the Bavli's authorship's interest in the key verses, Lev. 23:35ff., and, e.g., the authorship of Pesiqta deRab Kahana. A given verse's point of interest to one authorship bears nothing in common with what, in that same verse, captures the attention of another authorship. Our survey of Chapter Four will underline this result, for there we do have a biblical verse important both to the authorship of the Bavli-chapter and also to compilers of prior exegetical compilations. There we shall see no material point of intersection whatsoever – and that not in a minor detail but in protracted discourse on the part of several distinct authorships. I simply did not anticipate how casual and inconsequential would be the points of contact or intersection between and among treatments of verses important in our Bavli passage and the reading of those same verses in other documents. The sole exception to this statement – commonalities of interest in a given verse on the part of the authorships of other tractates of the Bavli or of the Yerushalmi – need not detain us for the reasons already worked out. We come now to the issues we raised at the outset.

Let us in conclusion consider the questions just as we originally asked them.

1. *The topical program* of prior writings on the subject as compared to the topical program of the Bavli on the same subject, with attention to questions such as these: does the Bavli follow the response to the Mishnah characteristic of the authorship of the Tosefta? Not systematically, only episodically. As to the Sifra, Sifré to Numbers or Sifré to Deuteronomy, these documents have little in common with ours. Does the Bavli follow the response to

relevant passages of Scripture that have caught the attention of compilers of Midrash-exegeses in Genesis Rabbah, Leviticus Rabbah, Pesiqta deRab Kahana, and other documents generally thought to have come to closure prior to the Bavli? Quite to the contrary, apart from the Yerushalmi and other authorships within the Bavli itself, our authorship turns out to define unique and uncommon points of interest in verses treated both in the Bavli and in some other document.

2. *The Bavli's use or neglect of the available treatments ("sources") in the prior literature*: if the Bavli does make use of available materials, does it impose its own issues upon those materials or does it reproduce those materials as they occur elsewhere? The answer to these questions for the present sample is negative. The Bavli does not make extensive use of available materials. Most of what we have reviewed turns out to be unique to the Bavli. Where there are materials that occur both here and in other documents, they provide mere facts, not a point of generative discourse. Has the authorship of the Bavli carried forward issues important in prior writings, or has it simply announced and effected its own program of inquiry into the topic at hand? Our authorship has made its own statement in its own way.

3. *The traits of the Bavli's canonical statement, that is, derivative and summary at the end, or essentially fresh and imputed retrospectively?* In consequence of the detailed examination of the Bavli's authorship's use of and response to available sources, for the sample at hand we may characterize the statement of the Bavl as a whole in comparison to prior statements as original, fresh, and self-defined. And, since that statement is canonical by the definition of the entire history of Judaism, we ask about the upshot: the shape and character of a canonical statement on a given subject. The answer, for the sample we have considered, yields a negative finding: the canonical statement does not aim at drawing together available materials and restating a long-term and (assessed in terms of the extent writings) broadly-circulated consensus. Data that constitute evidence for documentary traditionality do not appear to the naked eye – or even to a vision educated to discern literary traits and concerns. Quite to the contrary, the pages of plain type, not the bold face indicative of a passage deriving from a prior compilation, testify to the plain truth that our document does not cite or quote or attempt to summarize and recast available materials, reaching a later authorship out of an earlier and on-going process of tradition. True, individual sayings may have circulated and may have undergone a process of continuous tradition. But the

Bavli as we have it, the work of its penultimate and ultimate authorship, makes its own statement in its own way on its own agenda. It gives us not a tradition out of a remote past but a system of its own, composed, quite obviously, in substantial measure from received materials and in accord with received conventions, but, in all and in essence, a singular, autonomous, and, by its nature, unprecedented statement: a system. We shall now survey two more samples of the same tractate, persistently performing the same inquiry and at the end asking exactly the same questions.

Chapter Four

The Bavli and its Sources in the Case of Tractate Sukkah Chapter Two

I

Tradition or System in the Case of a Complete Chapter

I claim that the authorship of the Bavli makes a sustained and cogent statement of its own, using for its own purposes whatever received materials it chooses to use, bound only to the Mishnah's structure. The way to assess that claim is to follow the unfolding of a complete chapter. In this way the reader will look for signs of a reworking of completed and received materials, such as I claim a systemic statement accomplishes, in a cogent and utterly rational, topical and orderly way. If the chapter proves to be mainly constructed as a commentary on some other document (exclusive of the Mishnah), if the program of a prior writing, for example, the Tosefta, serves to dictate the interests of the authorship of the Bavli, if what we have does not hang together in the aggregate but looks to be more of a scrapbook of this and that, now lovingly preserved as tradition, then my characterization is false.

In claiming that, in the Bavli, reason reigns, supreme and alone, revising the received materials and restating, in its own powerful and rigorous logic into a compelling statement, the entirety of the prior heritage of information and thought, I have identified criteria for assessing that same claim. If the marks of the received heritage of information and thought persist and govern the statement as a whole, then the Bavli is a traditional document. If the unfolding of the topical program and the momentum of discussion, the dialectic of argument and inquiry strike the reader as fundamentally self-defined and self-sustained by the authorship before us, then the Bavli does not repeat a tradition but freshly states a system, merely referring to or making adventitious use of, such received materials as the authorship for its own reasons finds interesting. These questions the reader may pursue through a patient perusal of the complete chapter presented here.

As in the preceding chapter, I call attention to the character of the units of sustained discourse signified by a Roman numeral, e.g., 2:1.I, II, and so on. These form the building blocks of the whole, and they impart to the Bavli the character of the document as we know it. The question the reader will want to answer is simple: do I find these units of discourse sustained or episodic? Do I discern the program of a fully-worked out inquiry or the collection and arrangement of bits and pieces of information? As between the choice of seeing received materials as strung together into a chain, or woven together into a tapestry, my judgment is that the received materials – whether verses of Scripture, sentences of the Mishnah or imputed to authorities of the time of the Mishnah, statements of named authorities of the Bavli's setting itself – ordinarily come together into a tapestry, not a necklace. The movement is not merely from saying to saying but from an opening to a concluding proposition. From the perspective at hand, however, I do not comment on the data before us.

II

The Text: Bavli to Mishnah-Tractate Sukkah Chapter Two

As in the preceding chapter, I give the text in my own translation[1] and mark the text to indicate the presence of materials shared with prior documents (excluding the Yerushalmi, for reasons spelled out in Chapter Two). That is the sole purpose of this survey. As before, the Mishnah-passage is given in italics. Then I use bold-face type to indicate that a passage occurs in an earlier compilation. I do not pay attention to the appearance of a passage in another tractate of the Bavli, in the theory that all of the Bavli's thirty-seven tractates came to their present state in more or less the same determinate period of time. It would follow that the appearance of a passage in more than one tractate will tell us nothing about how the same general authorship has made use of materials produced in a prior period. My comments on each passage are limited to some redactional issues and addressed mainly to the question at hand. My sample of Chapter Two covers the entirety of Mishnah-tractate Sukkah Chapter Two.

As in my survey of the intersecting passages utilized by the Bavli's authorship in their treatment of M. Sukkah 1:1 (2a-9a), so for the present sample, I have followed a simple procedure to assess the points of intersection with the documents redacted prior to the Bavli. First I surveyed the cross-references given in the Bavli itself. Where Bavli's editors referred to a Tosefta passage, I give that passage in bold face type, even though the wording is not exactly the same as that which we find in the Tosefta. Then, following A. Hyman, *Torah hakketubah vehammesurah* (Tel Aviv, 1937), I reviewed references in prior compilations of scriptural exegeses to key verses cited in the Bavli. I surveyed, in particular, Sifra, the two Sifrés, Fathers According to Rabbah Nathan, Genesis Rabbah, Leviticus Rabbah, Pesiqta deRab Kahana, Pesiqta Rabbati, and the other compilations closed by A.D. 600, in all instances accepting the view of the dating of documents as given by M. D. Heer in his authoritative table in *Encyclopaedia Judaica, s.v., Midrash.* In this way I was

---

[1]*The Talmud of Babylonia. An American Translation.* VI. *Tractate Sukkah* (Chico, 1984: Scholars Press for Brown Judaic Studies).

able to determine the extent to which the authorship of the Bavli drew upon that available exegetical literature in their larger composition.

2:1

    A. *He who sleeps under a bed in a sukkah has not fulfilled his obligation.*

    B. *Said R. Judah, "We had the practice of sleeping under the bed before the elders, and they said nothing at all to us."*

    C. *Said R. Simeon, "M'SH B: Tabi, Rabban Gamaliel's slave, slept under the bed.*

    D. *"And Rabban Gamaliel said to the elders, 'Do you see Tabi, my slave — he is a disciple of a sage, so he knows that slaves are exempt from keeping the commandment of dwelling in the sukkah. That is why he is sleeping under the bed.'*

    E. *"Thus we learned that he who sleeps under bed has not fulfilled his obligation."*

I.

    A. But lo, [how can the bed be deemed to constitute a tent within the sukkah and so to intervene between a person sleeping under it and the sukkah-roofing, when the bed is not] ten handbreadths high?

    B. Samuel interpreted [the rule to speak] of a bed that is ten handbreadths high.

II.

    A. We have learned in the following passage of the Mishnah:

    B. *All the same is the hole dug by water or reptiles or which salt-petre has eaten through, and so a row of stones, and so [a hollow space formed by] a pile of beams: all these constitute Tents and interpose before uncleanness, [preventing its egress or entry if they are a cubic handbreadth in area].*

    C. *R. Judah says, "Any tent which is not made by man is no tent." [But he agrees concerning the power to constitute an overshadowing tent imputed to clefts and overhanging rocks] [M. Oh. 3:7V-Y].*

    D. What is the scriptural basis for the view of R. Judah?

    E. [21A] He derives the meaning of the word "tent" from its use in connection with the tabernacle in the wilderness.

    F. Here it is written, "This is the Torah. As to a man, when he dies in a tent" (Num. 19:14).

    G. And elsewhere it is written, "And he spread the tent over the tabernacle" (Ex. 40:19).

    H. Just as, in that later passage, the tent qualifies only if it is made by man, so here, it qualifies only if it is made by man.

    I. And as to rabbis [of B. (M. Oh. 3:7), why do they not reach the same conclusion]? They regard the recurrence of the word "tent" to serve to encompass [tents deriving both from human and from natural action].

    J. [Now we come to the point of the foregoing citation.] Is it then the case that R. Judah takes the position that any tent which is not made by man is no Tent?

    K. The following objection was raised from a pertinent passage of the Mishnah:

L. *There were courtyards in Jerusalem, built on rock, and under them was a hollow, which served as a protection against a grave in the depths. And they bring pregnant women, who give birth there, and who raise their sons there. And they bring oxen, and on them are wooden saddles, and the youngsters sit on top of them, with cups of stone in their hands. When they reached the Siloam, they descended and filled them, mounted and sat on top of them. R. Yose says, "From his place did he let down and fill the cup without descending" [M. Par. 3:2].*

M. And in this connection it has been taught on Tannaite authority: **R. Judah says, "They did not make use of wooden saddles but rather of oxen [with broad bellies]"** [T. Par. 3:2G].

N. Now oxen constitute [for the purpose of the law at hand] a tent [since they clearly serve to interpose between the children riding them and any grave in the depths over which they may ride,] yet [they are] a tent not made by man, and lo, it has been taught on Tannaite authority. **R. Judah says, "They did not make use of wooden saddles but rather of oxen"!**

O. When R. Dimi came, he said R. Eleazar [said], "R. Judah concurs concerning a [tent] that is of the size of a fist [that is, larger than a handbreadth. Even though a tent of such size is not made by man, it nonetheless constitutes a valid tent.]" [That would then harmonize the two passages. In the case in which Judah does not regard a hole as a tent, as at M. 3:7V-W's hole dug by water or insects, it is because it is a small hole not made by man. In the case where he does, it is because it is a big one.]

P. So too it has been taught on Tannaite authority:

Q. *R. Judah concurs in the case of clefts and overhanging rocks [M. Oh. 3:7Y].*

R. Yet there is the case of the wooden saddles, which are many times the size of a fist [and so should be regarded as adequate to serve as tents to intervene against the effects of a grave in the depths], and yet in that regard, it has been taught:

S. **R. Judah says, "They did not bring wooden saddles but rather oxen"** [T. Par. 3:2G]. [So the oxen served instead of wooden saddles, which should surely be large enough.]

T. Said Abayye, "[His sense is that] they did not have to bring wooden saddles [because they could make do merely with the oxen, contrary to the story told in the Mishnah's version]."

U. Raba said, "They did not bring wooden saddles at all, for, since a child is thoughtless, he might poke out his head or one of his limbs and contract corpse-uncleanness [21B] from a grave in the depths."

V. It has been taught on Tannaite authority in accord with the view of Raba:

W. R. Judah says, "They did not bring wooden saddles at all, for, since a child is thoughtless, he might poke out his head or one of his limbs and contract corpse-uncleanness from a grave in the depths. Rather, they bring Egyptian oxen, which have broad bellies, *and the children sit on top of them, with cups of stone in their hands. When they reached the Siloam, they descended and filled them, mounted and sat on top of them."*

X. [Now reverting to the Mishnah-passage at hand, we ask:] Lo, a bed is any number of fists in height, and yet we have learned in the Mishnah: *Said R. Judah, "We had the practice of sleeping under the bed before the elders..." [M. Suk. 2:1B].* [So a bed is no tent but it should be regarded as one in line with the foregoing.]

Y.   A bed is different [from the case at hand], because it is made [so that someone can sleep] on top of it. [Sleeping underneath it then changes the normal practice and is not taken into account. The bed used in an unusual way does not constitute a tent.]

Z.   But oxen also are used [to be sat upon], [so that is no proper distinction between the two cases, which contradict one another].

AA. When Rabin came, he said R. Eleazar [said], "The oxen are different, for they serve as protection against the sun for shepherds in the hot season, and against rain in the rainy season [so it would be usual to sit underneath, not only on top of, an ox, unlike the case of a bed.]"

BB. If that is the argument, then the same may be said of the bed, which covers up [serves as a tent over] shoes and sandals that are placed underneath it.

CC. Rather, said Raba, "The case of oxen is different, since their bellies serve to afford shelter for their intestines [so forming a tent beneath], as it is written, 'You have clothed me with skin and flesh and covered me with bones and sinews' (Job 10:11). [Slotki, p. 92, n. 8: "Covered" implies "shelter," "tent."]

DD. If, on the other hand, you prefer, I may propose [a different explanation for Judah's view that it is all right to sleep under a bed in a tent namely], R. Judah is consistent with his position stated elsewhere.

EE. For he has said that, for a sukkah, we require a permanent dwelling, while a bed provides at best only a temporary dwelling. Since a sukkah is a permanent Tent, a temporary Tent, namely, the bed, cannot come along and invalidate a permanent tent.

FF. And lo, it is R. Simeon who has also said, "A sukkah is to be a permanent dwelling, but, [nonetheless, Simeon maintains at M. 2:1C-E] that a temporary tent – a bed – may indeed come along and invalidate a permanent tent.

GG. This is what is at issue between the two [at M. 2:1]:

HH. One authority [Simeon] takes the view that a temporary Tent does come along and invalidate a permanent Tent, and the other master [Judah] takes the position that a temporary Tent may not come along and invalidate a permanent Tent.

III.

A.   Said R. Simeon, "M'SH B: Tabi, Rabban Gamaliel's slave..." [M. 2:1C]:

B.   It has been taught on Tannaitic Authority: said R. Simeon, "From the day to day remarks of Rabban Gamaliel we learned two lessons.

C.   "We learned that slaves are exempt from the religious requirement of dwelling in a sukkah.

D.   "And we learned that he who sleeps under a bed has not fulfilled his obligation" [M. 2:1E].

E.   And should one not say, "From the teachings of Rabban Gamaliel" [rather than "from the day-to-day remarks..."]?

F.   In phrasing matters as he did, he tells us a tangential lesson.

G. What he says is in accord with that which Rab Aha bar
    Adda [said] – and some say that Rab Aha bar Adda said Rab
    Hamnuna said Rab said, "How do we know that even the
    day-to-day remarks of disciples of sages require close
    study?

H. "As it is said, 'And whose leaf does not wither' (Ps. 1:3)."
    [Slotki, p. 93, n. 3:   The righteous man is compared to
    the tree and his casual talk to the leaf.]

M. 2:1A's theory, in line with M. 1:2's, is that the bed constitutes a tent
within the sukkah. One has thus not slept in the sukkah – under its roofing –
but under the tent constituted by the bed. The dispute, B, C-E, then consists of
contradictory precedents. Unit I provides a minor clarification of the passage at
hand. Unit II investigates the position of Judah on what constitutes a valid tent.
The issue is pertinent, since the Mishnah-rule will not accept as valid a sukkah –
that is, a tent – inside of another one, and yet, we see, Judah allows sleeping
under a bed. The pertinent passages are nicely harmonized. Unit III moves on to
Simeon's statement, in contradiction to Judah's. So the three units proceed in
order from M. 2:1A, to M. 2:1B, to M. 2:1C-E.

2:2 A-B

A. *He who props his sukkah up with the legs of a bed – it is valid.*

B. *R. Judah says, "If it cannot stand on its own, it is invalid."*

I.

A. What is the reason for the view of R. Judah [at M. 2:2B]?

B. There was a dispute on this matter between R. Zira and R. Abba bar
    Mammel.

C. One said, "It is because [if the sukkah cannot stand on its own], it does
    not enjoy permanence."

D. The other said, "It is because one thereby holds up the sukkah with
    something that is susceptible to uncleanness [if he leans it against a
    wall]."

E. What is the practical difference between the two positions?

F. It would be the case of someone who knocked iron stakes into the ground
    and spread sukkah-roofing over them."

G. In the view of him who has said that the reason is that the sukkah lacks
    permanence, lo, in this case there really is permanence.

H. In the view of him who has said that it is because one holds up the
    sukkah with something that is susceptible to uncleanness, lo, in this
    case one indeed holds up the sukkah with something that is susceptible
    to uncleanness. [So the former would validate the arrangement, the latter
    would invalidate it, both doing so in Judah's name.]

I. Said Abayye, "What has just now been said applies only if one has
    leaned [the legs of a bed against a wall].   But if one spread sukkah
    roofing on the bed itself [so that the bed provides the walls, but the roof
    is supported on independent poles, which do not receive uncleanness], it
    is a valid arrangement.

J. "What is the operative consideration?

K. "In the view of him who has said that the reason is that the former arrangement lacks permanence, lo, here there is permanence.

L. "In the view of him who has said that the operative consideration is that one holds up the sukkah with something that receives uncleanness, lo, [as just now defined], here the householder does not set up the sukkah with something that receives uncleanness."

The Talmud does a first rate job of both explaining the position of Judah and also explaining the implications of the adduced explanations.

2:2 C-H

C. *[22A] A sukkah [the roofing of which] is loosely put together,*

D. *but the shade of which is greater than the light,*

E. *is valid.*

F. *The [sukkah] [the roofing of which] is tightly knit like that of a house,*

G. *even though the stars cannot be seen from inside it,*

H. *is valid.*

I.

A. What is the meaning of [a sukkah, the roofing of which is] loosely put together?

B. Said Rab, "It is an impoverished sukkah."

C. And Samuel said, "It is a sukkah in which one reed is above another, [so that the reeds are not on the same level]."

D. Rab repeated [the opening clauses, C-E] as a single phrase, and Samuel repeated them as two phrases.

E. Rab repeated it as a single phrase: "A sukkah, the roofing of which is loosely put together, [and] what is the meaning of loosely put together? Loosely put together, but the shade of which is greater than the light, is valid."

F. Samuel repeated them as two phrases: "What is the meaning of loosely put together? And the passage provides two distinct rulings. A sukkah, the roof of which is loosely put together, is valid, and one, the shade of which is greater than its light, likewise is valid."

II.

A. Said Abayye, "The teaching [I. C, concerning a sukkah whose roof is made of reed that lie on different levels] applies only to a case in which there is not a [horizontal] gap between one reed and another of more than three handbreadths but if there is a gap between one and the next of more than three handbreadths, [the sukkah-roofing] is invalid."

B. Said Raba, "Even if there is a [horizontal] gap of more than three handbreadths between one reed and another, we do not rule [that the arrangement is invalid], unless [a section of the] roof is not a handbreadth [wide]. But if a reed is a handbreadth, the sukkah-roofing [arranged in this way] is in any case valid [even if it is three handbreadths higher than the lower reed]. [The reason is that we invoke the rule of fictively regarding the upper sections of the roof as] forced downward and treated as level [with the rest of the roof]." [Slotki, p. 94, n. 11: A legal fiction whereby a plane is regarded as though it were placed at a lower level. The section of the roof (i.e. a bunch of reeds) which is raised above the others is regarded as though it were lying on the same level as the lower ones. The necessity of a handbreadth of width is explained forthwith.]

C. Said Raba, "How do I know that when [the upper section of the roof] is a handbreadth, we invoke the fictive principle that it is forced downward and levelled, and that when [the upper section of thereof] is not a handbreadth, we do not invoke the fictive principle that the reed is forced downward and levelled?

D. "For we have learned in the following passage of the Mishnah:

E. *"The beams, each a square handbreadth, of the house and of the upper room, on which there is no plaster, and which lie exactly in line with one another – if uncleanness is under one of the lower ones, space under it is unclean. If uncleanness is between a lower and an upper beam, only the space between them is unclean. Uncleanness is on an upper one – space directly above it up to the firmament is unclean. If the upper ones lay directly above and opposite the gaps between the lower ones, if uncleanness is under one of them, the space under all of them is unclean. If uncleanness is on top of them, the space directly above it up to the firmament is unclean [M. Oh. 12:5].*

F. "In this regard it has been taught on Tannaite authority:

G. "Under what circumstances? When they have a square handbreadth [forming a tent] and between them is the space of a handbreadth. And if they do not have a square handbreadth between them, if uncleanness is located underneath one of them, [the space] underneath it is unclean. [The space] between the boards and on top of them is clean [cf. T. Ah. 13:7].

H. "It follows, therefore, that where there is a handbreadth [in one of the beams] we do invoke [the principle of fictively regarding the beam] as forced downward and treated as level [with the other beams], and where there is not a handbreadth [in one of the beams], we do not invoke [the principle of fictively regarding the beam] as forced downward and treated as level [with the other beams]."

I. That indeed does prove [Raba's case].

J. R. Kahana was in session and cited this tradition [of Raba about the requisite breadth of the bunch of reeds or beam]. Said R. Ashi to R. Kahana, "And is it the case that, wherever there is not a handbreadth [in the dimensions of the reed or beam], we do not invoke [the principle of fictively regarding the beam] as forced downward and treated as level [with the other beams or reeds]?

K. "And has it not been taught on Tannaite authority:

L. "In the case of a beam projecting from one wall [of an alley way toward the other, which we wish to regard as forming a cross beam for purposes of forming a fictive gateway to close off the alleyway and treat it as a single domain for purposes of carrying on the Sabbath], which does not reach the opposite wall,

M. "and so too two beams, one protruding from one wall and the other protruding from the other wall, which do not touch one another –

N. "[if there is a distance of] less than three [handbreadths between them], one does not have to bring another [beam to close off the space].

O. "[If there is a space] of three [handbreadths between them], one does have to bring another [beam to close off the space].

P. "Rabban Simeon b. Gamaliel says, '[22B] If it is less than four handbreadths, one does not have to bring another [beam]. If it is four handbreadths [or more], one does not have to bring another [beam].

Q. "So in the case of two beams which run parallel to one another, and in the one there is not enough breadth to hold a half-brick, nor in the other enough breadth to hold a half brick,

R. "if they can hold a half-brick placed breadthwise, [on their breadth of an entire handbreadth,] it is not necessary to bring another [beam], and if not, it is necessary to bring another [beam].

S. "Rabban Simeon b. Gamaliel says, 'If they can hold a half brick placed lengthwise, over a distance of three handbreadths, it is not necessary to bring another [beam], and if not, it is necessary to bring another [beam].'

T. "If one was above and one was below, R. Yose b. R. Judah says, 'They regard the lower one as if it goes upward, and the upper one as if it goes downward, on condition that the upper one not be more than twenty cubits from the ground, and the lower one not lower than ten handbreadths from the ground' [T. Er. 1:4-6, with different wording].

U. "[What follows from the cited passage?] Lo, if both protruding beams lay within twenty cubits of the ground, we do invoke [the fictive principle that] the upper beam is regarded as forced down and levelled with the lower one, [and that is the case even though the distance between one beam and the other was more than three cubits], even though [in the beam] is not a handbreadth [contrary to Raba's view, H].'"

V. He said to him, "This is how to respond: And I invoke the rule on condition [now revising the language of T] that the upper one not be more than twenty cubits from the ground, and the lower one at least three handbreadths from the upper one.

W. "Or, alternatively: On condition that the lower one not be within ten handbreadths of the ground but rather above ten handbreadths, and the upper one be within at least three handbreadths of it.

X. "But [if they were] three handbreadths apart, if one of the beams is not a handbreadth, we do not invoke [the principle of fictively regarding the upper beam] as being forced down and levelled [with the lower one]."

III.

A. *But one, the shade of which is greater than the light, is valid [M. 2:2D-E]:*

B. But if the light and shade areas are equivalent, it is invalid.

C. But lo, we have learned in the Mishnah of the earlier chapter: *If the light is greater than the shade, it is invalid [M. Suk. 1:1E-F].*
D. That would indicate, therefore, that if they are equivalent, it is valid.
E. There is no real contradiction, since the former [in which case, if the areas are of equal size, the sukkah is invalid] is when the sukkah is seen from above [that is, from the perspective of the roofing], the latter [in which the sukkah is valid], is when the sukkah is seen from below. [Slotki, p. 97, n. 5: If in the roof there is as much open as covered space, then it is invalid, since the sun appears on the floor in broader patches than the shade; if on the floor (below) there is as much sunshine as shade, it is evident that there is more of the roof covered than open. The idea is that the beams of the sun widen from the roof to the floor.]
F. Said R. Pappa, "This is in line with what people say: 'What is the size of a zuz above becomes the size of an issar [a much larger coin] below.'"

IV.

A. *[The sukkah,] the roofing of which is tightly knit like that of a house... [M. 2:2F]:*
B. Our rabbis have taught on Tannaite authority:
C. *[The sukkah,] the roofing of which is tightly knit like that of a house, even though the stars cannot be seen from inside it, is valid [M. 2:2F-H]:*
D. If the rays of the sun cannot be seen through [the roofing],
E. the House of Shammai declare it invalid.
F. And the House of Hillel declare it valid.

So long, M. 2:2C-E, F-H, as the roofing conforms to the basic requirement, M. 1:1E, the sukkah is valid. Unit II is continuous with unit I, which begins with the exegesis of the language of the Mishnah, so the whole forms a protracted inquiry into the fundamental principles of the law, underlying both the passage at hand (as Samuel and Abayye explain it) and the quite distinct materials of tractate Erubin. The long citation of materials similar to what we find in the Tosefta is needed only for what occurs at the very end. Unit III compares the present passage to M. 1:1, and unit IV provides a minor clarification along the same lines as unit III, now in the names of earlier authorities.

2:3

A. *He who makes his sukkah on the top of a wagon or a boat – it is valid.*
B. *And they go up into it on the festival day.*
C. *[If he made it] at the top of the tree or on a camel, it is valid.*
D. *But they do not go up into it on the festival day.*
E. *[If] two [sides of a sukkah] are [formed by] a tree, and one is made by man,*
F. *or two are made by man and one is [formed by] a tree,*
G. *it is valid.*
H. *But they do not go up into it on the festival day.*
I. *[If] three are made by man and one is [formed by] a tree, it is valid.*

J. *And they do go up into it on the festival day.*

K. *[23A] This is the governing principle: In the case of any [sukkah] in which the tree may be removed, and [the sukkah] can [still] stand by itself, it is valid.*

L. *And they go up into it on the festival day.*

I.

A. In accord with which authority is the rule of the Mishnah-paragraph [M. 2:3A]?

B. It accords with the view of R. Aqiba. For it has been taught on Tannaite authority:

C. He who makes his sukkah on the deck of a ship –

D. Rabban Gamaliel declares it invalid.

E. And R. Aqiba declares it valid.

F. There is a precedent involving Rabban Gamaliel and R. Aqiba, who were traveling on a boat. R. Aqiba went and made a sukkah on the deck of the ship. On the next day the wind blew and tore it away. Said to him Rabban Gamaliel, "Aqiba, where is your sukkah!"

II.

A. Said Abayye, "All parties concur in a case in which a sukkah cannot withstand an ordinary land breeze, that such a sukkah is null.

B. "If a sukkah can stand in an uncommon land breeze, all parties concur that it is a valid sukkah.

C. "Where there is a dispute, it concerns a sukkah that can stand in a commonplace land breeze but cannot stand in a [supply:] commonplace sea breeze.

D. "Rabban Gamaliel takes the view that a sukkah is meant to be a permanent dwelling, and since this one cannot stand in a commonplace sea breeze, it is null.

E. "R. Aqiba takes the position that we require merely a temporary dwelling, and since this sukkah can withstand an ordinary land breeze [even though it cannot withstand a sea breeze], it is valid."

III.

A. *[If he made it at the top of a tree] or on a camel, it is valid [M. 2:3C]:*

B. In accord with which authority is the rule of the Mishnah-paragraph [at M. 2:3C]?

C. It is R. Meir, for it has been taught on Tannaite authority:

D. He who makes his sukkah on a beast –

E. R. Meir declares [the sukkah] valid.

F. And R. Judah declares it invalid.

G. What is the scriptural basis for the view of R. Judah?

H. Scripture has stated, "You shall keep the feast of Sukkot for seven days" (Deut. 16:13).

I. A sukkah that is suitable for use for seven days is regarded as a sukkah.

J. A sukkah that is not suitable for use for seven days is not regarded as a sukkah.

K. And R. Meir? In his view, from the perspective of the law of the Torah, such a sukkah likewise may serve [even though it would not be ideal]. It is merely the rabbis who have made a precautionary decree against such a sukkah.

IV.

A. If one made a beast as a wall for a sukkah, R. Meir declares it invalid.

B. And R. Judah declares it valid.

C. For R. Meir would say, "Of anything that is animate people may not make use either for the wall of a sukkah, the sidebeam for an alley [for use in fictively turning the alleyway into an enclosed space for common carrying on the Sabbath], boards around wells [for the same purpose], or a stone for covering a grave."

D. In the name of R. Yose the Galilean they said, "Also they do not write on an animate creature a writ of divorce for a woman." [Cf. Unit VIII for exposition of this item.]

E. What is the reason for the position of R. Meir [that an animate object may not serve as a wall for a sukkah]?

F. Abayye said, "Lest the beast die [and deprive the sukkah of its services]."

G. R. Zira said, "Lest the beast escape [with the same effect]."

H. [In the case of a shackled elephant,] all parties concur [that the sukkah is valid], for, should it die, its carcass [nonetheless will form a wall of at least] ten handbreadths in height.

I. Where there is a dispute, it concerns an elephant that is not shackled.

J. From the viewpoint of him who has said, "... lest the beast die," we do not take account of that possibility, [since even in death the beast will continue to serve, as just now stated].

K. From the viewpoint of him who has said, "We make a precautionary decree lest the beast escape," we surely should take account of the possibility that [the unshackled beast] will escape.

L. But in the view of him who has said that the operative consideration is that the beast may die, should we not take account of the possibility that it may escape?

M. Rather [revising H-K], in the case of an elephant that is not shackled, all parties concur [that the sukkah relying upon such an elephant for one of its walls would be invalid].

N. Where there is a dispute, it concerns a beast [of commonplace size, not so large as an elephant], that is shackled.

O. In the view of him who has said that the operative consideration is a precautionary decree, lest the beast die, here too we take account of that possibility.

P. In the view of him who has said that we make a precautionary decree lest the beast escape, we do not take account of that possibility [since the beast is properly shackled and cannot escape. Hence the wall remains firm.]

Q. But in the view of him who has said that the operative consideration is lest the beast escape, should we not take account of the possibility that it may die? [Surely that remains a consideration, even while the probability of escape is nil.]

R. Death is not so commonplace, [that we have to take that possibility into account in the case of the shackled beast.]

V.

    A. But is there not too much open space between the animal's legs [so that the animal cannot form a valid wall]?

    B. We deal with a case in which the space is stuffed with branches of palms and bay-trees.

    C. But the animal might lie down [and crush the filling]?

    D. We deal with a case in which the animal was suspended with ropes from above [!] [and will not lie down and crush the filling or diminish the height of the wall that it constitutes].

    E. Now in the view of him who has said that we make a precautionary decree to take account of the possibility that the beast will die, [and that is why a sukkah with a wall formed by a beast is invalid], lo, one suspends the beast with ropes from above. [So why take account of the death of the beast? After all, being suspended, the carcass will still perform its service to the sukkah.]

    F. There may be a case in which, when the beast is alive, it is set up three handbreadths from the sukkah-roofing [hence in a valid position], but [23B], when the beast dies, its carcass will shrink, and that possibility will not have been taken into account by the owner [and so the sukkah will become invalid without the owner's knowledge].

VI.

    A. Now did Abayye say [IV F] that it is R. Meir who takes account of the possibility of the beast's dying, and R. Judah who does not take account of such a possibility?

    B. And have we not learned in the Mishnah:

    C. *An Israelite girl married to a priest whose husband went overseas eats priestly rations in the assumption that her husband is alive [M. Git. 3:3G-I].*

    D. Now the following objection was raised in this regard:

    E. "Lo, here is your writ of divorce, to take effect one hour before I die," – the wife is forbidden to eat priestly rations forthwith [since we do not know when the husband will die].

    F. [Now, in dealing with the contradiction between the cited passage of the Mishnah and the following statement,] said Abayye, "There is no contradiction. The one case represents the view of R. Meir, who does not take account of the possibility that the husband may die while overseas,] and the other case represents the view of R. Judah, who does take account of the possibility that the husband may die [suddenly].

    G. *For it has been taught on Tannaite authority:*

    H. *He who purchases wine among Samaritans [in a situation in which he cannot separate tithes right away, but wishes to drink the wine], says, "Two logs out of one hundred which I shall separate, behold, these are made priestly rations, and the following ten logs are made first tithe, and the following nine logs are made second tithe." He regards the wine as unconsecrated produce and drinks it [M. Dem. 7:4, Sarason, Demai, p. 243],* the words of R. Meir [T. Dem. 8:7AA].

    I. [24A] R. Judah, R. Yose, and R. Simeon prohibited [doing so] [T. Dem. 8:7BB].

J. The attributions then should be reversed. R. Meir takes account of the possibility of death, and R. Judah does not take account of the possibility of death. [We reverse Abayye's attributions.]

K. For it has been taught on Tannaite authority:

L. If one made a beast into a wall for a sukkah,

M. R. Meir declares it invalid.

N. And R. Judah declares it valid.

O. Nonetheless, is there not a contradiction between what R. Meir says [concerning the conditional designation of tithes and priestly rations, in which case he disregards the possibility that some sort of accident – whether the breaking of the wineskin, which will make it impossible later on to do what the man now declares he will do, or whether the death of the man, which will have the same effect – will take place, and the matter of the use of the beast for a wall of a sukkah, in which case he takes full account of the possibility of some sort of disqualifying accident].

P. R. Meir may reply to you, "The accident of death is commonplace, [the accident of] the breaking of the wine skin is not commonplace. It is possible to hand it over to a watchman [to make sure that the wine remains available. But the case of the sukkah is different.]"

Q. [We proceed to address the same question to Judah.] There is a contradiction between what R. Judah says [concerning the conditional designation of tithes and the like, in which case he takes account of the possibility of an untoward accident, and the matter of the use of the beast for a wall for the sukkah, in which case he does not take account of the possibility of an accident].

R. The operative consideration for R. Judah's views [in the matter of the conditional designation of the tithes and priestly rations of wine in the wineskin] is not the matter of the possibility of an untoward accident, namely, the splitting of the wineskin [which will leave no wine available for the actual fulfillment of the man's original condition, but a quite separate principle]. Specifically, R. Judah does not concede the principle of post facto selection. [That is, some hold that we retrospectively apply the results of a selection made only later on in produce to be assigned to the several tithes. In Judah's view what one will do later on has no retroactive validity. That is why he prohibits the entire procedure.]

S. But does R. Judah not take account of the possibility of the splitting of the wineskin? [Is the only issue retrospective selection, which he denies?]

T. And lo, note what is taught on Tannaite authority at the end of the same passage:

U. They said to R. Meir, "Do you not concede that if his wineskin bursts after he has drunk the wine but before he has separated tithes from the remainder, he has drunk fully untithed produce?"

V. He said to them, "Only when it actually bursts. But we do not scruple from the outset, since this is not a common occurrence" [T. Dem. 8:7CC-DD, Sarason, Demai, p. 249].

W. Would this passage not present the implication, then, that R. Judah does take account of the possibility that the skin may break?

X. [Not really, for] in that case, it is R. Judah who is addressing R. Meir in this wise: "In my view, I maintain that we do not invoke the principle of retrospective selection [such as you would hold], but by your own reasoning, by which we do invoke the principle of retrospective selection, do you nonetheless not concur that, in any event, the wine skin may burst?"

Y. At that point, [Meir then] replied to him, **"Only when it actually bursts..."**

Z. But does R. Judah not take account of the possibility of untoward death?

AA. And lo, we have learned in the Mishnah:

BB. *[Seven days before the Day of Atonement... they appoint another priest as the high priest's possible substitute, lest some cause of invalidation overtake him.] R. Judah says, "Also: they appoint another woman as a substitute for his wife, lest his wife die..." [M. Yoma 1:1D-E].*

CC. [No, that poses no problem, for] it has been stated in this regard: Said R. Huna, son of R. Joshua, "Sages imposed a higher requirement on the [Day of] Atonement [and normally would not take account of the possibility of sudden death]."

VII.

A. Both the one who maintains that the operative consideration is that the beast might die, and the one who holds that the criterion is that the beast might flee, [will concur that,] viewed from the aspect of the law of the Torah, a beast constitutes a perfectly acceptable partition, and it is only rabbis who made a precautionary decree. [Accordingly, we now ask about the status of the issue at hand.]

B. If that is the case, then, in the view of R. Meir, the beast should impart uncleanness when it serves as a rolling stone to seal a grave. [Slotki, p. 102, n. 7: Since according to Pentateuchal law it is a valid partition, it ought to contract uncleanness, even if the rabbis decreed later that it is no valid partition. With regard to sukkah and the alley the rabbinical decree might well be upheld, since it restricts the law, but in the case of uncleanness, where it leads to a relaxation of the Pentateuchal law, the rabbinical decree must obviously be disregarded.]

C. Why, then, have we learned in the Mishnah:

D. *[R. Judah declares that] An animate creature which is used to cover up the entrance of a tomb imparts uncleanness as a sealing-stone [M.'s text lacks "R. Judah declares"]. But R. Meir declares it insusceptible to uncleanness when used for that purpose [M. Er. 1:7D-E]. [Meir could not maintain that the uncleanness at hand is pentateuchal in authority and must then hold that it is a decree of rabbis that is involved.]*

E. Rather, said R. Aha bar Jacob, "R. Meir takes the view that any partition that [Slotki:] is upheld by wind is no partition."

F. There are those who report the matter as follows: Said R. Aha bar Jacob, "R. Meir takes the view that any partition which is not made by human action is no partition."

G. What is at issue between these two versions [of Meir's view]? At issue is a case in which one set up [the wall] with an inflated wineskin.

H. In the view of the one who holds that a partition that is upheld by wind is no partition, lo, in this case we have a partition that is upheld by wind [and it is unsuitable in Meir's view].

I.   In the view of one who holds that if it is not made by human action [it is no partition,] [24B] lo, this one is made by human action."

VIII.

A.   A master has stated: "In the name of R. Yose the Galilean they said, 'Also they do not write on it [i.e., an animate object] a bill of divorce for a woman.'" [See 2:3 IV D.]

B.   What is the scriptural basis for the position of R. Yose the Galilean?

C.   It is in accord with that which has been taught on Tannaite authority:

D.   "[He will write her] a writ [of divorce]," (Deut. 24:1) –

E.   I know only that one may use a writ. How do I know that the law encompasses anything?

F.   Scripture states, "He will write for her..." – in any manner.

G.   If so, why does Scripture state, "A writ..."

H.   It is to indicate to you that just as a "writ" is something which is inanimate and does not consume [produce], so anything that is inanimate and does not consume produce [may be used, thus excluding animate creatures].

I.   And rabbis?

J.   If the Scripture had stated, "... in a writ...," matters would have been as you claim. But now that it is written, "... a writ...," the purpose is so as to make known matters in general.

K.   And as to the language, "... write..." how do rabbis interpret it?

L.   They require that expression to indicate that it is through the act of writing [the bill of divorce] that a woman is divorced, and it is not through the payment of money [owing on the occasion of the divorce] that the woman is divorced.

M.   [Why would someone have thought otherwise?] It might have entered your mind to rule that, since the leaving of the marriage is compared to the establishment of the marriage, just as the relationship at the outset is established through the payment of money, so at the end the relationship may be broken off through the payment of money. Accordingly we are informed that that is not the case.

N.   Now how, for his part, does R. Yose the Galilean attain that same principle, [since he interprets the language of the verse at hand for another purpose]?

O.   He derives that lesson from the language, "a writ of divorce," meaning, "A writ is what cuts the relationship, and no other consideration cuts the relationship."

P.   And the other party?

Q.   That formulation is required to indicate that the relationship is broken off through something that effectively severs the tie between him and her.

R.   For it has been taught on Tannaite authority:

S.   [If the husband said], "Lo, here is your writ of divorce, on the condition that you not drink wine, that you not go to your father's house for ever," this is not an act of totally severing the relationship.

T.   [If he said,] "... for thirty days...," lo, this is an act of severing the relationship. [The husband cannot impose a permanent condition, for if he could do so, then the relationship will not have been completely and finally severed.]

U. And the other party?

V. He derives the same lesson from the use of the language, "total cutting off" as against merely "cutting off."

W. And the other party?

X. The rabbis do not derive any lesson from the variation in the language at hand.

The operative principle is that one may not make use of a tree or a camel on the festival day (M. Bes. 5:2). The restrictions then are the same as they are on the Sabbath. The contrast between M. 2:3A-B and C-D is therefore quite clear. E-L then form a secondary, and rather extended, expansion of the same point as is made about C. If the sukkah depends upon the tree, then it may not be used on the festival day. If it stands on its own and does not depend on the tree, then it may be used on the festival, as M. 2:3K-L explain. So what we have is a primary statement, in rather trivial terms, and then a secondary development, somewhat overblown, given the obvious point to be made here. Units I and II provide routine clarification for the Mishnah, with the former discovering the authority behind the Mishnah's anonymous rule, the latter clarifying the details of the law. The real action is at unit III, which serves to introduce units IV-VIII. Now we take up the slightly silly possibility that someone uses a beast to form the wall of a sukkah, a conception that the framer of the Mishnah cannot imagine, e.g., at M. 2:3C. The discussion of the issue of not using a beast is really focused upon the operative considerations, and this leads us to identify the authority behind the two distinct criteria. Once we have determined that a given authority espouses one of the two principles, we forthwith investigate whether or not that authority remains consistent through other cases in which the same principle applies. The discussion thus is continuous, protracted, and beautifully composed, even though we can identify a number of distinct subunits. Unit VIII then takes up a matter introduced, to begin with tangentially, in unit IV.

2:4A

A. *He who makes his sukkah among trees, and the trees are its sides – it is valid.*

I.

A. Said R. Aha bar Jacob, "Any partition that cannot stand in an ordinary wind is not regarded as a valid partition."

B. We have learned in the Mishnah: *He who makes his sukkah among trees, and the trees are its sides – it is valid [M. 2:4A].*

C. And lo, they go back and forth.

D. Here with what do we deal? It is with a strong tree [which does not sway].

E. But lo, there are the branches [which do sway]?

F. We deal with a case in which he wove the branches with shrubbery and bay trees [to make them solid].

G. If that is the case, what purpose is there in stating the rule [since the partition in this case would be entirely valid]?

H. What might you have said? We should make a precautionary decree against such an arrangement, lest someone come and make use of the tree [e.g., to support objects on the festival day, which would be forbidden]?

I. So we are informed [that we make no such decree].

J. Come and take note: **If there was a tree, fence or a partition of reeds, these are regarded as equivalent to a corner piece [of boards] [T. Er. 1:15A].** [These partitions would move with the wind, yet are valid].

K. We deal here too with a case where it is valid because the owner has woven the branches with shrubbery and bay trees [to make them solid].

L. Come and take note: *A tree which overshadows the ground — if its foliage was not three handbreadths above the ground, they carry under it [in the theory that it forms a partition and designates a distinct domain thereby] [M. Er. 10:8A-C].*

M. Why should that be the case? Lo, the branches move back and forth [with the wind and so should not be regarded as a valid partition]?

N. Here too, it is valid, because the owner has woven the branches with shrubbery and bay trees.

O. If so, then a person should be permitted to carry throughout the area. On what account then did R. Huna, son of R. Joshua, say, "People may carry there [25A] if the partitioned area is only over an area of two seahs"? [Why not permit carrying over the entire partitioned area, if it is a valid partition at all?]

P. It is because here we deal with a fictive abode which is meant to be used in the open air, and in the case of any dwelling which is meant to be used in the open air [that is, lacking fixed roof and walls], people may carry only in an area of two seahs [and no more, despite the provision of valid partitions that ordinarily would allow for a greater area of movement than that].

Q. Come and take note: If one has taken as his place for Sabbath residence a hill that is ten handbreadths high and in extent from four cubits to two seahs, so also in a hole ten handbreadths deep and four cubits to two seahs in extent, or in a harvested area surrounded by areas of corn — he may walk freely over the entire area and for two thousand cubits beyond.

R. Now that is the case even though the walls formed of the sheaves of corn sway back and forth [in the wind].

S. In this case too we deal with his weaving the sheaves with shrubs and bay trees.

The reason for the Mishnah's rule is that the branches form partitions. This leads to Aha's qualification, and then an extensive secondary expansion, proving that that qualification is both valid and also worth stating. The rest allows us to review a sequence of cases to make the same point, with the good result of allowing us to review parallel cases of partitions that serve to set up the walls for the domain for Sabbath carrying.

2:4B-D

B. *Agents engaged in a religious duty are exempt from the requirement of dwelling in a sukkah.*

C. *Sick folk and those who serve them are exempt from the requirement of dwelling in a sukkah.*

D. *[People] eat and drink in a random manner outside of a sukkah.*

I.

A. How do we know on the basis of Scripture [that the rule at M. 2:4B is correct]?

B. It is in line with that which he have learned on Tannaite authority:

C. "When you sit in your house" (Deut. 6:7) serves to exclude one who is engaged in carrying out a religious duty.

D. "And when you walk by the way" (Deut. 6:7) serves to exclude a newly-married groom [who likewise does not have to carry out the religious duty of reciting the Shema, to which the cited verse refers].

E. On this basis they have stated: He who marries a virgin is exempt from the requirement to recite the Shema, and he who marries a widow is liable.

F. What is the sort of evidence that implies the stated distinction?

G. Said R. Huna, "...on the way..." – Just as the [taking of a trip] on the way is an optional matter, so too anything that is an optional matter [would have to be set aside for the saying of the Shema,] thus excluding one who is engaged in the performance of a religious duty.

H. But does the cited language not refer to one who is going along the way to carry out a religious duty, and lo, the All-Merciful has said that such a one should recite the Shema?

I. If so, Scripture should have said, "... in sitting... and in going..." What is the sense of "in your sitting... in your going..." [which Scripture does state]? It refers to going on your own business. Under such circumstances you are liable. Lo, if you are going on the purpose of carrying out a religious duty, however, then you will be exempt.

J. If that is the case, then even he who marries a widow also should be exempt [from the requirement of reciting the Shema].

K. He who marries a virgin is preoccupied, he who marries a widow is not preoccupied.

L. Is that to suggest that whenever a person is preoccupied, he also will be exempt from the requirement of reciting the Shema?

M. Then what about the case of one whose ship is sinking in the ocean, who is surely preoccupied. Is this a case in which one also would be exempt?

N. And if you wish to say that that indeed is the case, has not R. Abba bar Zabeda said Rab said, "A mourner is liable to carry out all of the religious duties that are stated in the Torah except for the religious duty involved in putting on the phylacteries.

O. "For lo, in their regard, the word 'beauty' is stated [at Ez. 24:17] [and a mourner should not don something of beauty]."

P. In the case at hand [involving a virgin] one is preoccupied with the carrying out of a religious duty, while in the other case [where the ship is sinking], he is preoccupied with an optional matter.

II.

   A. Now does the law derive from the cited passage [see I, Deut. 6:7] that he who carries out a religious duty is exempt from the obligations to carry out some other religious duty?

   B. Surely it derives [not from what served above but] from the following proof-text, for it has been taught on Tannaite authority:

   C. "And there were certain men who were unclean on account of a human corpse" (Num. 9:6). [These men were occupied with a religious duty and could not keep the Passover celebrated in Nisan, so they kept it in Iyyar, a month later, and hence observed what was the second Passover. This proves that those occupied in carrying out a religious duty involving the corpse were exempt from the religious duty involving the Passover sacrifice, and the cited generalization follows.]

   D. Who indeed were these men?

   E. "They were the ones who were carrying Joseph's bier," the words of R. Yose the Galilean.

   F. [25B] R. Aqiba says, "They were Mishael and Elzaphan, who were busy taking care of the bodies of Nadab and Abihu."

   G. R. Isaac says, "If they were carrying Joseph's bier, they could have had sufficient time to attain cultic purity [prior to Passover]. If they were Mishael and Elzaphan, they also should have had sufficient time to attain cultic cleanness. [So who were they, and why were they unclean with corpse-uncleanness?]

   H. "But they were people who were busy dealing with a neglected corpse [which religious duty takes priority over all others], and the seventh day [beyond their contracting corpse uncleanness in that connection] coincided with the eve of Passover, as it is said, 'They could not keep the Passover on that day' (Num. 9:6).

   I. "The sense is that that particular day they could not observe, but they could have kept the day following."

   J. [Now that we have shown that there are two distinct texts that prove a person involved in carrying out one religious duty is exempt from having to carry out others, the one regarding the Shema (Deut 6:7), the other regarding Passover (Num. 9:6), we ask why both proof-texts are necessary.] It is necessary [to have both proof-texts]. For had we derived the law only from the latter case [Num. 9:6], [I should have reached the conclusion that the reason is that] the occasion on which the obligation to keep the Passover had not yet come. But in the former case [Deut. 6:7, see I], where the occasion for reciting the Shema has arrived, I might have said that one would not be exempt.

   K. It is necessary [to have both proof-texts (Deut. 6:7 and Num. 9:6)]. And had I derived the proof only from the former case, [namely, the recitation of the Shema], I might have supposed that it is because violation of the requirement is not subject to the penalty of extirpation. But in the latter case [namely, Passover], in which failure to carry out the religious duty of observing the Passover sacrifice is penalized by extirpation, I might have reached the conclusion that the remission of the obligation does not apply.

   L. Accordingly, it was necessary to supply two proof-texts.

III.

A. [Returning to the] cited [passage from I.N, which is]:   Said R. Abba bar Zabeda said Rab, "A mourner is liable to carry out all of the religious duties that are stated in the Torah except for the religious duty involved in putting on the phylacteries.

B. "For lo, in their regard, the word 'beauty' is stated."

C. [How so?] Since the All-Merciful said to Ezekiel, "Bind your beauty on you" (Ez. 24:17), [his sense is that] "You are the one who is obligated, but everyone else [who is in mourning] is exempt.   [Ezekiel, in particular, is admonished to give up the normal rites of mourning. So he is told to put on his phylacteries. Other mourners are exempt from doing so.]

D. That rule pertains to the first day [of mourning], since it is written, "And the end thereof as a bitter day" (Amos 8:10). [Slotki, p. 109, n. 20: The beginning of the verse is, "And I will make it as the mourning for an only son." Since "day" in the singular is used, it follows that actual mourning is limited to one day.]

E. And R. Abba bar Zabeda said Rab said, "A mourner is liable to the religious duty of dwelling in the sukkah."

F. That fact is self-evident.

G. What might you have said?

H. Since R. Abba bar Zabeda said Rab said, "One who is in distress is exempt from the religious duty of dwelling in a sukkah," this one also is in the category of one who is in distress. So we are informed that that is not the case.

I. The exemption of one who is in distress applies to a person who suffers distress on account of some objective fact, but in this case [that is, the one of the mourner], he is the one who causes distress for himself. He has, therefore, to regain his composure.

J. And R. Abba bar Zabeda said Rab said, "A groom and the groomsmen and all the members of the wedding are exempt from the religious duty of dwelling in a sukkah all seven days of the Festival."

K. What is the reason for that exemption?

L. Because they have to rejoice [in the marriage].

M. But let them eat their festive meals in the sukkah and rejoice in the sukkah?

N. True rejoicing is only under the marriage canopy.

O. But let them then eat in the sukkah and rejoice under the marriage canopy?

P. True rejoicing takes place only where a meal is eaten.

Q. Then let them set up the marriage canopy in the sukkah?

R. Abayye said, "[They do not do so] because of considerations of privacy. [The sukkah was isolated. Should the groom have to leave, the bride would be left alone and a stranger might enter.]"

S. Raba said, "Because of the anguish of the groom [who will not want to show affection in so public a place, which has, after all, only three walls]."

T. What is the practical issue between the two explanations?

U. At issue is a case in which people routinely go out and come in [to the place at which the sukkah is located].

V. In the view of him who has said that the operative consideration is the possibility of [the bride's being left alone with a stranger], there is no such possibility.

W. In the view of him who has said that the issue is the anguish of the groom, that consideration remains valid.

X. Said R. Zira, "I ate in the sukkah and rejoiced in the marriage canopy, and my heart was all the happier, because I thereby kept two religious duties [at once]."

IV.

A. Our rabbis have taught on Tannaite authority:

B. The groom, the groomsmen, and all the members of the wedding are exempt from the religious duty of [reciting] the Prayer, and the phylacteries, but are liable to recite the Shema.

C. [26A] In the name of R. Shila they said, "The groom is exempt, but the groomsmen and all the members of the wedding are liable."

V.

A. It has been taught on Tannaite authority:

B. Said R. Hanania b. Aqabia, "Those who write scrolls, phylacteries, and parchments for *mezuzot* – they, their employees, and employees of their employees,

C. "and all those who are engaged in the work of Heaven –"

D. (this includes those who sell blue –)

E. "are exempt from the religious requirement of reciting the Shema, the Prayer, the phylacteries, and all religious duties that are listed in the Torah."

F. This serves to second the view of R. Yose the Galilean.

G. For R. Yose the Galilean would say, "He who is occupied with one religious duty is exempt from the obligation of carrying out another religious duty."

VI.

A. Our rabbis have taught on Tannaite authority:

B. **Wayfarers by day are exempt from the religious duty [of dwelling in the sukkah] by day and liable to carry it out at night.**

C. **Those who are on a trip by night are exempt from the religious duty of dwelling in a sukkah by night and liable by day.**

D. **Those who make their journey by day and by night are exempt from the religious duty of dwelling in a sukkah both by day and by night.**

E. **Those who are going to carry out a religious duty are exempt both by day and by night [cf. T. Suk. 2:3F].**

F. This is illustrated by the behavior of R. Hisda and Rabba bar R. Huna. When they went to visit the exilarch's establishment of the Sabbath of the festival [of Sukkot], they would sleep on the river bank at Sura. They said, "Since we are engaged as agents to carry out a religious duty, we are exempt [from the religious duty of sleeping in the sukkah]."

G. Our rabbis have taught on Tannaite authority:

H. City guards by day are exempt from the religious requirement of dwelling in a sukkah by day, but they are liable by night.

I. City guards [cf. M. 2:5B] by night are exempt from the religious requirement of dwelling in a sukkah by night, but they are liable by day.

J. City guards by day and by night are exempt from the religious requirement of dwelling in a sukkah by day and by night.

K. Garden-guards and orchard-guards are exempt by day and by night [T. Suk. 2:3C-G].

L. [As to the case of the last-named,] why not build a sukkah there and dwell in it [out in the fields or orchards]?

M. Said Abayye, "You shall dwell... (Lev. 23:42) as you ordinarily live."

N. Raba said, "The hole in the fence is an invitation to the thief. [Thieves will know where the guards are.]"

O. What is the practical difference between the two explanations?

P. At issue is a case in which the guard is in charge of a pile of fruit. [Abayye still will not approve building a sukkah there, Raba will.]

VII.

A. *Sick folk and those who serve them [M. 2:4C]:*

B. And [this is the case] not only of one who is seriously ill,

C. but even if someone has a headache or a pain in the eye.

D. Said Rabban Simeon b. Gamaliel, "M'SH W: I had a pain in the eye in Caesarion, and R. Yose b. Rabbi permitted me to sleep, along with my servant, outside of the sukkah" [T. Suk. 2:2B-D, in T.'s version].

E. Rab permitted R. Aha Bardela to sleep in a sukkah in a tester-bed [Slotki, p. 112, n. 11: which is ten handbreadths high and has a roof and is ordinarily forbidden], so as to keep out gnats.

F. Raba permitted R. Aha bar Adda to sleep outside of the shade of the sukkah on account of the stench of the clay.

G. Raba is consistent with views stated elsewhere, for Raba has said, "One who is in anguish is exempt from the religious duty of dwelling in a sukkah."

H. And lo, we have learned in the Mishnah: *Sick folk and those who serve them are exempt from the requirement of dwelling in a sukkah [M. 2:4C]* – which bears the implication that the exemption applies to sick folk and not to those who are [merely] distressed!

I. [We may interpret the sense of the passage in this way:] In the case of one who is sick, he and his attendants are exempt, but in the case of one who is in distress, while he is exempt, those who attend him are not.

VIII.

A. *People eat and drink in a random manner outside of a sukkah [M. 2:4D]:*

B. And what falls into the category of a random meal?

C. Said R. Joseph, "Two or three eggs."

D. Said Abayye to him, "And yet, on many occasions a person finds enough nourishment in such a meal, and it would then fall into the category of a regular meal."

E. Rather, said Abayye, "It is about as much as a snack of a [disciple] of a master's household before he goes into the study-session."

IX.

A. Our rabbis have taught on Tannaite authority:

B. People may eat a random meal outside of a sukkah but they may not take a snooze outside of a sukkah.

C. What is the reason for this distinction?

D. Said R. Ashi, "It is a precautionary decree, so that someone not fall into a deep sleep."

E. Said Abayye to him, "But along these same lines, it has been taught on Tannaite authority: 'A man make take a snooze while wearing his phylacteries but he may not take a regular nap.' [Surely we should take precautions] lest he fall into a deep sleep [in this case too]!"

F. R. Joseph, son of R. Ilai, said, "[It is permitted to snooze while wearing phylacteries] in a case in which one hands over to others responsibility for waking him up out of his sleep. [In that case we need not take precautions of another sort.]"

G. To this explanation R. Mesharshia objected. "Who will watch the watchman?"

H. Rather, said Rabbah bar bar Hana said R. Yohanan, "We deal [in the case of one who may snooze while wearing phylacteries] with one who does so while simply putting his head between his knees."

I. Raba said, "[As to the sukkah], there is no issue of distinguishing regular sleep from a snooze. [Both sorts are not to be done outside of the sukkah.]"

J. One Tannaite teaching holds: A man may take a snooze while wearing his phylacteries, but not fall into deep sleep.

K. A second Tannaite teaching holds: Whether a snooze or deep sleep, [one may do so while wearing phylacteries].

L. Yet a third: Whether a snooze or a deep sleep, one may not [do so while wearing phylacteries].

M. There is no contradiction among the three versions of the rule. In the third case, the man holds the phylacteries in his hand, [and if he falls asleep at all, the phylacteries will fall down]. In the first case, he leaves them on his head [in which case we distinguish a snooze from deep sleep]. In the second he spreads a cloth under him [so that, should the phylacteries fall, they will not hit the ground].

N. What is the length of a snooze [as distinct from deep sleep]?

O. Rami bar Ezekiel taught on Tannaite authority, "Enough time to walk a hundred cubits."

P. It has been taught on Tannaite authority along these same lines:

Q. "He who falls asleep while wearing his phylacteries, and, [when he wakes up,] sees that he has ejaculated [so must remove the phylacteries], takes hold of the strap [of the phylacteries], [26B] but not of the box thereof," the words of R. Jacob.

R. And sages say, "A man may sleep in his phylacteries only to take a snooze but not to fall into a deep sleep [so such an event will not take place].

S. "And how long is a snooze?

T. "Sufficient time to walk a hundred cubits."

U. Said Rab, "It is forbidden for a person to sleep by day any longer than a horse ever sleeps."

V. And how long does a horse ever sleep?

W. For sixty breaths.

X. Said Abayye, "The length of time that the master [Rabbah] sleeps is the same as the time that Rab sleeps, and Rab sleeps as long as Rabbi, and Rabbi sleeps as long as [King] David, and David sleeps as long as a horse, and a horse sleeps for sixty breaths."

Y. During the day time Abayye would snooze as long as it takes to go from Pumbedita to Be Kube. In his regard R. Joseph recited this verse: "How long will you sleep, O lazy man, when will you get up?" (Prov. 6:9).

X.

A. Our rabbis have taught on Tannaite authority:

B. "He who goes in to sleep by day may, if he wishes, take off his phylacteries, and may, if he wishes, leave them on.

C. "But if he does so by night, he must remove them and may not leave them on," the words of R. Nathan.

D. R. Yose says, "Youngsters must always remove them and may not leave them on, because they routinely become unclean [when asleep, from nocturnal emissions]."

E. May we then draw the conclusion that R. Yose takes the view that one who has had a seminal emission is prohibited from putting on phylacteries?

F. Abayye replied, "In this case we deal with youngsters who go to sleep with their wives, [and we impose a precautionary decree, that the man must remove his phylacteries] lest the couple do what comes naturally [which may not be done while wearing phylacteries]."

G. Our rabbis have taught on Tannaite authority:

H. If someone forgot and had sexual relations while wearing his phylacteries, he does not take hold either of the strap or the box [of the phylacteries] until he washes his hands. Only then may he remove the phylacteries. The reason is that the hands are always busy [and may have touched some unclean thing].

The Talmud provides a rather full account of the three topics of the Mishnah-paragraph at hand, following the order as well. Unit I presents a proof for M. 2:4B, unit II presents a second and then justifies the need for both. Unit III clarifies a passage adduced in evidence in the foregoing, and this leads us back to the main theme, allowing us to proceed directly to M. 2:4C – a fine and artful transition. Unit IV takes up the underlying principle – exemption from religious duty in general. At issue now are categories of persons to which unit III has made reference. Unit V proceeds to the same issues. Unit VI then turns to Tosefta's complement to the Mishnah-passage at hand. Unit VII cites the

Mishnah – M. 2:4C – and moves on to Tosefta's complement. Unit VIII cites M. 2:4D and provides definitions relevant to the matter. Unit IX then carries forward the exposition of the rule of M. 2:4D. But the theme now investigated – the wearing of phylacteries while one is asleep – takes over and the Talmud's remaining materials deal with that secondary question. Overall, therefore, what we have is exposition of the Mishnah, then secondary expansion of the exposition, carefully organized and in a straight-line from start to finish.

2:5

    A. *M'SH W: They brought Rabban Yohanan b. Zakkai some cooked food to taste, and to Rabban Gamaliel two dates and a dipper of water.*

    B. *And they said, "Bring them up to the sukkah."*

    C. *And when they gave to R. Sadoq food less than an egg's bulk, he took it in a cloth and ate it outside of the sukkah and said no blessing after it.*

I.

    A. Does the precedent [of M. 2:5] mean to contradict the rule [of M. 2:4D]? [We have just been told that people may eat a casual snack outside of the sukkah. What is the point of M. 2:5A-B?]

    B. There is a lacuna in the tale, and this is how it should be told:

    C. "If someone wishes to impose upon himself a more strict rule, he may do so, and there is no element, in his doing so, of self-aggrandisement [or presumptuousness].

    D. *"And M'SH W: They brought Rabban Yohanan b. Zakkai some cooked food to taste, and to Rabban Gamaliel two dates and a dipper of water, [27A], and they said, 'Bring them up to the sukkah.'"*

II.

    A. *And when they gave to R. Sadoq less than an egg's bulk, he took it in a cloth and ate it outside of the sukkah and said no blessing after it [M. 2:5C]:*

    B. Does this then bear the implication that if it had been of the bulk of an egg, he would have had to eat it in the sukkah?

    C. Then this precedent would constitute a refutation of the view of R. Joseph and Abayye [who define a casual meal as two or three eggs, or a student's snack, a bulk of an egg. Here such a meal would appear to belong in a sukkah only, contrary to their view of a random snack.]

    D. No, the point is that food of less than the bulk of an egg does not require the washing of hands and the saying of a blessing, while food of the bulk of an egg would require the washing of the hands and the saying of a blessing.

At unit I the Talmud clarifies the relationship of the case to the law that it is supposed to illustrate, and in unit II the secondary implications of the second precedent are brought into line with an established rule. So the whole constitutes Mishnah-exegesis.

2:6

A. R. Eliezer says, "Fourteen meals is a person obligated to eat in the sukkah,

B. "one by day and one by night."

C. And sages say, "There is no fixed requirement, except for the first two nights of the festival alone."

D. And further did R. Eliezer say, "He who has not eaten his meal in the Sukkah on the first night of the festival should make up for it on the last night of the festival."

E. And sages say, "There is no way of making it up.

F. "Concerning such a case it is said, That which is crooked cannot be made straight, and that which is wanting cannot be reckoned (Qoh. 1:15)."

I.

A. What is the scriptural basis for the opinion of R. Eliezer?

B. "You will dwell" (Lev. 23:42) as you usually dwell. Just as in a dwelling a person [eats] one [meal] by day and one by night, so the sukkah must serve both by day and by night [as the setting for a meal].

C. And sages [concur that the sukkah is] like a dwelling, [drawing a different conclusion from the analogy, namely:]

D. Just as in the case of a dwelling, if one wants, he eats a meal, and if one wants, he does not eat a meal, so in the case of a sukkah, if one wants, he eats a meal, and if one wants, he does not eat a meal.

E. If that is the case, then even in the first night of the festival [there should] also [be no obligation to eat in the sukkah, contrary to M. 2:6C].

F. Said R. Yohanan in the name of R. Simeon b. Yehosedeq, "'The fifteenth' (Lev. 23:39) is stated here [with reference to the festival of Sukkot], and elsewhere it is stated, 'the fifteenth' (Lev. 23:6) with respect to the festival of unleavened bread.

G. "Just as, in that latter instance, on the first night there is a fixed obligation [to eat unleavened bread], while from that point onward in the holy week, it is an optional matter,

H. "so here too in the case of the first night it is a fixed obligation [to eat in the sukkah], while from that time onward it is an optional matter."

I. In the case of Passover, how do we know [that it is a formal obligation to eat unleavened bread on the first night of Passover]?

J. Scripture states, "In the evening you will eat unleavened bread" (Ex. 12:18).

K. In this way Scripture imposes a fixed obligation in this regard.

II.

A. And further did R. Eliezer say [etc.] [M. 2:6D]:

B. But did R. Eliezer not say, Fourteen meals is a person obligated to eat in the sukkah, one by day and one by night [M. 2:6A-B] ? [Slotki, p. 117, n. 13: And since the last day is not subject to the obligation, and any person sitting in the sukkah on that day in fulfillment of the commandment is guilty of adding to the commandments, how can that day compensate for the first?]

C. Said Bira said R. Ami, "R. Eliezer retracted [that view]."

D. How does one make up [the meal of the first night, if he misses it]?

E. If one might propose that he does so with bread, then he thereby eats the meal of the festival day [that he is obligated to eat anyhow, so how can that make up for the day he has missed]?

F. What then is the sense of "make up"?

G. One makes up the missing meal with various kinds of desserts.

H. It has been taught along these lines on Tannaite authority:

I. If one has made up [a missing meal] with various kinds of desserts, he has carried out his obligation.

III.

A. The butler of Agrippas the king asked R. Eliezer, "In the case of a person such as I, who am used to eat only a single meal a day, what is the law as to my eating only a single meal in the sukkah and thereby carrying out my obligation?"

B. He said to him, "Every day you go along and eat various sorts of desserts for your own honor, and now shouldn't you add one additional savory in the honor of your creator?"

C. And he further asked him, "And what about me, for I have two wives, one in Tiberias and one in Sepphoris, and I have two sukkahs, one in Tiberis and one in Sepphoris. What is the law on my going from one sukkah to the other and thereby carrying out my obligation [even though one is supposed to carry out his obligation to dwell in a sukkah by doing so in a single sukkah during the seven days of the holiday]?"

D. He said to him, "No, [you may not do so.] For I rule that whoever goes out from one sukkah to another loses out on the religious duty he has performed through the first of the two."

IV.

A. It has been taught on Tannaite authority:

B. R. Eliezer says, "[27B] People may not go out from one sukkah to another, and they may not erect a sukkah to begin with on the intermediate days of the festival [but it must be built in advance of the first holy day of the festival week]."

C. And sages say, "People may go from one sukkah to another, and they may also erect a sukkah on the intermediate days of a festival."

D. And all parties concur that if the sukkah falls down, the owner may go and rebuild it on the intermediate days of the festival.

E. What is the scriptural basis for the position of R. Eliezer?

F. Scripture has said, "You shall keep the feast of Sukkot for seven days" (Deut. 16:13), which is to say, make a sukkah that is suitable for seven days.

G. And rabbis?

H. This is the sense of Scripture: "Make a sukkah for the festival" [without specification as to how long it must last].

I. "And all parties concur that if the sukkah falls down, the owner may go and rebuild it on the intermediate days of the festival."

J. That is self-evident!

K. Not so, for what might you have said? This really is another sukkah, and it is not for seven days [and so not acceptable].

L. So we are informed that [even in Eliezer's view] that is not the case.

V.

A. It has been taught on Tannaite authority:

B. R. Eliezer says on the first festival day of the Festival, "Just as a man may not fulfill his obligation to take hold of a lulab by using that of his fellow, for it is written, 'And you shall take hold for yourself on the first day of the fruit of goodly trees, branches of palm trees' (Lev. 23:40), meaning, such as belong to you,

C. "so on the first festival day of the Festival a man may not carry out his obligation to dwell in the sukkah by doing so in the sukkah of his fellow, for it is written, 'The festival of Sukkot you shall keep for yourself for seven days' (Lev. 23:42), meaning, making use of a sukkah that belongs to you yourself."

D. And sages say, "Even though they have said, 'On the first festival day of the Festival a man may not fulfill his obligation to take hold of the lulab by using that of his fellow,'

E. "nonetheless, on the first festival day of the Festival he may carry out his obligation to dwell in the sukkah by doing so in the sukkah of his fellow, for it is written, 'All that are homeborn in Israel shall dwell in sukkahs' (Lev. 23:42), teaching that every Israelite may dwell in a single sukkah. [Obviously it will then be a sukkah that some of them do not own.]"

F. Now how do rabbis interpret the specific reference, at Lev. 23:42, to "for yourself"?

G. They require that reference to prove that one may not make use of a stolen sukkah, but, with reference to one that is merely borrowed, they point to the verse of Scripture that speaks of "all that are homeborn" (Lev. 23:42).

H. And as to R. Eliezer, how does he deal with that same reference?

I. He requires it to treat the categories of the proselyte, who converted it in the intervening days [between the first and last days of the Festival], and the minor who reached maturity in the intermediate days, [showing that they too must make a sukkah for themselves, even from the point at which the obligation came to apply to them, in the middle of the festival week].

J. And as to rabbis?

K. Since they have said that people may make a sukkah on the intermediate days of the festival, they take the view that no scriptural proof is needed, [in addition, to indicate that the named categories may build a sukkah for themselves during those days].

VI.

A. Our rabbis have taught on Tannaite authority:

B. There was the precedent involving R. Ilai, who went to greet R. Eliezer, his master, in Lud, on the Festival.

C. He said to him, "Ilai, are you not among those who observe the Festival by remaining at rest?"

D. For R. Eliezer maintained, "I praise those who take their ease and do not leave their homes on the Festival, for it has been written, 'You shall rejoice, you and your household' (Deut. 14:26) [including your wife, hence you must stay home on an occasion of rejoicing]" [T. Suk. 2:1C].

E. Is this the case? And did not R. Isaac say, "How do we know that a man is liable to greet his master on the Festival?

F. "As it is said, 'Why will you go to him today? It is neither the New Moon nor the Sabbath' (2 Kgs. 4:23), which bears the implication that on the New Moon and on the Sabbath one is liable to greet his master" [and hence Ilai did the right thing].

G. There is no contradiction. The one verse [which indicates one is liable to do so] speaks of a trip which one can make in one day, and the other speaks of a trip one cannot make in one day.

H. Our rabbis have taught on Tannaite authority:

I. There was the precedent, in which R. Eliezer spent the Sabbath [during the Festival] in Upper Galilee in the sukkah of Yohanan, son of R. Ilai at Caesarea, and, some say, in Caesarion. The sun came into the sukkah. [Thinking of avoiding the glare], he said to him, "What is the law as to my spreading a sheet over [the sukkah]?"

J. He said to him, "You have no tribe in Israel that did not produce a judge."

K. The sun now shone half the height of the sukkah. He said to him, "What is the law as to my spreading a sheet over it?"

L. He said to him, "You have no tribe in Israel from which prophets did not go forth. The tribe of Judah and Benjamin produced kings on the instructions of prophets."

M. The sun reached the feet of R. Eliezer [as it climbed into the sky]. Yohanan took a sheet and spread it over the sukkah.

N. R. Eliezer threw his cloak over his back and left.

O. It was not because [Eliezer wished to] evade answering the questions, he had said, but because [Eliezer] never made a statement that he had not heard from his master.

P. Now how did [Eliezer] act in this way [going out from his own sukkah to keep the Festival at Yohanan's sukkah]? And did not R. Eliezer say, "One may not go forth from one sukkah to another sukkah"? [So surely he should have stayed home and used his own sukkah the entire time.]

Q. It was on a different festival [not Sukkot, and the purpose of sitting in the sukkah had nothing to do with observing the Festival of Sukkot].

R. But did not R. Eliezer himself say, "I praise those who take their ease and do not leave their homes on the Festival"?

S. It was the Sabbath [and not a festival].

T. But he could have inferred the answer to the questions from a ruling that he himself had made, for we have learned in the Mishnah:

U. *As to the window-shutter [a stopper of a skylight] – R. Eliezer says, "When it is tied on and suspended, they shut the window with it, and if not, they do not shut the window with it." And sages say, "One way or the other, they shut the window with it" [M. Shab. 17:7].* [Slotki, p. 122, n. 2: Now since the question was whether spreading the cloth over the sukkah would be regarded as adding to it on the Sabbath, why did not R. Eliezer deduce from this analogous case that the answer was in the affirmative?]

V.   [28A] In that other case [involving the shutter, one may not do so,] because [in doing so,] one deprives [the shutter of its distinct identity as an object and so ends up simply adding to the building when he closes the shutter.   That is, the shutter is regarded as simply part of the building].   But in the former case [involving a sheet on the sukkah], one does not deprive [the sheet of its identity, because no one can regard it as part of the sukkah itself, and the sheet will be removed.   Slotki, p. 122, n. 6:   The window-shutter becomes part of the frame, but the cover does not become part of the sukkah.]

VII.

A.   There was the story concerning R. Eliezer, who spent the Sabbath in the Upper Galilee.   People asked him questions about thirty matters of law concerning the sukkah.   In the case of twelve of them he said to them, "I have heard the answer."

B.   In the case of eighteen of them, he said to them, "I have not heard the answer."

C.   R. Yose b. R. Judah says, "The matters were reversed.   In the case of eighteen of them, he said to them, 'I have heard the answer.'   In the case of twelve of them, he said to them, 'I have not heard the answer.'"

D.   They said to him, "Is it the case that everything you say derives only from what you have heard?"

E.   He said to them, "You have tried to make me say something that I did not hear from my masters.   In my life, no one ever came to the study house before me, I never slept in the study house, either a real nap or a snooze, I never left anybody behind me when I left, I never engaged in idle chatter, and I never said anything that I did not hear from my master."

F.   They said about Rabban Yohanan ben Zakkai: He never engaged in idle chatter, he never went four cubits without words of Torah and without wearing his phylacteries, no one ever got to the study house before him, he never slept in the study house, either a real nap or a snooze, he never reflected upon holy matters while in filthy alleys, he never left anyone behind him in the study house when he went out, no one ever found him sitting and dreaming, but only sitting and repeating traditions, only he himself opened the door of his house for his disciples, he never said anything that he had not heard from his master, and he never said, "Time has come to arise from studying in the study house," except for doing so on the eve of Passover and on the eve of the Day of Atonement.

G.   And that is how R. Eliezer, his disciple, conducted himself after him.

VIII.

A.   Our rabbis have taught on Tannaite authority:

B.   Hillel the Elder had eighty disciples, thirty of whom were worthy that the Presence of God should rest upon them as upon Moses, our master, thirty of whom who were worthy that the sun stand still for them as it did for Joshua b. Nun, and twenty of whom were of middle rank.

C.   The greatest among them all was Jonathan b. Uzziel, and the least among them was Rabban Yohanan ben Zakkai.

D.   They said concerning Yohanan ben Zakkai that he never in his life left off studying Mishnah, Gemara, laws and lore, details of the Torah, details of the scribes, arguments a minori ad majus, arguments based on analogy, [Slotki:] calendrical computations, gematrias, the speech of the ministering angels, the speech of spirits, the speech of palm-trees, fullers' parables and fox fables, great matters and small matters.

E. "Great matters" refers to the Works of the Chariot.

F. "Small matters" refers to the reflections of Abayye and Raba.

G. This serves to carry out that which is said in Scripture: "That I may cause those who love me to inherit substance and fill their treasuries" (Prov. 8:21).

H. Now since the least of them was this way, how much the more so was the greatest of them!

I. They say concerning Jonathan ben Uzziel that when he was in session and occupied with study of Torah, every bird that flew overhead was burned up.

Unit I provides a scriptural basis for Eliezer's opinion. The inquiry opens the underlying issue of which potential analogy we invoke, with sages comparing the rule of the Festival of Sukkot to that applying to Passover. Unit II goes on to Eliezer's second rule. Unit III augments the foregoing, with a story that makes the same point as the rule. Unit IV introduces a further rule in Eliezer's name, relevant to the topic of the Mishnah-paragraph only in general terms. Unit V contributes yet another dispute on Eliezer's view of a rule for Sukkot, one that signals what will be coming before us at M. 3:1. Unit VI proceeds with yet another item on Eliezer and the Festival. Units VII-VIII conclude with secondary augmentations of unit VI's details. So the entire construction presents a pastiche of materials on Eliezer and the Festival of Sukkot, appropriate in theme even when irrelevant in detail to the Mishnah-paragraph at hand.

2:7-8

A. *He whose head and the greater part of whose body are in the sukkah, but whose table is in the house –*

B. *the House of Shammai declare invalid.*

C. *And the House of Hillel declare valid.*

D. *Said the House of Hillel to the House of Shammai, "Was not the precedent so, that the elders of the House of Shammai and the elders of the House of Hillel went along to pay a sick-call on R. Yohanan b. Hahorani, and they found him sitting with his head and the greater part of his body in the sukkah, and his table in the house, and they said nothing at all to him!"*

E. *Said the House of Shammai to them, "Is there proof from that story? But in point of fact they did say to him, 'if this is how you act, you have never in your whole life fulfilled the religious requirement of dwelling in a sukkah!'"*

M. 2:7

A. *Women, slaves, and minors are exempt from the religious requirement of dwelling in a sukkah.*

B. *A minor who can take care of himself is liable to the religious requirement of dwelling in a sukkah.*

C. *M'SH W: Shammai the Elder's daughter-in-law gave birth, and he broke away some of the plaster and covered the hole with sukkah-roofing over her bed, on account of the infant.*

M. 2:8

I.

A. How do we know on that basis of Scripture [the rule at M. 2:8A]?

B. It is in accord with that which our rabbis have taught:

C. "Homeborn" (Lev. 23:42) by itself [without "the" and "every"] would have included every homeborn [encompassing women and minors].

D. [Since it says,] "The homeborn," it means to exclude women, and "Every..." serves to encompass minors. [That explains M. 2:8A, B].

E. A master has said, "'The homeborn' (Lev. 23:42) serves to exclude women."

F. Does this then imply that the word, "homeborn" [without the] applies both to women and to men?

G. And has it not been taught, "The homeborn" (Lev. 16:29) [in regard to observance of the Day of Atonement] serves to encompass homeborn women, indicating that they are liable to undertake the distress [of the fast].

H. Therefore when the word "homeborn" is used [without the "the"] it means to refer only to males.

I. Said Rabbah, "[In fact] these are matters of received law, and the purpose of rabbis was simply to find scriptural support for the received law."

J. Which [of the two laws, the one referring to the sukkah or the one about the fasting on the Day of Atonement then] is based on Scripture and which is a received law?

K. And further, what need do I have to make reference either to a received law or to Scripture? In the case of the requirement to dwell in a sukkah, that is a religious duty calling for an act of commission and based upon a particular time, and any religious duty calling for an act of commission and based upon a particular time leaves women exempt. [They do not have to keep a law which requires them to do something at a particular time, since they have prior obligations to their families.]

L. As to the Day of Atonement, it derives from a teaching in accord with that which R. Judah said R. Rab said.

M. For R. Judah said Rab said, and so too did a Tannaite authority of the house of R. Ishmael state, "Scripture has said, 'Man or woman' (Num. 5:6), [28B] so treating men and women as equal in regard to all those acts subject to penalty that are listed in the Torah." [Accordingly, both matters – sukkah, Day of Atonement, derive from secondary exegesis of the law. In no way do they depend upon either a received tradition or a primary exegesis or proof text.]

N. Said Abayye, "Under all circumstances, the sukkah [rule concerning women] is a received law, and it is necessary [to make the matter explicit as a received law].

O. "[Why so?] I might have thought to argue as follows: 'You shall dwell' (Lev. 23:42) in the manner in which you ordinarily dwell. Just as, in the case of an ordinary dwelling, a man and his wife [live together], so in the case of a sukkah, a man and his wife must live together. [Thus I might have reached the conclusion that a woman is liable to dwell in the sukkah.] So we are informed [that that is not the case.]"

P. Said Raba, "It indeed was necessary to provide such a proof [but it is different from Abayye's argument in the same regard]. For I might have said that we shall derive the rule governing the fifteenth [of Tishri, that is, Sukkot] from the fifteenth [of Nisan,] that is the festival of unleavened bread.

Q. "Just as, in the latter case, women are liable [to eat unleavened bread], so in the present case, women are liable [to dwell in a sukkah]. So we are informed [that that is not the case]."

R. Now that you have maintained that the rule about women's exemption from the sukkah is a received law, what need do I have for a Scriptural proof-text?

S. It is to encompass proselytes [within the requirement to dwell in a sukkah].

T. You might have said, "The home born in Israel" (Lev. 23:34) is what the All-Merciful has said, thus excluding proselytes.

U. So we are informed that that is not the case, [and proselytes come under the obligation].

V. As to the Day of Atonement, since what R. Judah said what Rab said has provided an adequate proof, [that women must fast on the day of atonement, what need do we have for further proof]?

W. The proof-text encompasses additional affliction [on the eve of the Day of Atonement, prior to nightfall. The fast begins even before sunset. That additional time is added to the fast, and it applies to women as much as to men.]

X. You might have thought that since the All-Merciful has excluded the additional affliction from the penalties of punishment and admonition [so that, if one does not observe that additional period of fasting, he is not punished on that account], women are not obligated to observe that additional period at all.

Y. Accordingly, we are informed [that that is not the case, and women are obligated as much as are men.]

II.

A. A master has said, "Every" [homeborn] serves to encompass minors."

B. And have we not learned in the Mishnah:

C. *Women, slaves, and minors are exempt from the religious requirement of dwelling in a sukkah [M. 2:8A]?*

D. There is no contradiction [between the exegesis that proves minors must observe the requirement of living in a sukkah, and the Mishnah that states that they need not do so.]

E. In the case of the exegesis, we speak of a minor who has reached the age at which he becomes educable, while in the Mishnah's case we speak of a minor who has not reached that age.

F. But is it not the case that the rule that a minor who has reached the age at which he is educable must dwell in the sukkah derives from the authority only of rabbis?

G. [True enough, but] the verse of Scripture supplies support for their view.

III.

A. *A minor who can take care of himself... [M. 2:8B]:*

B. What is the definition of a minor who can take care of himself?

C. Members of the household of R. Yannai said, "It is any child who defecates and does not need to have his mother wipe him."

D. Rabbi says, "It is any child who wakes up from his sleep without crying for his mother."

E. But adults may also cry out for their mothers!

F. Rather, it is any who wakes up from his sleep and does not call, "Mother! mother!"

IV.

A. *M'SH W: Shammai the Elder's daughter-in-law... [M. 2:8C]:*

B. Does the precedent not contradict the rule [that the minor is exempt (M. 2:8A-B)]?

C. There is a lacuna in the tale, and this is how it is to be repeated:

D. "And Shammai imposes a strict rule upon himself.

E. *"And there also was the precedent that Shammai the Elder's daughter-in-law gave birth, and he broke away some of the plaster and covered the hole with sukkah-roofing over her bed on account of the infant [M. 2:8C]."*

The Talmud ignores M. 2:7 entirely. Unit I provides an elaborate account of the scriptural basis for M. 2:8A. Unit II works through the same matter. Units III and IV gloss the Mishnah's statements.

2:9

A. *All seven days a person treats his sukkah as his regular dwelling and his house as his sometime dwelling.*

B. *[If] it began to rain, at what point is it permitted to empty out [the sukkah]?*

C. *From the point at which the porridge will spoil.*

D. *They made a parable: To what is the matter comparable?*

E. *To a slave who came to mix a cup of wine for his master, and his master threw the flagon into his face.*

I.

A. Our rabbis have taught on Tannaite authority:

B. *All seven days a person treats his sukkah as his regular dwelling and his house as his sometime dwelling [M. 2:9A].*

C. How so?

D. If he had handsome garments, he brings them up to the sukkah, [if he had] lovely spreads, he brings them up to the sukkah. He eats and drinks and walks about in the sukkah.

E. What is the Scriptural basis for this rule?

F. It is in accord with that which our rabbis have taught on Tannaite authority:

G. "You shall dwell" (Lev. 13:42) in the manner in which you ordinarily dwell.

H. On this basis, they have said: *All seven days a person treats his sukkah as his regular dwelling and his house as his sometime dwelling [M. 2:9A].* How so? If he had handsome garments, he brings them up to the sukkah, lovely spreads, he brings them up to the sukkah. He eats and drinks and walks about in the sukkah.

I. And he should repeat his traditions in the sukkah.

J. Is this so? And has not Raba said, "One may recite Scripture and repeat Mishnah-teachings in the sukkah, but he reviews his Talmud-learning [following Rashi] outside of the sukkah.

K. There is no contradiction, the first of the two statements alludes to merely reviewing, the second to deep reflection.

L. [29A] That is in line with what Raba bar Hama did, when he was standing in session before R. Hisda. First they reviewed the Talmud together, and then they went and engaged in deep reflection on it.

II.

A. Said Raba, "Drinking cups are to be in the sukkah, food dishes are to be outside of the sukkah. Earthenware pitchers and wooden pails are to be outside of the sukkah.

B. A lamp may be in the sukkah, and some say, outside of the sukkah.

C. There is no dispute in the two versions, the one speaks of a large sukkah [in which one may keep the lamp], the other, a small sukkah [which should not be crowded by needless objects].

III.

A. *If it began to rain... [M. 2:9B]:*

B. It was taught on Tannaite authority: *[From the point at which a porridge] of beans [will spoil] [M. 2:9C].*

C. Abayye was in session before R. Joseph in a sukkah. The wind blew, and chips fell [from the roofing, into their food].

D. R. Joseph said to them, "Clear my dishes out of here."

E. Said to him Abayye, "And lo, we have learned: *From the point at which the porridge will spoil [M. 2:9C],* [and we are far from that]!

F. He said to him, "So far as I am concerned, since I am sensitive, it is as if the porridge was spoiled."

IV.

A. Our rabbis have taught on Tannaite authority:

B. **[If] one was eating in a sukkah, and it rained, and he went and stood somewhere else [cf. M. 2:9B],**

C. **even though the rain let up,**

D. **they do not obligate him to go back, until he completes his meal.**

E. **If he was sleeping in a sukkah and it rained and he got up and went away,**

F. **even though the rain let up,**

G. **they do not obligate him to go back, until it is dawn [T. Suk. 2:4].**

H. As to the preceding sentence, the question was asked:

I. Do we read the final word's spelling so that it means "until he wakes up" or "until dawn"?

J. Come and take note: "Until dawn and the morning star appears."

K. Why say the same thing twice? Rather, "Until he wakes up, and the morning star appears."

V.

A. *They made a parable: To what is the matter comparable [M. 2:9D]:*

B. They asked, "Who poured [in line with M. 2:9E] upon whom?"

C. Come and take note, for it has been taught on Tannaite authority:

D. His master threw the flagon into his face [M. 2:9E] and said to him, "I don't want your service any more."

VI.

A. Our rabbis have taught on Tannaite authority:

B. [In T.'s version:] When the lights are in eclipse, it is a bad omen for the whole world.

C. It is to be compared to a mortal king who built a palace and finished it and arranged a banquet, and then brought in the guests. He got mad at them and said to the servant, "Take away the light from them," so all of them turned out to be sitting in the dark.

D. It has been taught on Tannaite authority: R. Meir did say, "When the lights of heaven are in eclipse, it is a bad omen for Israel, for they are used to blows.

E. "It is to be compared to a teacher who came into the school house and said, 'Bring me the strap.' Now who gets worried? The one who is used to being strapped" [T. Suk. 2:6H-D].

VII.

A. Our rabbis have taught on Tannaite authority:

B. [In Tosefta's version] When the sun is in eclipse, it is a bad omen for the nations of the world.

C. [When] the moon is in eclipse, it is a bad omen for Israel,

D. since the gentiles reckon their calendar by the sun, and Israel by the moon.

E. When it is in eclipse in the east, it is a bad omen for those who live in the east.

F. When it is in eclipse in the west, it is a bad omen for those who live in the west.

G. When it is in eclipse in-between, it is a bad omen for the whole world.

H. When it turns red, it is a sign that punishment by the sword is coming into the world.

I. When it is like sack-cloth, it is a sign that punishment by pestilence and famine are coming into the world.

J. If they are smitten at its entry [into sunset], the punishment will tarry. [When they are smitten] when they rise, the punishment is coming fast.

K. And some say matters are reversed.

L. You have no nation in the whole world which is smitten, the god of which is not smitten right along with it,

M. as it is said, And against all the gods of Egypt I will execute judgments (Ex. 12:12).

N. When Israel do the will of the Omnipresent, they do not have to worry about all these omens,

O. as it is said, Thus says the Lord, Do not learn the way of the gentiles, nor be dismayed at the signs of the heavens, for the nations are dismayed at them (Jer. 10:2) [T. Suk. 2:6E-R].

P. So idolators will be dismayed, but Israelites should not be dismayed.

VIII.

A. Our rabbis have taught on Tannaite authority:

B. For four reasons is the sun eclipsed:

C. Because a head of a court has died and has not been properly mourned,

D. because a betrothed girl has cried out in a town and none goes to her assistance,

E. because of pederasty,

F. and because of two brothers whose blood is spilled simultaneously.

G. [In Tosefta's version] And because of four reasons are the lights of heaven eclipsed:

H. because of counterfeiters, perjurers, people who raise small cattle in the land of Israel and people who cut down good trees.

I. And because of four sorts of bad deeds in the property of Israelite householders handed over to the government:

J. because of holding on to writs of indebtedness which have already been paid,

K. because of lending on interest,

L. [29B] because of pledging funds to charity but not paying up, and

M. because of having the power to protest and not protesting [wrong-doing] [T. Suk. 2:5].

N. Said Rab, "For four reasons is the property of householders confiscated for taxes:

O. "because of those who hold back the wages of a hired hand,

P. "because of those who oppress a hired hand,

Q. "because of those who remove the yoke from their shoulders and put it on their fellow,

R. "and because of arrogance.

S. "But arrogance outweighs all the others.

T. "And with reference to humble people, it is written, 'But the humble shall inherit the earth and delight themselves in the abundance of peace' (Ps. 37:11)."

After carefully explaining the law of the Mishnah in units I-IV, the Talmud amplifies the matter of M. 2:9D-E. Since the weather is taken to present a bad omen, the matter of other omens, with special reference to eclipses of the sun, moon, and stars, enters in. This occupies the remainder of the discussion, with abundant materials from Tosefta used to fill the space at hand.

III

The Result

These units have no counterparts and are made up to serve the interests of the present authorship alone: **2:1**: I, II, III; **2:2A-B**: I; **2:2C-H**: I, III, IV; **2:3**: I, II, III, IV, V, VI, VII, VIII; **2:4A**: I; **2:4B-D**: III, IV, V, VIII, IX, X; **2:5**: I, II; **2:6**: I, II, III, IV, V; **2:7-8**: I, II, III, IV; **2:9**: I, II III, V.

These units are built upon citation and exegesis of a passage of the Tosefta: **2:1** (mere citation: II), **2:2A-B**: none; **2:2C-H**: II; **2:3** (mere citation: VI); **2:4A**: none; **2:4B-D**: VI; (VII: cited to amplify the Mishnah-paragraph, not as the structural basis for the discourse); **2:5**: none; **2:6**: VI (here the entire discourse focuses upon the exposition of the cited passage of Tosefta); **2:7-8**: none; **2:9**: IV, VI, VII, VIII. These final three passages consist of Toseftan statements, with little discussion of them. Once more we conclude that the Tosefta's program for our Mishnah-chapter has served as a resource for our authorship but has not dictated the exegetical program to that authorship. The Bavli's treatment of the Mishnah-chapter initially works out a program particular to the authorship at hand, which, to be sure, has found of interest materials critical to the programs of the prior authorships of the Tosefta and, in substantially lesser measure as we saw earlier, the Yerushalmi. So, once more, not a traditional process of reworking received materials, but an essentially fresh reading of the Mishnah, informed to be sure by received materials, has generated the documentary statement before us.

These units are built upon citation and exegesis of a passage of Scripture: **2:4B-D**: I, Deut. 6:7; III: amplification of Num. 9:6: those who were unclean on account of a human corpse, who they were, what they were doing. The interest of our authorship is in proof that one who carries out one religious duty is exempt from the obligation to carry out some other. But the focus is on the cited verse and its amplification. Here is a fine example of how exegesis of Scripture essentially in its own terms accounts for the cogency of a discourse, while the discourse as a whole is cited as an example of a proposition of interest to the Bavli's authorship. By contrast **2:6**.I resorts to Scripture to prove a proposition of the Mishnah's authority, but does not build discourse on the exegesis of Scripture or even derive its generative problem from the interpretation of Scripture or from prior interpretations of Scripture. **2:7-8**.I is built on the interpretation of Scripture as the basis for the rule of the Mishnah-passage.

Once again, from the perspective of this chapter of Bavli the important exegetical program pertains to Lev. 23:35ff. But the treatment by those verses in other extant compilations bears only tangential relevance to the importance of those verses to very specific – and few – passages in our chapter. That is a result which will be definitively confirmed in Bavli Sukkah Chapter Four, as we shall see presently. **2:6.** I derives from the words, "You will dwell," the details important to Eliezer's position; Lev. 23:39, speaking of Tabernacles, and Lev. 23:6, speaking of Passover, provide information for a proposition important here as well. These items have no important connections to the reading of the verses in other compilations, so far as I can see. The same is so for Deut. 16:13 at **2:6.IV.F.**

The point throughout is not that the exegetical traditions on the cited verses are mostly particular to the documents in which they occur, though that seems to be the case. The point is that the available exegetical traditions have not suggested to our authorship any substantial point of inquiry; some important compositions are built upon the exegesis of particular verses, and these passages are not particular to our tractate. *But their very irrelevance to the main point of the passage, in our chapter, in which they occur proves probative.* The treatment, e.g., of Num. 6:9 – at some length and in a systematic way – when utilized in our chapter is essentially illustrative, not generative or part of a large-scale and sustained discourse of inquiry. That fact, rather rathan the obviously limited use of available materials of prior writings, seems to me to make the case at hand that our authorship has made no systematic effort – and, really, no effort at all – to follow an available agendum in its large-scale work of composition.

This unit is built around names and deeds of sages: **2:6:** VII, VIII. What we have noted with respect to the use of exegeses of Scriptures available in extant compilations applies here as well – all the more so.

We revert to the issues we raised at the outset. Let us consider the questions just as we originally asked them. The topical program of the Bavli is set by the Mishnah. Passages of the Tosefta come under discussion. There is no other program to which the authorship of our chapter responds. It follows that available treatments ("sources") in the prior literature play no role, and our authorship in no way imposes its own issues upon those materials. The authorship of the Bavli has simply announced and effected its own program of inquiry into the topic at hand. I see no traits of the chapter at hand that suggest an interest in supplying an encompassing statement, covering all available treatments of a given topic. What we have is not derivative and summary but fresh and independent. We have not a reworking of sources but an essentially fresh statement – hardly the mark of a traditional document within a traditional system.

Chapter Five

The Bavli and its Sources in the Case of Tractate Sukkah Chapter Four

I

Traditions of, or Ad Hoc Decisions on, Scripture-Exegesis

What is important in this sample is the appeal to verses of Scripture. We shall see that there is a sustained effort to read Scripture in light of facts important to the Mishnah. We have considerable evidence on how in other, earlier documents, these same verses of Scripture were received. Since we know what was important in these shared verses in our document and in prior ones, we have the opportunity to see whether and how a received tradition of Scripture-interpretation has made its impact upon the authorship of the Bavli. What we shall now see is that that authorship had its interests, which it worked out in its own way, not finding itself bound to the program or even the topic deemed critical, in a given verse, by a prior authorship.

II

The Text: Bavli to Mishnah-Tractate Sukkah Chapter Four

I give the text in my own translation[1] and mark the text to indicate the presence of materials shared with prior documents (excluding the Yerushalmi, for reasons spelled out in Chapter Two). That is the sole purpose of this survey. As before, the Mishnah-passage is given in italics. Then I use bold-face type to indicate that a passage occurs in an earlier compilation. I do not pay attention to the appearance of a passage in another tractate of the Bavli, in the theory that all of the Bavli's thirty-seven tractates came to their present state in more or less the same period of time. It would follow that the appearance of a passage in more than one tractate will tell us nothing about how the same general authorship has made use of materials produced in a prior period. My comments on each passage are limited to some redactional issues and addressed mainly to the question at hand. I cover the entirety of Mishnah-tractate Sukkah Chapter Four, Bavli folios 42b-50a.

---

[1]*The Talmud of Babylonia. An American Translation.* VI. *Tractate Sukkah* (Chico, 1984: Scholars Press for Brown Judaic Studies).

As in my survey of the intersecting passages utilized by the Bavli's authorship in their treatment of M. Sukkah 1:1 (2a-9a), so for the present sample, I followed a simple procedure to assess the points of intersection with the documents redacted prior to the Bavli. First I surveyed the cross-references given in the Bavli itself. Where Bavli's editors referred to a Tosefta passage, I give that passage in bold-face type, even though the wording is not exactly the same as that which we find in the Tosefta. Then, following A. Hyman, *Torah hakketubah vehammesurah*, I reviewed references in prior compilations of scriptural exegeses to all verses cited in the Bavli. I surveyed, in particular, Sifra, the two Sifrés, Fathers According to Rabbah Nathan, Genesis Rabbah, Leviticus Rabbah, Pesiqta deRab Kahana, Pesiqta Rabbati, and the other compilations closed by A.D. 600, in all instances accepting the view of the dating of documents as given by M. D. Heer in his authoritative table in *Encyclopaedia Judaica* s.v., *Midrash*. In this way I was able to determine the extent to which the authorship of the Bavli drew upon that available exegetical literature in their larger composition. What is new in this chapter is the occasion to compare exegesis of a verse of the written Torah important both to the authorship of the Bavli and also to the compilers of major midrash-compilations, Sifra, Leviticus Rabbah and Pesiqta deRab Kahana. We may therefore settle a very considerable question of how influential upon the Bavli's authorship is a received exegetical tradition pertaining to a verse of Scripture – at least so far as our sample is probative.

4:1-4

A. *[The rites of] the lulab and the willow branch [carried by the priests around the altar, M. 5:5] are for six or seven [days].*

B. *The recitation of the Hallel-Psalms and the rejoicing are for eight [days].*

C. *[The requirement of dwelling in the] sukkah and the water libation are for seven days.*

D. *And the flute-playing is for five or six.*

M. 4:1

A. *The lulab is for seven days: How so?*

B. *[If] the first festival day of the Festival coincided with the Sabbath, the lulab is for seven days.*

C. *But [if it coincided] with any other day, it is for six days.*

M. 4:2

A. *The willow branch [rite] is for seven days: How so?*

B. *[If] the seventh day of the willow branch coincided with the Sabbath, the willow branch [rite] is for seven days.*

C. *But [if it coincided] with any other day, it is for six days.*

M. 4:3

A. *The religious requirement of the lulab [on the Sabbath]: How so?*

B. *[If] the first festival day of the Festival coincided with the Sabbath, they bring their lulabs to the Temple mount.*

C. *And the attendants take them from them and arrange them on the roof of the portico.*

D. *But the elders leave theirs in a special room.*

E. *They teach them to make the following statement: "To whomever my lulab comes, lo, it is given to him as a gift."*

F. *On the next day they get up and come along.*

G. *And the attendants toss them before them.*

H. *They grab at lulabs and hit one another.*

I. *Now when the court saw that this was leading to a dangerous situation, they ordained that each and every one should take his lulab in his own home.*

M. 4:4

I.

A. But why [would it be forbidden to carry the lulab on the Sabbath if that does not coincide with the first day of the Festival (M. 4:2B-C)]? After all, it is merely an act of moving the object, and it should override the restrictions of the Sabbath [without the imposition of such a strict rule as is indicated by the law].

B. Said Rabbah, "It is indeed a precautionary decree, lest a person take the lulab in hand and go to an expert [in the laws governing the rite] so as to learn [what is to be done] [43A], and, in so doing, carry the lulab for four or more cubits in the public domain [which must not be done].

C. "That accounts also for the rule pertaining to the shofar [which is not to be carried or blown on the Sabbath] and the scroll of Esther [which id not to be carried or read on the Sabbath]."

D. If that is the operative consideration, then even when the first day [of the Festival coincides with the Sabbath], the prohibition likewise [should apply].

E. As to the first day, lo, rabbis have made an ordinance covering it, requiring that the rite be performed at home [M. 4:41] [and the possibility of law-violation then does not exist].

F. That solves the problem, to be sure, for the period after the ordinance [to which M. 4:41 refers] had been laid down, but what is there to say about the situation prior to that ordinance?

G. As to conduct on the first day of the Festival, which is governed by the authority of the Torah-law so that even in the outlying areas [not in the Temple], taking the lulab is done on the authority of the Torah, rabbis made no such decree.

H. But as to the other days, on which taking the lulab in the outlying areas is not done on the authority of the law of the Torah, the rabbis made their precautionary decree [even pertaining to the Temple].

I. If that is the operative consideration, then at the present time also [the law should be the same]. [Slotki, p. 195, n. 8: The command to take the lulab should override on the first day the Sabbath even now when the Temple is no longer in existence.]

J. We [in Babylonia] are not able precisely to establish the lunar calendar [and so do not know for sure that, in taking up the lulab on the Sabbath day, we are not violating the sanctity of the Sabbath without proper justification].

K. If that is the case, then, since they [in the Land] are precise in setting the lunar calendar, for them [in the Land of Israel] the taking of the lulab should surely override the restrictions on the Sabbath.

L. That is indeed the case, for we learn in the Mishnah: *If the first festival day of the Festival coincided with the Sabbath, all the people bring their lulabs to the Temple mount [M. 4:4B].*

M. A further version of the matter on Tannaite authority states: "to the synagogue."

N. That would then produce the inference that in the one case we speak of the age in which the Temple stood [that is, at M. 4:4B], while in the other case [M] we speak of the age in which the Temple is no longer standing.

O. That inference indeed emerges.

II.

A. How do we know that taking the lulab on the Sabbath in the outlying districts is done on the authority of the Torah?

B. It is in accord with that which is taught on Tannaite authority:

C. **"And you shall take" (Lev. 23:40) – indicating that the act of taking should be carried out by each and every one.**

D. **"For yourselves" – something that belongs to you, excluding one that is borrowed or stolen [Sifra Emor Pereq 16:2].**

E. "On the day" (Lev. 23:40) – even if it is the Sabbath.

F. "First" – even in the outlying districts.

G. **"The first" – This teaches that doing so overrides the restrictions of the Sabbath only on the first festival day of the Festival alone [loc. cit., cf. also Lev. R. XXX:VIII.1].**

III.

A. A master has said, "'On the day ... – 'even if it is the Sabbath."

B. "But it is merely an act of moving the object [and it should override the restrictions of the Sabbath]. Is a verse of Scripture really required to permit carrying on that occasion?"

C. Said Raba, "It is necessary to produce such a verse only with respect to carrying, in addition, the things that are used in connection with the carrying of the lulab [but not the lulab itself].

D. "And the proof text is required in accord with the view of the Tannaite authority who stands behind the following teaching of Tannaite origin:

E. "'Carrying not only the lulab but also whatever is needed in connection with it overrides the restrictions of the Sabbath,' the words of R. Eliezer."

F. What is the scriptural basis for the position of R. Eliezer?

G. Scripture has said, "On the day ..." even if it is the Sabbath.

H. And as to rabbis [who reject Eliezer's position], how do they deal with the phrase, "On the day ..."?

I. They require that phrase to prove the proposition:

J. "By day" – and not by night. [The lulab is taken by day but not by night.]

K. And how does R. Eliezer prove the same point?

L. He derives the same proposition from the end of the verse at hand, as follows:

M. "And you shall rejoice before the Lord your God for seven days" (Lev. 23:40) – days, not nights.

N. And as to rabbis?

O. If the proof derived from that verse, I might have reached the false conclusion that I should derive the sense of the word "days" from the use of the word "days" in connection with dwelling in the sukkah itself.

P. Just as the use of the word "days" in that latter connection means that even the nights are involved, so the word "days" used in the present connection likewise means that the nights are involved. [To avoid reaching that incorrect conclusion, rabbis will not invoke the proof-text at hand to demonstrate the point they wish to make.]

IV.

A. And as to the sukkah itself, how do we know [that the word "days" encompasses even the nights, so that one must dwell in the sukkah both by day and by night]?

B. It is in line with that which rabbis have taught on Tannaite authority:

C. "You shall dwell in sukkot for seven days" (Lev. 23;42) – "days" means, "and even nights."

D. You say that days means, "And even nights." But perhaps the sense is "days and not nights."

E. It [D] is a matter of logic. Here the word "days" is used, and the word "days" is used in connection with the lulab.

F. Just as in that latter context, the sense is that the lulab is to be carried by day but not by night, so here too the sense should be that people must dwell in sukkot by day and not by night.

G. Or take the following route: Here it is stated, "Days." In connection with [the seven days of] consecrating [the priesthood] the word "days" is used.

H. Just as in that latter case, when [at Lev. 8A:35] the word "days" appears, it means, "even the nights," so here too the word "days" means "and even the nights."

I. Let us then see which analogy applies.

J. We should reason concerning a matter the religious requirement of which applies all day long, from another matter the religious requirement of which applies all day long, but let not proof derive from a matter the religious requirement of which applies for only a single hour [namely, the lulab, which is properly dealt with in a brief span of time. People do not have to carry the lulab around all day long.]

K. Alternatively let us derive the analogy from something the religious requirement of which applies for all generations [that is, the taking of the lulab, the dwelling in the sukkah] from another matter the religious requirement of which applies for all generations. But let not the rite of consecration of the priesthood provide the governing analogy, for that rite does not apply for all generations [but only for the very first act of consecrating the priestly caste, in the time of Aaron].

L. Scripture twice states, [43B] "You shall dwell" (Lev. 23:42) so as to provide grounds for constructing an analogy.

M. Here "You shall dwell" is stated, and with regard to the rite of consecration of the priesthood, "You shall dwell" is used [at Lev. 8:33, 35].

N. Just as in that latter case, when the word "days" is used, it encompasses even the nights, so here too, when the word "days" is used, it encompasses even the nights.

V.

A. *The willow branch rite is for seven days: How so [M. 4:2A]:*

B. As to conducting the rite of the willow branch on the Sabbath if that day coincides with the seventh day of the Festival why should the rite on that day override the restrictions of the Sabbath?

C. Said R. Yohanan, "It serves to make it public that the rite derives from the authority of the Torah [and so is carried out when the seventh day of the Festival coincides with the Sabbath. Thus overriding the rules of the Sabbath constitutes a demonstration that the rite itself rests upon scriptural authority]."

D. If that is the case, why not carry the lulab on the Sabbath even when the first day of the Festival does not coincide with the Sabbath, as a means of publicizing the fact that carrying the lulab is done on the authority of the Torah?

E. The lulab is not carried on the intermediate days when they coincide with the Sabbath on account of the present precautionary decree made for the reasons given by Rabbah [I B].

F. If that is the case, should we not make an equivalent decree governing the rite of the willow branch?

G. In the case of the rite of the willow branch, agents of the court are the ones who bring the necessary willow branches [and they will not make an error], while, as to the lulab, the task of bringing it is given over to everyone [and the concern of Rabbah is well justified in such a situation].

H. If it is the case [that the willow is taken all seven days of the Festival on the authority of the Torah], then let the willow-rite override the Sabbath, whatever day it falls [and not only on the seventh occasion of performing the rite, as M. 4:3B has specified].

I. [If such favor were shown to the willow-rite] then people would imagine that the basis for carrying the lulab [not accorded similar recognition] was dubious.

J. But [at least] let the willow-rite override the restrictions of the Sabbath on the first day of the Festival [as is the case with the lulab that overrides the restrictions of the Sabbath, [and the willow is there only because it is part of the lulab, not because of the willow-rite itself].

L. But why then should the willow-rite not override the restrictions of the Sabbath on any of the other days [apart from the seventh? Why should we rule that the willow-rite overrides the restrictions of the Sabbath only when the seventh time the rite is done and the Sabbath coincide?]

M. Once you have removed the rite from the first day [of the festival, should it coincide with the Sabbath], you might as well reset it at the seventh occasion for doing the rite [even if it should coincide with the Sabbath].

N. If that is the operative consideration, then at the present time, why should [the willow-rite] not override the restrictions of the Sabbath [when the seventh occasion of the rite coincides with the Sabbath]?

O. The reason is that we are not able precisely to establish the lunar calendar [as above].

P. If that is the case, then since they [in the Land of Israel] are precise in setting the lunar calendar, the rite should override the restrictions of the Sabbath.

Q. When Bar Hadeh came, he said, "It never happened. [Slotki, p. 199, n. 3: The date of the beginning of the month was so arranged that the seventh day of the Festival never coincided with the Sabbath. This was effected by adding a day to the previous month or to any other of the preceding months.]"

R. When Rabin and all those who go down [from the Land of Israel] came, they said, "It did actually happen, and [the rite of the willow] did not override the restrictions of the Sabbath."

S. Then is there not a question [as proposed just now at L]?

T. Said R. Joseph, "Who will tell us that the rite of the willow branch is done by taking it up [which would involve overriding the restrictions of the Sabbath]? Perhaps it is done by setting up [the willow along the sides of the altar, and that can be done in advance of the Sabbath]."

U. Abayye objected to this explanation, *"The rites of the lulab and the willow branch are for six or seven days [M. 4:1A].*

V. "Does this not yield the comparison of the rite of the willow branch to that of the lulab? Just as the rite of the lulab is carried out by taking the lulab in hand [which then means the rite must override the restrictions of the Sabbath], so the rite of the willow branch must be carried out by taking the willow branch in hand [not just setting it up by the altar]?"

W. What makes you say so? This rite is done in accord with its rule, and that one in accord with its rule.

X. Abayye objected, *"Every day they walk around the altar one time ... and on that day [the seventh day of the willow branch] they walk around the altar seven times [M. 4:5D, F].*

Y. "Is this not done while carrying the willow branch?

Z. No, it is done while carrying the lulab.

AA. And lo, R. Nahman said Rabbah bar Abbahu said, "It is with the willow branch."

BB. He said to him, "He may have told you that it is done with the willow branch, but I maintain that it is done with the lulab."

CC. It has been stated on Amoraic authority:

DD. R. Eleazar says, "It is done carrying the lulab."

EE. R. Samuel bar Nathan said R. Hanina [said], "It is done with the willow branch."

FF. And so R. Nahman said Rab bar bar Abbuhah said, "It is done with the willow branch."

GG. Said Raba to R. Isaac, son of Rabbah bar bar Hanan, "True son of Torah, come and let me tell you a lovely teaching that your father said:

HH. "Lo, as to that which we have learned in the Mishnah: *Every day they walk around the altar one time and on that day they walk around the altar seven times [M. 4:5D, F],* this is what your father said in the name of R. Eleazar, 'It is done with the lulab.'"

II.   It was objected:

JJ.   The rite of the lulab overrides the prohibitions of the Sabbath at the beginning of the Festival of Sukkot [that is, when the Sabbath coincides with the first festival day of Sukkot], and the rite of the willow branch at the end [when the rite of the willow branch carried out for the seventh time is supposed to be done on the Sabbath].

KK.   One time the seventh occasion for the rite of the willow branch coincided with the Sabbath, so people brought on the eve of the Sabbath willow saplings and left them in the courtyard.

LL.   The Boethusians found out about them and took them and hid them under boulders.

MM. The next day the common folk found out about the matter and dragged the branches out from under the stones and the priests brought them, and they set them up around the altar.

NN.   The Boethusians did this because they did not concede that the rite of beating the willow branches against the altar overrides the restrictions of the Sabbath [T. Suk. 3:1A-E].

OO.   What follows from this passage is that the rite of the willow branch is carried out by taking the willow branch itself.

PP.   That refutes the proposition under discussion.

QQ.   Why, then should taking the willow on the seventh day of the Festival not override the Sabbath [in the Land of Israel, where the lunar calendar is accurately reported]?

RR.   Since we [in Babylonia] do not overlook the restrictions of the Sabbath in connection with that rite they too will not overlook those restrictions.

SS.   But what about the first day of the Festival, on which, for us, we do not overlook the restrictions of the Sabbath [for we do not take up the lulab on that day], while they do overlook the restrictions of the Sabbath and take up the lulab?

TT.   [44A] One may say: For them [in the Land of Israel] the restrictions of the Sabbath should not be set aside.

UU.   But then these two Tannaite teachings contradict one another.

VV.   One maintains the wording, *All the people bring their lulabs to the Temple Mount [M. 4:4B]* and the other phrases matters, " *... to the synagogue."*

WW. Now we replied, "The one speaks of the time in which the house of the sanctuary stood, the other when it is no longer standing."

XX.   That is not the case.   Both passages refer to the time that the house of the sanctuary was standing, but, nonetheless, there is still no contradiction.   One speaks of the sanctuary, the other of how matters are done in outlying districts.

VI.

A.   Said Abayye to Raba, "How is it the case that, in respect to the lulab, we do carry out the rite for seven days as a memorial to the Temple, while in the case of the willow-rite, we do not carry out the rite for seven days as a memorial to the sanctuary [since the willow-rite is carried out nowadays for only one day]?"

B. He said to him, "It is because a man fulfills his obligation by means of the willow branch that is contained in the lulab in any event [so there is no need for a further such commemoration with the willow branch]."

C. He said to him, "But that is done on account of the lulab itself [and not for the express purpose of making use of the willow branch in commemoration of the destruction of the Temple].

D. "And if you should maintain that one lifts up the lulab one time [in regard to the lulab] and yet another time [in regard to the willow branch], but lo, there are occasions every day on which we do not do things that way."

E. [Replying to the original question,] said R. Zebid in the name of Raba, "As to the lulab, which is carried on the authority of the Torah, we make use of the object for seven days as a memorial to the sanctuary.

F. "As to the willow branch, which rests only upon the authority of rabbis, we do not carry out the rite for seven days as a memorial to the sanctuary."

VII.

A. In accord with whom [is the view that the authority of the rite of the willow branch is only rabbinical and not derived from the Torah]?

B. Of one should propose that it accords with Abba Saul, has he not said, the following:

C. "'Willows of the brook' (Lev. 23:40 [in the plural] indicates that there are two, one to be used in the lulab, the other to be used in the rite of the sanctuary [and both, then, deriving from the authority of Scripture]."

D. Nor could it be in accord with the view of rabbis, for, in their view, it is a law transmitted [from Sinai, and hence enjoying the same standing as Torah-law].

E. For R. Assi said R. Yohanan said in the name of R. Nehunia of the Plain of Bet Hawartan, "The laws governing the ten plants the willow branch and the water-offering [of the rite of the Festival] constitute laws revealed to Moses from Sinai [as explained above, 34A]."

F. But, said R. Zebid in the name of Raba, "In the case of the lulab, which enjoys a foundation in the authority of the Torah for its utilization on the first day of the Festival which coincides with the Sabbath even in the outlying districts, we carry it for seven days as a memorial to the sanctuary.

G. "In the case of the willow branch, which does not enjoy a foundation in the authority of the Torah for its utilization in the outlying districts, we do not carry it for seven days as a memorial to the sanctuary."

VIII.

A. Said R. Simeon b. Laqish, "Blemished priests [who may not ordinarily serve] may enter the area between the hall [leading to the interior of the Temple (Slotki)] and the altar so as to carry out the religious duty of the willow branch."

B. "Said R. Yohanan to him, "Who said this?"

C. 'Who said it? He is the very one who said it, for R. Assi said R. Yohanan said in the name of R. Nehunia of the Plain of Bet Hawartan,

"The laws governing the ten plants, the willow branch, and the water-offering [of the rite of the Festival] constitute laws revealed to Moses from Sinai."

D. But [the issue is], who said that this is done by actually taking up the willow? Perhaps it is done by standing them up [by the altar].

E. Who has made this statement with reference, in particular, to blemished priests? Perhaps it applies to unblemished ones alone.

IX.

A. It has been stated on Amoraic authority:

B. Yohanan and R. Joshua b. Levi —

C. One of them said, "The rite of the willow branch is an institution established by the prophets."

D. The other said, "The rite of the willow branch is a mere custom carried on by the prophets."

E. You may conclude that it is R. Yohanan who has said that the rite of the willow branch is an institution established by the prophets.

F. For R. Abbahu said R. Yohanan said, "The rite of the willow branch is an institution established by the prophets."

G. You may indeed reach that conclusion.

H. Said R. Zira to R. Abbahu, "Did R. Yohanan make such a statement at all?

I. "And has not R. Yohanan said in the name of R. Nehunia of the Plain of Bet Hawartan, 'The laws governing the ten plants, the willow branch, and the water-offering [of the rite of the Festival] constitute laws revealed to Moses from Sinai.'"

J. He was struck dumb for a moment, and then he said, "The laws were forgotten and the prophets came along and re-established them."

K. But did R. Yohanan maintains that [laws were forgotten during the exile in Babylonia]?

L. And did not R. Yohanan say, "As to what is yours that I have reported, in fact it belongs to them. [Slotki, p. 203, n. 12: The knowledge of the Law which he first thought was the possession of the Palestinians was in fact in the hands of the Babylonians. How then could it be said that he held that the Torah was forgotten during the Babylonian exile?]"

M. There is no contradiction. [44B]In the one case we speak of the rite carried on in the sanctuary [and that is a law Moses received at Sinai], in the other, the practice of the rite in the outlying districts [and that is what only the prophets instituted].

X.

A. Said R. Ammi, "As to the willow branch, it is subject to a minimum measure.

B. "It may be taken only by itself.

C. "A person does not carry out his obligation [to take up the willow branch] by doing so with the willow branch that is in the lulab."

D. Since the cited authority [Ammi] has said that it may be taken only by itself [and not in conjunction with other species], is it not self-evident that a person does not carry out his obligation by doing so with the willow branch that is in the lulab?

E. What might you have said? The former rule applies only to a case in which the householder did not lift up the lulab, containing the willow branch, and then go and lift it up a second time [thus once for the lulab, inclusive of the willow branch, the other time for the willow branch on its own]. But in a case in which one has lifted up the lulab and then gone and done so a second time, I might have said that that is not the case.

F. So we are informed that we make no such supposition.

G. And R. Hisda said R. Isaac [said], "A person does carry out his obligation [to take up the willow branch] by doing so with the willow branch that is in the lulab."

H. And what is the minimum measure for the lulab [A]?

I. Said R. Nahman, "It must have three twigs with fresh leaves."

J. And R. Sheshet said, "Even one leaf and one twig."

K. "One leaf and one twig?!" How can you think so?

L. Rather, I should phrase matters, "Even one leaf on one twig."

XI.

A. Said Aibu, "I was standing before R. Eleazar b. R. Sadoq, and someone brought a willow branch to him. He took it and shook it and did so again, but did not say a blessing.

B. "He took the position that the matter is simply a custom that the prophets introduced."

C. Aibu and Hezekiah, sons of the daughter of Rab, brought a willow branch before Rab. He beat it and did so again, but he did not say a blessing over it.

D. He took the position that the matter is simply a custom that the prophets introduced.

E. Said Aibu, "I was standing before R. Eleazar b. R. Sadoq, and someone came to him and said to him, 'I own villages, vineyards, and olive groves. The villagers come and hoe in the vineyards, and [as payment] they eat the olives [and this is done in the Seventh Year, when the land is treated as if it is ownerless.]

F. "Is this proper or improper [for them to take as payment for hoeing the vineyards the olives that they eat]?'

G. "He said to him, 'It is not proper.'

H. "As the man was leaving, [Eleazar] said, 'I have been living in this land for forty years, and I have never seen a man walking in the right paths the way this one does.'

I. "The man came back and said to him, 'What should I do?'

J. "He said to him, 'Declare the olives to be ownerless property for those in need, and pay money for those who do the hoeing.'"

K. Now it is permitted to hoe [in the Seventh Year]?

L. And has it not been taught on Tannaite authority:

M. "But the seventh year you shall let [the land] rest and lie still" (Ex. 23:11).

N. "You shall let it rest" from hoeing,

O. "and lie still" from having stones removed.

P.   Said R. Uqba bar Hama, "There are two kinds of hoeing. In one kind one closes up the holes [around the roots of a tree], and in the other, he aerates the soil [around the roots of a tree].

Q.   "Aerating the soil is forbidden, closing up the holes is permitted [since the former serves the roots of the tree, the latter merely protects the tree (Slotki)]."

R.   Said Aibu in the name of R. Eleazar bar Sadok, "A person should not walk on the eve of the Sabbath [Friday] more than three parasangs [for fear he may not reach his destination prior to the Sabbath]."

S.   Said R. Kahana, "The statement at hand applies only to someone going home [where people might have food ready for him, if he is not expected]. But as to going to his inn, he depends upon what he has in hand [for food, so there is no problem]."

T.   There are those who report matters as follows:

U.   Said R. Kahana, "The statement at hand was necessary only to apply even to one who was going to his home."

V.   Said R. Kahana, "Such an incident happened to me, and [at home] I did not find even a fish-pie [because I came in unexpectedly]."

XII.

A.   *The religious requirement of the lulab on the Sabbath: how so [M. 4:4A]:*

B.   A Tannaite teacher repeated the following Tannaite teaching before R. Nahman: *They arrange them on the roof of the portico [M. 4:4C].*

C.   He said to him, [45A] "But do they have to dry them out [that they should be arranged up there? [If they dry out, the lulabs are invalid.]"

D.   But say, " ... on the portico."

E.   Said Rahba said R. Judah, "The Temple Mountain had a double colonnade, one within the other."

M. 4:2 and M. 4:3 take up the items of M. 4:1A and explain why they may be done either on six or on seven days. Only if the first festival day of the Festival coincides with the Sabbath are these rites carried out on the Sabbath. If the first festival day of the Festival is on any other day, then for the Sabbath which falls in the intermediate days of the festival these rites are suspended (compare M. 3:12). That is the point repeated at M. 4:2 and M. 4:3. It will not be relevant to M. 4:1B or C, since there is no problem with the Sabbath for these rites, or to M. 4:1D, because there is no basis for permitting the flute-playing to override the restrictions of the Sabbath in any event. The supplement at M. 4:4, to M. 4:2 goes over the ground of M. 3:12-13. The narrative is complete at B-F +G. H-I are jarring, just as the consideration of E is surprising in light of the certainty of M. 3:13 on a quite different theory. In all, this is an odd item, contradicting M. 3:12 at I and M. 3:13 at E-F. Unit I proceeds directly to the issue of not carrying the lulab on the Sabbath when the Sabbath and the first day of the Festival do not coincide, that is, the premise of the entire construction. Unit II is continuous with the foregoing, I G. Unit III still goes over the same issue, and unit IV is continuous with the foregoing, supplementing and completing its discussion. Unit V moves us to M. 4:2 and seeks the needed proof for the law. The issue of the basis for the rite of the willow branch, and its relationship to the rite of the lulab, persists to the end. Unit VI reverts back to the issue of the memorial to the destroyed sanctuary, accomplished with the latter and not the former, and explains why that is the case. Unit VII proceeds to the issue of the scriptural basis once more. Because of VII E, VIII, IX are appended, though the latter is in place. Unit X introduces fresh material, relevant to the theme at hand. The issue of the basis for the willow-rite recurs at XI, now in quite novel materials. Since Aibu-Eleazar b. R. Sadoq stands at the head of the lot, other materials, not relevant to the opening issue, are gathered together, which indicated that the materials were formed as a unit around the name of the authority at hand, not the Mishnah-paragraph under discussion. Unit XI then proceeds to M. 4:4A.

4:5-7

A. *The religious requirement of the willow branch: How so?*

B. *There was a place below Jerusalem, called Mosa. [People] go down there and gather young willow branches. They come and throw them up along the sides of the altar, with their heads bent over the altar.*

C. *They blew on the shofar a sustained, a quavering, and a sustained note.*

D. *Every day they walk around the altar one time and say, "Save now, we beseech thee, O Lord! We beseech thee, O Lord, send now prosperity (Ps. 118:25)."*

E. *R. Judah says, "[They say], 'Ani waho, save us we pray! Ani waho, save us we pray!'"*

F. *And on that day [the seventh day of the willow branch] they walk around the altar seven times.*

G. *When they leave, what do they say?*

H. *"Homage to you, O altar! Homage to you, O altar!"*

I. *R. Eliezer says, "For the Lord and for you, O altar! For the Lord and for you, O altar!"*

M. 4:5

A. *As the rite concerning it [is performed] on an ordinary day, so the rite concerning it [is performed] on the Sabbath.*

B. *But they would gather [the willow branches] on Friday and leave them in the gilded troughs [of water], so that they will not wither.*

C. *R. Yohanan b. Beroqah says, "They would bring palm tufts and beat them on the ground at the side of the altar,*

D. *"and that day was called the 'day of beating palm tufts.'"*

M. 4:6

A. *They take their lulabs from the children's hands and eat their citrons.*

M. 4:7

I.

A. It has been taught on Tannaite authority:

B. [The place named at M. 4:5B] was Kolonia.

C. As to the Tannaite authority at hand, why does he call it Mosa?

D. Since it was exempt from the royal tax, he calls it Mosa [removed, that is, removed from the tax rolls].

II.

A. *They come and set them up along the sides of the altar [M. 4:5B]:*

B. It was taught on Tannaite authority: They [willows] were sizable and long, eleven cubits high, so that they would bend over the altar by one cubit.

C. Said Maremar in the name of Mar Zutra, "That statement implies that people would leave them at the base of the altar [but not on the ground].

D. "For if you should imagine that they left them on ground, [take note of the following]: *[The altar] rose by one cubit and drew in by one cubit [on every side]. This is the foundation ... It rose by five cubits and drew in by one cubit. This is the circuit [M. Mid. 3:1B-F]. It rose three cubits, and this was the place of the horns [Cf. M. Mid. 3:1H].*

E. "Now how then can the willows have bent over the altar [if they were set on the ground? [Slotki, p. 208, n. 6: The willow branch, placed in a slanting position against the altar nine cubits in height and removed sufficiently from its base to allow for the horizontal distance of two cubits from the side of the base to the top of the altar would not project at all beyond the top of the altar. What then would remain for bending over?]

F. "Does this not imply that the people placed them at the base of the altar [and not on the ground]?"

G. It does indeed bear that implication.

H. Said R. Abbahu, "What verse of Scripture makes that same point [that the boughs bent over the altar]? It is as it is said, 'Order the festival procession with boughs, even unto the horns of the altar' (Ps. 118:27). [Slotki, p. 208, n. 9: The height of the horns was one cubit above the top of the altar, and boughs that reached to the top of the horns naturally bent one cubit over the altar top.]"

III.

A. Said R. Abbahu said R. Eleazar, "Whoever takes up a lulab with its binding and a willow branch with its wreath is regarded by Scripture as if he had built an altar and sacrificed an offering on it.

B. "For it is said [45B] 'Order the festival procession with boughs, even unto the horns of the altar' (Ps. 118:27)."

C. Said R. Jeremiah in the name of R. Simeon b. Yohai, and R. Yohanan in the name of R. Simeon of Mahoz in the name of R. Yohanan of Makkut, "Whoever makes an addition [Slotki] to the festival by eating and drinking is regarded by Scripture as if he had built an altar and sacrificed an offering on it.

D. "For it is said, 'Order the festival procession with boughs, even unto the horns of the altar' (Ps. 118:27)."

IV.

A. Said Hezekiah said R. Jeremiah in the name R. Simeon b. Yohai, "In the case of things used in carrying out all religious duties, a person is able to fulfill his obligation only by using those objects in the manner in which they grow [with the natural bottom at the bottom, the natural top of the top],

B. "as it is said, 'Acacia wood standing up,' (Ex. 26:15)."

C. It has been taught along these same lines on Tannaite authority:

D. "Acacia wood standing up" (Ex. 26:15) means that the wood is arranged so that it stands up in the manner in which it grows [with the grain perpendicular to the ground].

E. Another interpretation: "Standing" in the sense that they had up[right] the golden plating [that is affixed to them].

F. Another interpretation of "Standing:"

G. Should you say, "Their hope is lost, their prospects null," Scripture to the contrary says, "Acaia wood standing up" (Ex. 26:15), meaning that they stand for ever and ever.

H. And Hezekiah said R. Jeremiah said in the name of R. Simeon b. Yohai, "[Because of the troubles I have known], I can free the entire world from punishment from the day on which I was born to this very moment, and were my son, Eliezer with me, it would be from the day on which the world was made to this moment, and were Yotam b. Uzziah with us, it would be from the day on which the world was made to its very end."

I. And Hezekiah said R. Jeremiah said in the name of R. Simeon b. Yohai, "I have myself seen the inhabitants of the upper world, and they are only a few. If they are a thousand, my son and I are among their number. If they are only a hundred, my son and I are among their number. If they are only two, they are only my son and I."

J. But are they so few in number? And lo, Raba said, "The row [of the righteous] before the Holy One, blessed be He, is made up of eighteen thousand,

K. "as it is said, 'There shall be eighteen thousand round about' (Ez. 48:35)."

L. There is [few] no contradiction [between the two views]. The former number refers to those [few] who see Him through a bright mirror, the latter [larger] number, through a dirty mirror.

M. But are those who see him through a bright mirror so few? And has not Abayye said, "There are in the world never fewer than thirty-six righteous men who look upon the face of the Presence of God every day.

N. "For it is said, 'Happy are those who wait for him' (Is. 30:18), and the numerical value of the letters in the word 'for him' is thirty-six"?

O. There is no contradiction. The latter number [thirty-six] speaks of the ones who may come in with permission, the former [two, Simeon and his son] are the ones who may come in without even asking for permission].

V.

A. *When they leave, what do they say [M. 4:5G]:*

B. And lo, [in saying, *"For the Lord and for you, O altar" [M. 4:5I]*, they will be joining the Name of heaven and something else.

C. And it has been taught on Tannaite authority: Whoever [in seeking salvation] joins the Name of heaven and something else will be uprooted from the world,

D. as it is said, "Except for the Lord entirely by himself" (Ex. 22:19).

E. This is the sense of the statement: "To the Lord we give thanks and to you we give praise, to the Lord we give thanks, and to you we give hommage."

VI.

A. *As the rite concerning it is performed on an ordinary day, so the rite concerning it is performed on the Sabbath [M. 4:6A-B]:*

B. Said R. Huna, "What is the scriptural basis for the rule as framed by [involving a distinct rite of the lulab performed at the altar] R. Yohanan b. Beroqah [M. 4:6C-D]

C. "It is because the word for branches is written in the plural [at Lev. 23:40], thus indicating that there are to be willows, one for the lulab and the other for use in beating on the altar [as at M. 4:6C].

D. "But rabbis point out that the word is written defectively [without the customary signification of the plural, hence only a single one is involved]."

E. R. Levi says, "The matter is compared to a date-palm. Just as a date palm has only one heart, so Israel has only one heart – for their Father in heaven."

VII.

A. Said R. Judah said Samuel, "[A blessing is said over] the lulab for seven days but for the sukkah only one [the first day of the festival].

B. "What is the reason for this distinction?

C. "In the case of the lulab, the nights [on which the lulab is not taken up] break up the days, so that taking up the lulab each day constitutes the commission of a distinct religious duty.

D. "But in case of the sukkah, in which the nights do not form divisions between the days [since the sukkah is to be used by night as much as by day], all seven days are regarded as a single protracted interval of one day."

E. And Rabbah bar bar Hana said R. Yohanan said, "The sukkah is to be given a blessing seven days, but the lulab only one.

F. "What is the reason for this distinction?

G. "The sukkah derives use of the sukkah for seven days derives from the authority of the Torah.

H. "But use of the lulab for the other days of the Festival derives only from the authority of a rabbis, so saying a blessing only on the first day is entirely sufficient."

I. When Rabin came, he said R. Yohanan [said], "The same rule applies to both this and that: the blessing is to be said all seven days."

J. Said R. Joseph, "Select the position stated by Rabbah bar bar Hana, for all the Amoraic authorities stand with him in respect to the sukkah [and insist that a blessing be said all seven days]."

K. The following objection was raised:

L. [46A]One who makes a lulab for himself says, "Praised [be Thou, O Lord ...], who gave us life and preserved us and brought us to this occasion."

M. When he takes it [in hand] to carry out his obligation, he says, "Praised [be Thou, O Lord ...] who has sanctified us through his commandments and commanded us concerning the taking of the lulab."

N. And though he has said a blessing on the first day, he just recite the benediction over [the lulab] all seven [days of the festival].

O. [B. omits:] One who performs any of the commandments must recite a benediction over them.

P. One who makes a sukkah for himself says, "Praised [be Thou, O Lord ...] who has brought us to this occasion."

Q. [One who] enters to dwell in it says, "Praised [be Thou, O Lord ... [who has sanctified us through his commandments and commanded us to dwell in the sukkah."

R. Once he recites a benediction over it on the first day, he need not recite the benediction again [or remaining days of the festival] [T. Ber. 6:10, 6:9, trans. T. Zahavy].

S. There is a contradiction between one statement and another on the lulab [for Rabbah b. b. Hana wants the benediction for the lulab only on the first day, not all seven] and likewise between the two statements on the sukkah [since Rabbah b. b. Hana requires a blessing over the sukkah all seven days and the cited passage of Tosefta has the blessing only on the first day].

T. Now indeed there really is no contradiction between the two statements concerning the lulab, since the one [requiring a daily blessing] refers to the time in which the house of the sanctuary was standing, the other to the time when the house of the sanctuary was no longer standing.

U. But there really is a disagreement between the two statements concerning the sukkah.

V. It in fact represents a point under dispute among Tannaite authorities.

W. For it has been taught on Tannaite authority:

X. "As to the phylacteries, every time one puts them on, he must say a blessing over them," the words of Rabbi.

Y. And sages say, "One says a blessing only when he puts them on in the morning alone. [Later on in the day he need not do so]."

Z. It has been stated on Amoraic authority:

AA. Abayye says, "The decided law accords with the view of Rabbi."

BB. And Raba said, "The decided law accords with the view of rabbis."

CC. Said R. Mari, son of the daughter of Samuel, "I saw that Raba did not in fact act in accord with his own tradition [that one says the blessing only once]. Rather, he would get up early and go into the privy, then come out and wash his hands, and only then put on his phylacteries, and say the requisite blessing.

DD. "But if he should need to make use of the privy again during the day, he would go into the privy and come out and wash his hands and put on his phylacteries and say another blessing.

EE. "And we too act in accord with the view of Rabbi and say a blessing [for the sukkah] all seven days."

FF. Said Mar Zutra, "I saw R. Papi, who would say a blessing every time he put on his phylacteries."

GG. Rabbis of the household of R. Ashi, whenever they touched them, would say a blessing for them.

VIII.

  A. Said R. Judah said Samuel, "The religious duty of taking the lulab applies all seven days."

  B. And R. Joshua b. Levi said, "On the first day it is a religious duty to take up the lulab. From that point forth, it is a religious requirement imposed only by the elders."

  C. And R. Isaac said, "On every day of the festival, it is merely a religious requirement imposed by elders, and that applies even to the first day."

  D. But lo, we have it as an established fact that the first day's [observance of the rite] is based upon the authority of the Torah.

  E. Then I should formulate the statement, "Exclusive of the first day."

  F. If so, then, that [E] is just what R. Joshua b. Levi has said [B].

  G. Then I should formulate the matter, "And so has R. Isaac said."

  H. And Rab also takes the view that the religious duty of carrying the lulab applies for all seven days of the Festival.

  I. For R. Hiyya bar Ashi said Rab said, "he who lights the Hanukkah light has to say a blessing." [Since the lighting of the Hanukkah lamp is only on the authority of rabbis, it must follow that Rab will concur likewise in the case of the lulab, carried on the last six of the seven days solely on the authority of the rabbis, also requires a blessing, and the rest follows].

  J. R. Jeremiah said, "He who says the Hanukkah light has to say a blessing."

  K. What blessings does he say,"?

  L. Said R. Judah, "On the first day, the one who lights the flame says three blessings and the one who sees it says two. From that night onward, the one who lights the light says two blessings, and the one who sees it says only one blessing."

  M. What blessing does one say?

  N. "Blessed ... who has sanctified us by his commandments and commanded us to light the Hanukkah light."

  O. And where did he so command us?

  P. [The commandment concerning Hanukkah, a rabbinically ordained rite, derives from the verse,] "You shall not turn aside" (Deut. 17:11). [Even what rabbis require enjoys the authority of the Torah.]

  Q. And R. Nahman bar Isaac said, "'Ask your father and he will tell you' (Deut. 32.7). [The point is the same.]

  R. R. Nahman bar Isaac repeated this matter explicitly, "Rab said, 'All seven days it is a religious duty to carry the lulab.'"

IX.

  A. Our rabbis have taught on Tannaite authority:

  B. **He who makes a sukkah for himself says, "Praised who has kept us in life ..."   One who enters to dwell in it says, "Praised ... who has sanctified us   ..." [T. Ber. 6:9].**

  C. If the sukkah was ready-made and available, if the householder can do something new to it, he still says a blessing. But if not, when he goes in to dwell there, he says two blessings.

  D. Said R. Ashi, "I saw that R. Kahana said all of the blessings [for the sukkah] over the cup of wine used for the sanctification."

E.   Our rabbis have taught on Tannaite authority: He who has to carry out many religious duties says, "Blessed ... who has sanctified us by his commandments and commanded us concerning the religious duties [in general]."

F.   R. Judah says, "He says an individual blessing for each one" [cf. T. Ber. 6:9].

G.   Said R. Zira, and some say it in the name of R. Hanina bar Papa, "The decided law accords with the view of R. Judah."

H.   And R. Zira, and some say it in the name of R. Hanina bar Para, "What is the scriptural basis for the view of R. Judah?

I.   "It is because it is written, 'Blessed be the Lord day by day' (Ps. 68:20).

J.   "Now do people say a blessing for him by day, but by night they do not as say a blessing for him? [Surely not.]

K.   "But the verse comes to tell you that, day by day, one must give back to him appropriate blessings.

L.   "Here to, for each and every matter one should give back to him a blessing that is appropriate to that deed."

M.   And R. Zira said, and some say it was R. Hanina bar Papa, "Come and see that the trait of the Holy One, blessed be He, is not like the trait of mortal man.

N.   "In the case of mortal man, an empty vessel [46B] holds something, but a full vessel does not.

O.   "But the trait of the Holy One, blessed be He, [is not like that]. A full utensil will hold [something], but an empty one will not hold something.

P.   "For it is said, 'And it shall come to pass, if you will listen diligently' (Deut. 28:1). [One has to learn much and if he does, he will retain his knowledge.]

Q.   "The sense is, If you will listen, you will go on listening, and if not, you will not go on listening.

R.   "Another matter: If you hear concerning what is already in hand, you will also hear what is new.

S.   "'But if your heart turns away' (Deut. 30:17), you will not hear anything again."

X.

A.   *They take their lulabs from the children's hands [M. 4:7A]:*

B.   Said R. Yohanan, "A citron [that has been used for its religious purpose] may not [be eaten] on the seventh day [of the festival], but on the eighth, it may [be eaten].

C.   "But as to the sukkah, even on the eighth day it may not [be used for fuel]. [People may not burn up the wood that has been used in the sukkah, even after the seven days of use of the sukkah are over. They must wait until after the Eighth Day of Assembly.]"

D.   And R. Simeon b. Laqish said, "as to the citron, even on the seventh day it also may [be eaten, once it is no longer needed for its religious purpose]."

E.   What is at issue between the two authorities?

F.   One party holds that it was specifically for carrying out a religious duty that the citron was set aside. [Once that has been carried out, even on the seventh day, it may be eaten, thus Simeon b. Laqish.]

G. And the other party takes the view that it was set aside for the entire day
    [on which it is required for the performance of a religious duty, and not
    only for the religious purpose for which it is needed. Hence it may not
    be eaten on the whole of the seventh day, even after it has served its
    religious purpose, thus Yohanan.]

H. R. Simeon b. Laqish objected to R. Yohanan [by citing the Mishnah-
    passage at hand]: *"They take their lulabs from the children's hands and
    eat their citrons [M. 4:7].*

I. "Now would it not then be the case that the same rule applies to adults
    [which would support the view that people may eat the citron even on
    the seventh day of the Festival]?"

J. No, the rule applies only to children.

K. There are those who state matters in this way:

L. R. Yohanan objected to R. Simeon b. Laqish: *"They take their lulabs
    from the children's hands and eat their citrons [M. 4:7].*

M. "That rule then applies indeed to the children, but not to the adults [and
    that would support the view that people may not eat the citron on the
    seventh day of the Festival]."

N. No, the rule applies both to children and to adults. The reason that the
    passage refers specifically to children is that this is how things
    generally are.

O. Said R. Papa to Abayye, "In the view of R. Yohanan, what is the
    difference between the sukkah and the citron [that he objects to using the
    wood in the sukkah for fuel even on the eighth day]?"

P. He said to him, "[The sukkah may be needed until the very last moment
    of the seventh day and into the eighth. [For] the sukkah may well serve
    at twilight [at the end of the seventh day], since if the householder was
    eating a meal there, he would want to sit in the sukkah and eat there
    [right past sunset]. In this case the use of the sukkah was originally
    planned for twilight. Since the sukkah had been designated for use at
    twilight, it also was designated for use for the entirety of the eighth day.

Q. "But the citron, which serves no purpose at twilight [at the end of the
    seventh day of the Festival] has not then been designated for use at
    twilight, and, in consequence, likewise has not been designated for use of
    the whole of the eighth day either."

R. [Reverting to the issue raised at B], Levi said, "Even on the eighth day it
    is forbidden to eat the citron."

S. And the father of Samuel said, "On the seventh day it is forbidden to eat
    the citron, but on the eighth day it is permitted."

T. But the father of Samuel adopted the thesis of Levi. R. Zira adopted the
    thesis of the Father of Samuel.

U. For R. Zira said, "It is forbidden to eat a citron that has been invalidated
    for all seven days of the Festival, [but one may do so on the eighth
    day]."

XI.

A. Said R. Zira, "A person should not acquire possession for a child of a
    lulab on the first festival day of the Festival.

B. "What is the reason? It is that a child has the power to acquire
    possession [of an object] but not the power to impart the right of
    possession to another party, with the result that the man would end up

carrying out his obligation to make use of the lulab with a lulab that does not belong to him [which, we know, is not permitted]."

C. And R. Zira said, "Someone should not say to a child 'I'm going to give you something,' and then not give it to him.

D. "The reason is that the child will come to learn how to lie,

E. "for it is said, 'They have taught their tongues to speak lies' (Jer. 9:4)."

XII.

A. [Reverting to the issue of unit IX:] Now in the dispute between R. Yohanan and R. Simeon b. Laqish [we have the following parallel debate]:

B. It has been stated on Amoraic authority:

C. If one has set aside seven citrons for use [in carrying out his religious obligation] on the seven successive days of the Festival:

D. Said Rab, "With each one of them, in succession, he carries out his religious obligation, and then he eats that one forthwith."

E. But R. Assi said, "With each one of them, in succession, he carries out his religious obligation, but then only on the following day does he eat the citron that he has used."

F. What is at issue here?

G. One party holds that it was specifically for carrying out a religious duty with it that that citron was set aside. [Once that has been carried out, it may be eaten even on the same day, so Rab.]

H. The other party takes the view that it was set aside for the entire day [on which it is required for the performance of a religious duty, and not only for the religious purpose for which it is needed. Hence it may not be eaten on the selfsame day, even after it has served its religious purpose, so Assi.]

XIII.

A. Now how are we, who keep two days of the Festival, to do things?

B. Said Abayye, "As to the eighth day which might be the ninth day of the festival, it is forbidden [to eat the citron]. As to the ninth day, which might be the eighth day, it is permitted [to eat the citron]."

C. Maremar said, "Even on the eighth day which may be the seventh, it is permitted [to eat it]."

D. In Sura people act in accord with Maremar's position.

E. R. Shisha, son of R. Idi, acted in accord with Abayye's position.

F. And the decided law accords with Abayye's position.

XIV.

A. Said R. Judah, son of R. Samuel bar Shilat, in the name of Rab, "On the eighth day which may be the seventh, we treat it as the seventh day so far as use of the sukkah is concerned, and the eighth day so far as the requisite blessing is concerned. [One makes use of the sukkah, but does not say a blessing in that connection when one says the daily prayers, the grace after meals, and the sanctification over wine]."

B. And R. Yohanan said, "It is deemed equivalent to the eighth day for all purposes."

C. As to dwelling in the sukkah, all parties concur that people must dwell there on that day.

D. Where there is a dispute [47A] it concerns saying blessings [in connection with doing so, that is, "Praised ... who has commanded us to dwell in the sukkah"].

E. In the view of him who has said that day is regarded as the seventh day so far as the sukkah is concerned, people also must say the requisite blessing.

F. As to him who says, "It is treated as the eighth day for all purposes," people do not say the cited blessing.

G. Said R. Joseph, "Stick with the view of R. Yohanan.

H. "For R. Huna bar Bizna and all the great sages of the generation happened to come to a sukkah on the eighth day that may have been the seventh. They sat down in the sukkah but said no blessing. [That then accords with Yohanan's view of matters.]"

I. But perhaps they were in accord with the view of him who has said, "Once one says a blessing for sitting in the sukkah on the first festival day of the Festival, one does not have to say a blessing in that regard any more."?

J. There is a tradition in connection with this story that the sages had just then come in from the fields [and so had not yet sat in a sukkah during the entire festival, so that possibility cannot be invoked in explaining away the precedent at hand].

K. There are those who report that all parties concur [as against D] that one does not say the blessing in connection with sitting in the sukkah. Where there is a dispute, it is whether or not to begin with one has to sit in the sukkah at all on that day.

L. In the view of one who maintains that the day in doubt as is treated as the seventh day as regards the sukkah, one does have to sit in the sukkah.

M. In the view of him who maintains that the day in doubt is treated as to the eighth day for all purposes, one does not have to sit in the sukkah on the day that is subject to doubt.

N. Said R. Joseph, "Stick with the view of R. Yohanan.

O. "For who is the authority behind the statement [in the name of Rab]? It is R. Judah, son of R. Samuel bar Shilat, and on the eighth day which might be the seventh, he sat outside of a sukkah [contrary to the law as he cited it. So he himself did not believe the rule as he reported it.]"

P. The decided law is that people do sit in the sukkah on that day but do not say the requisite blessing in that connection.

XV.

A. Said R. Yohanan, "On the eighth day of the Festival "the Eighth Day of Solemn Assembly] people say the blessing of 'the season' [who has kept us in life and sustained us and brought us to this season"] but they do not say that blessing on the seventh day of Passover."

B. And R. Levi bar Hama, and some say, R. Hama bar Hanina, said, "You may know that that is the case [that the eighth day of the Festival is treated as a distinct festival, so requiring the distinct blessing of 'season,' as specified just now].

C. "For lo, it is distinct [from the preceding days of the Festival] in three aspects: in use of the sukkah, in waving the lulab, and in making the water-offering."

D. In the view of R. Judah, who has held that one would make the water-offering with a log of water on all eight days, the eighth day of the Festival is distinct from the preceding seven days in two aspects [and not three]."

E. If that is the principal consideration, then as to the seventh day of Passover, lo, it too is distinct from the preceding days, in regard, in particular, to the matter of the religious requirement of eating unleavened bread.

F. For a master has said, "On the first night of Passover it is a religious duty [to eat unleavened bread] and from that point onward it is an optional, but not an obligatory, matter."

G. How now! In that case [Passover] it is distinct from the first night only, but it is hardly distinct from the remaining days. But in the present case [of the eighth day of the Festival] the holy day is distinct even from the other days.

H. Said Rabina, "This one [namely, the eighth day of the Festival is distinct from the preceding day [and all the others], while that one [the seventh day of Passover] is distinct from the days preceding the day before.

I. [Slotki, p. 220, n. 6: The next three statements point out that in the section dealing with the sacrifices of the Festival, Num. 29:12-39, there are differences between the first seven days of the Festival of Sukkot and the eighth day, either in respect of the laws of the sacrifices or the expressions used in connection with them, proving that the latter is a separate festival. These differences are that (a) on each of the seven days a number of bullocks were sacrificed, while on the Eighth Day only one was offered [Num. 29:36]; (b) the descriptions of the sacrifices of the second to the seventh day begin with the word, and, suggesting continuity, while that of the Eighth Day commences, 'On the eighth day,' omitting the and; (c) on the seventh day it says, "According to their ordinance, "connecting it with the previous days, whereas the Eighth Day, has, "according to the ordinance."]

J. R. Nahman bar Isaac said, "Here [on the eighth day] it is written only, 'On the day,' while there it is written, 'And on the day.'"

K. R. Ashi said, "Here [concerning the eighth day] it is written, 'In accord with the ordinance,' while there [in the case of the seventh day] it is written, 'according to their ordinance.'"

L. May we say that the following passage supports the view of R. Yohanan [at A, that the blessing, "who has brought us to this season" is said on the Eighth Day of the Festival]:

M. The bullocks, rams, and lambs [offered on the Festival] impair one another [so that if one is not offered properly, the entire group of animals is invalidated and a new group must be offered up properly].

N. And R. Judah says, "They do not impair one another, for lo, they grow fewer in number as the days pass." [Slotki, p. 221, n. 1: As the number is in any case steadily diminished, the additional omission of one or more cannot affect the remainder.]

O. They said to him, "But is it not the case that all of them [including rams and lambs] are reduced in number on the eighth day [which thus should be regarded as a separate entity]?"

P. He said to them, "The Eighth Day [of Solemn Assembly] is an entity unto itself. For just as the seven days of the Festival require an offering, song, blessing, and lodging overnight in Jerusalem."

Q. [47B] Now does not the reference to "a blessing" in the foregoing passage not allude to that covering the season [as Yohanan has claimed. This then explicitly supports that view.]

R. No, it speaks of a separate reference, to the Eighth Day of Solemn Assembly, in the Grace after Meals and in the Prayer.

S. That conclusion, moreover, is reasonable, for if you think that reference here is made to the blessing for the season, is the blessing for the season stated at all on all seven days of the Festival? [No, it is not. So the sense of the allusion to "a blessing" cannot bear that meaning at all. It can only be what R. has said.]

T. No, there is no difficulty after all. For if someone did not say a blessing for the season on one day, he says it on the next day or on the day after that [with the result that the reference to "blessing" may well be to the blessing for the season, against A and Q.]

U. In any event, we require that the blessing over the season be recited over a cup of wine, [and people do not have a cup of wine on the intermediate days of the festival, so the problem indeed recurs].

V. [If then we assume that "blessing" in the cited passage refers to the blessing of the season, would this not] support the view of R. Nahman, for R. Nahman said, "As to the blessing of the season, one says it even in the market place [and not necessarily over a cup of wine]"?

W. Now if you maintain that we require a cup of wine in that connection, is there a requirement for a blessing over a cup of wine every day [of the Festival]? [Surely not!]

X. Perhaps we deal with a case in which a cup of wine came to hand only later on.

Y. [Reverting to the clarification of the cited passage, P, we ask:] Does R. Judah then take the view that the Eighth Day of Solemn Assembly imposes the requirement of lodging overnight of Jerusalem?

Z. And has it not been taught on Tannaite authority:

AA. R. Judah says, "How on the basis of Scripture do we know that as to the second Passover [in Iyyar, not Nisan], it is not necessary to stay overnight in Jerusalem? As it is said, 'And you shall turn in the morning and go into your tents' (Deut. 16:7) and, forthwith thereafter, it is written, 'Six days you shall eat unleavened bread' (Deut. 16:8).

BB. "What follows from the juxtaposition of these two verses is simple. In the case of the Passover that requires a six day observance of unleavened bread there also is the requirement of lodging overnight, and in the case of the Passover that does not require a six day observance of the rite of unleavened bread also does not require lodging overnight in Jerusalem."

CC. What then is excluded? Is it not to exclude, in addition, the Eighth Day of the Festival?

DD. No, it serves only to eliminate the second Passover, which is similar to [the First Passover. Other festivals are not under discussion.]

EE. That indeed is a reasonable conclusion, for we have learned in the following passage of the Mishnah:

FF. *The offering of the first fruits requires a sacrifice, song, waving of the produce, and lodging overnight in Jerusalem [M. Bik. 2:4].*

GG. Who then takes the view that the offering of the the first fruits requires an act of waving? It is R. Judah.

HH. And he also takes the view that lodging overnight in Jerusalem is required.

II. For it has been taught on Tannaite authority:

JJ. R. Judah says, "'And you shall set [the basket of first fruits] down' (Deut. 26:10).

KK. "This refers to waving the basket.

LL. "You say it refers to waving the basket, but perhaps the sense is that it is literally set down.

MM. "Since further on, it says, 'And set it down' (Deut. 26:4), that takes care of that action.

NN. "To what, then, does the cited verse, 'And you shall set ... down ...' refer? It can only refer to waving."

OO. But perhaps the cited passage of the Mishnah accords with the view of R. Eliezer b. Jacob [Slotki, p. 223, n. 4: and not with R. Judah, who may maintain that whatever rite lasts for less than six days requires neither the one nor the other.]

PP. For it has been taught on Tannaite authority:

QQ. "'And the priest shall take the basket out of your hand' (Deut. 26:4) teaches that the basket of first fruits has to be waved," the words of R. Eliezer b. Jacob.

RR. What is the reason for the view of R. Eliezer b. Jacob?

SS. There is an analogy drawn between the use of the word "hand" here and the use of the same word in connection with peace-offerings.

TT. Here it is written, "And the priest shall take the basket out of your hand" (Deut. 6 26:4), and there [with reference to the peace-offering] it is written, "His own hands shall bring the offering to the Lord (Lev. 7:30).

UU. Just as in the present case it is the priest who does the work, so there it is the priest who does it.

VV. Just as in that other passage, it is the owner who participates, so here too the owner participates.

WW. How is this possible [for both to be involved]? The priest puts his hand underneath the hand of the owner and waves [the basket of first fruits, just as he would do in the case of the animal brought as a sacrifice in the category of peace-offerings].

XX. What, at any rate, is the upshot of the issue?

YY. R. Nahman said, "People say the blessing for the season on the Eighth Day of the Festival."

AAA. The decided law is that people do say the blessing for the season on the Eighth Day of the Festival.

BBB. It has been taught on Tannaite authority in accord with the view of R. Nahman:

CCC. The Eighth Day [48A] of Solemn Assembly constitutes a festival unto itself for the matters of balloting to see which priest does what job, for the saying of the blessing for the season, for the character of the holiday

as distinct from the Festival of Sukkot [so the sukkah is not used], the
sacrifice, the psalm, and the benediction. [In all these aspects it is a
completely distinct holy day and not a continuation of the Festival of
Sukkot].

The most interesting aspect of the construction before us does not pertain to
the Mishnah-paragraph, but to the relationship between the seven days of the
Festival of Sukkot and the Eighth Day of Solemn Assembly, with which the
Festival concludes. Is this part of the Festival or a distinct holy day on its own?
My own inclination is to suppose that the protracted discussion – unit XV –
would better serve M. 4:8A-B, which follows. But it clearly is meant to
continue the units that come before it. These, after all, persistently refer to the
eighth day, specifically to the doubts concerning the designation, in the Exilic
communities, of the eighth day. So, overall, the construction appears to follow
a rather subtle program. Units I and II gloss the cited clauses of the Mishnah. I
take it unit III is inserted because it is joined through Abbahu's name to the
foregoing, and unit IV because of Jeremiah-Simeon b. Yohai. Unit V then
reverts to M., as indicated, along with unit VI. Unit VII opens a secondary
issue, the blessings said over the lulab and the sukkah and the comparison
between the two distinct rites. This leads directly to the issue of how we treat
religious rites repeated from day to day. Are they of the same status, or is the
important act only the first one, so unit VIII? The same issue is worked out in
unit IX. Unit X then directs attention to M. 4:7A. But the issue of the
relationship between two of the rites of the Festival, on the one side, and
successive days of the festival – particularly the seventh, then the eighth (the
Eighth Day of Solemn Assembly) is raised. That issue thus extends unit VII's
basic premise. Unit XI is inserted whole but plays no role; unit XII continues
unit X. Unit XIII forms a separate unit but ties in closely with the foregoing.
Unit XIV reverts to the established issue, the matter of doubt about the eighth
day of the Festival and its status. Then unit XV presents a massive and well-
composed discussion of the same issue. So, in all, units VIII-XV in the balance
appear to be continuous, an impressive feat of sustained argument.

4:8A-B

A. *The Hallel-Psalms and the rejoicing are for eight days: How so?*
B. *This rule teaches that a person is obligated for the Hallel-Psalms, for the
rejoicing, and for the honoring of the festival day, on the last festival
day of the Festival, just as he is on all the other days of the Festival.*

I.

A. How on the basis of Scripture do we know this rule?
B. It accords with that which our rabbis have taught on Tannaite authority:
C. "And you shall be altogether joyful" (Deut. 16:15) serves to encompass
the last nights of the festival.
D. Perhaps it refers only to the first Festival day.

E.   When Scripture says, "Altogether," the word serves to distinguish [one set of Festival days from the other].

F.   Why then encompass the last nights of the Festival and exclude the first ones?

G.   I encompass the last nights of the Festival, [on the days] before which there is an aspect of rejoicing, and exclude the first nights of the festival, [on the days] before which there is no aspect of rejoicing.

The Talmud provides a scriptural basis for the Mishnah's rules. The larger issues of the required conduct on the Eighth Day of Solemn Assembly have already been worked out in the preceding.

4:8C-F

C.   *The obligation to dwell in the sukkah for seven days: How so?*

D.   *[If] one has finished eating [the last meal of the festival], he should not untie his sukkah right away.*

E.   *But he brings down the utensils [only] from twilight onward –*

F.   *on account of the honor due to the last festival day of the Festival.*

I.

A.   [In line with M. 4:8E], if someone has no utensils to bring down, what is the law?

B.   If he had no utensils?! Then what did he use [in the sukkah]?

C.   Rather, the question is to be phrased as follows:

D.   If the householder had no place to which to bring down his utensils, what is the law? [What if he had nowhere else to eat?]

E.   R. Hiyya bar Ashi said, "He removes four handbreadths [of the roof of the sukkah itself, thus removing the sukkah from valid use]."

F.   R. Joshua b. Levi said, "He lights a lamp in it [which is not to be done in a valid sukkah. That indicates that the sukkah is no longer in use in connection with the Festival.]"

G.   And there is no difference between the two authorities, one referring to how we do things [here in Babylonia], and the other to how they do things there [in the Land of Israel]. [In Babylonia, the eighth day may be the seventh, so one cannot remove the sukkah-roofing, and kindling the lamp is the only reasonable procedure.]

H.   [Lighting a lamp] is suitable in the case of a small sukkah [where one may not bring a lamp], what is there to say?

I.   One may bring into the sukkah dishes for eating.

J.   For Raba said, "Dishes for eating are to be kept outside of the sukkah, dishes for drinking are to be kept in the sukkah." [Thus bringing the dishes into the sukkah indicates that the sukkah now is no longer preserved for sacred purposes.]

The Talmud clarifies a minor aspect of the rule, M. 4:8E.

4:9-10

A.   *The water-libation: How so?*

B.   *A golden flask, holding three logs in volume, did one fill with water from Siloam.*

C. *[When] they reached the Water Gate, they blow a sustained, a quavering, and a sustained blast on the shofar.*

D. *[The priest] went up on the ramp [at the south] and turned to his left [southwest].*

E. *There were two silver bowls there.*

F. *R. Judah says, "They were of plaster, but they had darkened because of the wine."*

G. *They were perforated [48B] with holes like a narrow snout,*

H. *one wide, one narrow,*

I. *so that both of them would be emptied together [one of its wine, flowing slowly, the other of its water, flowing quickly].*

J. *The one on the west was for water, the one on the east was for wine.*

K. *[If] he emptied the flask of water into the bowl for wine, and the flask of wine into the bowl for water, he has nonetheless carried out the rite.*

L. *R. Judah says "A log [of water] would one pour out as the water libation all eight days."*

M. *And to the one who pours out the water libation they say, "Lift up your hand [so that we can see the water pouring out]!"*

N. *For one time one [priest] poured out the water on his feet.*

O. *And all the people stoned him with their citrons.*

M. 4:9

A. *As the rite concerning it [was carried out] on an ordinary day, so was the rite [carried out] on the Sabbath.*

B. *But on the eve of Sabbath one would fill with water from Siloam a gold jug, which was not sanctified,*

C. *and he would leave it in a chamber [in the Temple].*

D. *[If] it was poured out or left uncovered, one would fill the jug from the laver [in the courtyard].*

E. *For wine and water which have been left uncovered are invalid for the altar.*

M. 4:10

I.

A. What is the scriptural source for the rule [at M. 4:9C about sounding the ram's horn]?

B. Said R. Ina, "It is that Scripture has said, 'Therefore with joy you shall draw water from the wells of salvation' (Is. 12:3).

II.

A. There were two heretics, one called Joy, the other, Gladness.

B. Said Joy to Gladness, "I am better than you, for it is said, 'They shall obtain Joy and Gladness' (Is. 35:10)."

C. Said Gladness to Joy, "I am better than you, for it is written, 'Gladness and Joy go to the Jews' (Est. 8:17)."

D. Said Joy to Gladness, "Some day they will take you and make you a courier, since it is said, 'For with gladness they shall go forth' (Is. 55:12)."

E. Said Gladness to Joy, "One day they will take you and fill you with water, as it is written, 'Therefore with joy you shall draw water' (Is. 12:3)."

III.

A. A heretic named Joy said to R. Abbahu, "You are destined to draw water for me in the world to come, for it is written, 'Therefore with joy you shall draw water' (Is. 12:3)."

B. He said to him, "If it were written, 'For joy,' matters would have you been as you maintain. But since it is written, 'With joy,' the sense is that with the skin of that man [you] people will make a water-bucket and will draw water with it."

IV.

A. The priest went up on the ramp at the south and turned to his left, southwestward [M. 4:9D]:

B. Our rabbis have taught on Tannaite authority:

C. All who go up to the altar go up on the right, that is, to the east, and walk around the altar and go down on the left, that is, of the west

D. except for those who go up for these three purposes, who go up on the left and turn around [going up at the west and going down at the west]:

E. those who go up for the water-offering, for the wine-offering, and for the burnt-offering of fowl when the east side of the altar is too busy [T. Zeb. 7:7].

V.

A. ...but they had darkened... [M. 4:9F]:

B. Now there is no problem regarding the one for wine, which will darken, but why should the one for water darken?

C. Since the authority at hand has said, If he emptied the flask of water into the bowl for wine, and the flask of wine into the bowl for water [M. 4:9K],

D. it turns out that the one for water may darken as well.

VI.

A. They were perforated with holes like a narrrow snout [M. 4:9G]:

B. May we conclude that the Mishnah's statement accords with the view of R. Judah and not that of rabbis?

C. For we have learned in the Mishnah:

D. R. Judah says, "A log of water would one pour out as the water libation all eight days" [M. 4:9L].

E. But it cannot accord with rabbis, for, from their viewpoint, why should the water and wine not pour out together? [In Judah's view the wine was, in volume, three logs, so a larger hole would be needed for the wine flask than for the water. So far as rabbis are concerned, each was three logs in volume.]

F. No, that is not a valid surmise. You may maintain that the passage accords even with the view of rabbis. Wine is thick, water is thin.

G. That view is a reasonable one, for so far as R. Judah is concerned, the language he should prefer would be "broad" and "narrow."

H. For it has been taught on Tannaite authority:

I. R. Judah says, "Two bowls were there, one for water, one for wine. *The mouth of the one for wine was broad, the mouth of the one for water was narrow, so that both of them would be emptied together [cf. M. 4:9G-I].* [The Tannaite teaching thus assigns M. 4:9G-I to the authority of Judah].

J. That is conclusive proof [for the proposition of F-G].

VII.

A. *The one on the west was for water [M. 4:9J]:*

B. Our rabbis have taught on Tannaite authority:

C. For there was the case of the Boethusian who poured out the water on his feet, and all the people stoned him with their citrons [M. 4:9N-O].

D. And the horn of the altar was damaged that day [so the sacred service was annulled for that day], until they brought a lump of salt and put it on it, not because the altar was once more validated, but so that the altar should not appear to be damaged.

E. [49A] For any altar lacking a horn, ramp, or foundation is invalid.

F. R. Yose b. R. Judah says, "Also the rim" [T. Suk. 3:16D-F].

VIII.

A. Said Rabbah bar bar Hanan said R. Yohanan, "The pits [under the altar, to which the wine of the libation-offering flowed] had been created in the six days of creation,

B. "for it is said, 'The roundings of your thighs are like the links of a chain, the work of the hands of a skilled workman' (Song 7:2).

C. "'The roundings of your thighs' – these are the pits.

D. "'Like the links of a chain' indicates that their cavity goes down to the abyss.

E. "'The work of the hands of a skilled workman' – this refers to the skillful handiwork of the Holy One, blessed be He."

IX.

A. A Tannaite authority of the house of R. Ishmael: "'In the beginning' (Gen. 1:1) is not to be read 'in the beginning,' but rather, 'he created the pit [of the altar].'"

X.

A. It has been taught on Tannaite authority:

B. R. Yose says, "'The cavity of the pits descended to the abyss, as it is said, Let me sing of my well-beloved, a song of my beloved touching his vineyard. My well-beloved had a vineyard on a very fruitful hill. And he digged it and cleared it of stones and planted it with the choicest vine and built a tower in the midst of it and also hewed out a vat therein' (Is. 5:1-2).

C. "'And he built a tower in the midst of it' – this is the sanctuary.

D. "'And [also] hewed out a vat therein' – this is the altar.

E. "'And also hewed out a vat therein' – this is the pits."

F. R. Eliezer b. R. Sadoq says, "There was a small passage-way between the ascent and the altar at the west side of the ramp.

G. "Once every seventy years the young priests would go down there and gather up the congealed wine, which looked like circles of pressed figs, and they burned it in a state of sanctity, as it is said, In the holy place shall you pour out a drink-offering of strong drink unto the Lord (Num. 28:7).

H. [49B] "Just as the pouring out must be in a state of sanctity, thus the burning of it must be in a state of sanctity" [T. Suk. 3:15C-I].

I. What evidence is there [for the statement of H]?

J. Said Rabina, "There is an analogy to be drawn between two uses of the word 'Holy.'

K. "Here it is written, 'In the Holy Place shall you pour out a drink-offering of strong drink to the Lord' (Num. 28:7), and it is written elsewhere, 'Then you shall burn the remainder with fire, it shall not be eaten, because it is holy' (Ex. 29:34)."

L. In accord with whose view does the following accord, as has been taught on Tannaite authority:

M. As to drink-offerings, at the outset the laws of sacrilege apply to them. Once they have poured down into the pits, the law of sacrilege do not apply to them.

N. May I maintain that it must be R. Eleazar bar Sadoq [Slotki, p. 231, n. 8: who holds that the pits reached only to the floor of the court and that the wine poured into them was retrievable]?

O. For it cannot be rabbis, who take the view that the pits descended to the abyss. [Slotki, p. 231, n. 9: No law, surely, is required for an object that is for ever lost in the abyss.]

P. You may take the view that it accords even with rabbis' position. We deal with the place where the wine was collected.

Q. There are those who repeat the matter in the following version:

R. May we say that it accords with rabbis and not R. Eleazar bar Sadoq?

S. For if the rule accorded with R. Eleazar, do the remnants not remain in their condition of sanctification?

T. You may maintain that the rule accords even with R. Eleazar.

U. You have nothing which has already served for the fulfillment of the religious duty concerning it and yet which remains subject to the laws of sacrilege.

XI.

A. Said R. Simeon b. Laqish, "When the priests pour wine out on the altar, they stop up the pits.

B. "This serves to carry out that which is said: 'In holiness you shall pour out a drink-offering of strong drink to the Lord' (Num. 28:7)."

C. What is the sense of the passage?

D. Said R. Papa, "'Strong drink' refers to drinking, satisfaction, and plenty."

E. Said R. Papa, "That then bears the implication that when a man has had enough wine, it is because his throat has had its fill."

F. Said Raba, "A young disciple of rabbis, who does not have much wine, should drink it in large mouthfuls [Slotki: since thereby he has the same satisfaction as if he drank much wine]."

G. Raba would swallow the wine of the cup of benediction in a big gulp.

XII.

A. Raba interpreted [Scripture as follows], "What is the sense of what is written, 'How beautiful are your steps in sandals, O prince's daughter' (Song 7:2)?

B. "How beautiful are the steps of Israel when they come up for a festal pilgrimage.

C. "'Prince's daughter' – daughter of Abraham, our father, who was called a prince, as it is said, 'The princes of the peoples are gathered together, the people of the God of Abraham' (Ps. 47:10).

D. "'The God of Abraham' and not the God of Isaac and Jacob?

E. "The sense is, 'The God of Abraham, who was first of the converts [to God].'"

XIII.

A. A Tannaite authority of the house of R. Anan taught, "What is the sense of Scripture's statement, 'The roundings of your thighs' (Song 7:2)?

B. "Why are the teachings of Torah compared to the thigh?

C. "It is to teach you that, just as the thigh is kept hidden, so teachings of Torah are to be kept hidden."

D. That is in line with what R. Eleazar said, "What is the sense of the verse of Scripture, 'It has been told you, O man, what is good, and what the Lord requires of you: only to do justly, to love mercy, and to walk humbly with your God' (Mic. 6:8)?

E. "'To do justly' refers to justice.

F. "'To love mercy' refers to doing deeds of loving kindness.

G. "'And to walk humbly with your God' refers to taking out a corpse for burial and bringing the bride in to the marriage-canopy.

H. "And is it not a matter of argument a fortiori:

I. "Now if, as to matters which are ordinarily done in public, the Torah has said, 'To walk humbly,' matters which are normally done in private, all the more so [must they be done humbly and in secret, that is, the giving of charity is done secretly]."

J. Said R. Eleazar, "Greater is the one who carries out an act of charity more than one who offers all the sacrifices.

K. "For it is said, 'To do charity and justice is more desired by the Lord than sacrifice' (Prov. 21:3)."

L. And R. Eleazar said, "An act of lovingkindness is greater than an act of charity.

M. "For it is said, 'Sow to yourselves according to your charity, but reap according to your lovingkindness' (Hos. 10:12).

N. "If a man sows seed, it is a matter of doubt whether he will eat a crop or not. But if a man harvests the crop, he most certainly will eat it."

O. And R. Eleazar said, "An act of charity is rewarded only in accord with the lovingkindness that is connected with it.

P. "For it is said, 'Sow to yourselves according to your charity, but reap according to your lovingkindness' (Hos. 10:12)."

XIV.

A. Our rabbis have taught on Tannaite authority:

B. In three aspects are acts of lovingkindness greater than an act of charity.

C. An act of charity is done only with money, but an act of lovingkindness someone carries out either with his own person or with his money.

D. An act of charity is done only for the poor, while an act of lovingkindness may be done either for the poor or for the rich.

E. An act of charity is done only for the living. An act of lovingkindness may be done either for the living or for the dead.

XV.

A. And R. Eleazar has said, "Whoever does an act of charity and justice is as if he has filled the entire world with mercy.

B. "For it is said, 'He loves charity and justice, the earth is full of the lovingkindness of the Lord' (Ps. 33:5).

C. "Now you might wish to say that whoever comes to jump may take a leap [Slotki: whoever wishes to do good succeeds without difficulty].

D. "Scripture accordingly states, 'How precious is your lovingkindness, O God' (Ps. 36:8). [Slotki, p. 233, n. 11: The opportunity of doing real, well deserved charity and dispensing it in a judicious manner is rare].

E. "Now you might wish to say that the same is the case for fear of Heaven [so that one who fears Heaven nonetheless has trouble in carrying out charity and justice].

F. "Scripture accordingly states, 'But the lovingkindness of the Lord is from everlasting to everlasting upon them that fear him' (Ps. 103:17)."

G. Said R. Hama bar Papa, "Every man who enjoys grace is assuredly a God-fearer.

H. "For it is said, 'But the lovingkindness of the Lord is from everlasting to everlasting upon them that fear him' (Ps. 103:17)."

I. And R. Eleazar said, "What is the sense of the following verse of Scripture: 'She opens her mouth with wisdom, and the Torah of lovingkindness is on her tongue' (Prov. 31:26)?

J. "Now is there such a thing as a Torah that is one of lovingkindness and a Torah that is not one of lovingkindness?

K. "But rather the study of Torah done for its own sake falls into the category of Torah of lovingkindness, and Torah not studied for its own sake falls into the category of Torah that is not of lovingkindness."

L. There are those who say, "Study of Torah in order to teach it is Torah of lovingkindness, while Torah learned not so as to teach it is Torah that is not of lovingkindness."

XVI.

A. *As the rite concerning it was carried out on an ordinary day, so was the rite carried out on the Sabbath [M. 4:10A]:*

B. But why [bring the water in a jug that was not sanctified] [M. 4:10B]?

C. Said Zeiri, "The framer of the passage takes the view that there is no minimum volume for the water-offering, while utensils of the Temple service serve to sanctify their contents even without the prior intent [of the one who uses them].

D. [50A] "Now if the priest should bring the water in a jug that had been sanctified, the water [being sanctified] will be made unfit through being left to stand over night. [There is nothing the priest can do to prevent the sanctification of the water, and what has been sanctified is subject to the prohibition against being left overnight. So the only solution is not to bring the water in a sanctified utensil to begin with.]"

E. Said Hezekiah, "Utensils of service sanctify their contents only with prior intent [of the one who uses them]. So the issue raised by Zeiri is of no bearing. But it is a precautionary decree, so that people will not think that the water was deliberately sanctified [and then left overnight]."

F. Said R. Yannai said R. Zira, "Even if you say that there is a minimum volume of water that is required for the water-offering, and, further, that utensils of service sanctify what is put in them only with the prior intention of the one who uses them, nonetheless the rule would be the same. [Why?]

G. "It is a precautionary decree lest people say that the priest filled the utensil for the purpose of sanctifying [through washing] the hands and feet. [Slotki, p. 235, n. 2: Such water must first be hallowed, and however large its quantity, it might still be regarded as intended to be used for this purpose. If the water were allowed to be used on the next day, wrong conclusions might be drawn.]"

XVII.

A. *If it was poured out or left uncovered [M. 4:10D]:*

B. Why [was the water not used]? One should simply pour the water through a strainer.

C. May I then say that the Mishnah-passage does not accord with the view of R. Nehemiah?

D. For it has been taught on Tannaite authority:

E. Water that has been passed through a strainer nonetheless is subject to the consideration that it has been left uncovered.

F. Said R. Nehemiah, "When is this the case? It is when the receptacle on the bottom has been left uncovered. But if the receptacle on the bottom has been covered, then even though the one on top [from which the fluid will pour out to be strained] has been left uncovered, there is no consideration of danger on account of the utensil's fluid being left uncovered.

G. "The reason is that the venom of a snake is like a fungus that floats to the surface and stands there [Slotki: in the strainer]."

H. You may say that the Mishnah-rule at hand [which does not take account of the possibility of straining the water that has been left uncovered] follows even the view of R. Nehemiah.

I.   R. Nehemiah would make such a rule when the liquid that has been left
     uncovered is for ordinary use, but for use for the Most High, would he
     make the same rule?

J.   For does not R. Nehemiah maintain the view: "Present it now to your
     governor, will he be pleased with you? Or will he accept your person?"
     (Mal. 1:8). [What is used for the divine service must be unblemished.]

Unit I provides a minor gloss to M. 4:9C, and units II, III are appended as
an anthology of materials on the cited proof-text. Unit IV proceeds to M. 4:9D,
V to M. 4:9F, VI to M. 4:9G, VII to M. 4:9J. Once the subject of the pits
under the altar is raised, it is pursued in its own terms at units VIII, IX, X, XI.
Since Raba occurs in XI, XII, which provides a further pertinent statement of
his, is appended. Then the exposition of Song 7:2 at XII A accounts for the
inclusion of XIII, on the same verse, a kind of running amplification, as
something in one item triggers the inclusion of the next. The same
consideration accounts for all that follows to the end of XV. Then units XVI-
XVII go on to complete the exposition of the Mishnah-passage. So there are
two principles of agglomeration: (1) exposition of the Mishnah, and (2)
amplification of materials used in the exposition of the Mishnah.

III

The Result

These units have no counterparts and are made up to serve the interests of
the present authorship alone: **4:1-4:** I, V, VI, VII, VIII, IX, X, XI, XII; **4:5-7:**
I, II, III, V, VI, VII, VIII, X, XI, XII, XIII, XIV, XV; **4:8A-B:** I; **4:8C-F:** I;
4:9-10: I, II, III, V, VI, VIII, IX, XI, XVI, XVII.

These units are built upon citation and exegesis of a passage of the Tosefta:
4:1-4: none (V.JJ-NN is cited in the context of an argument not focused on that
passage); **4:5-7** (VII is cited as an objection to an argument that develops along
its own lines), IX; **4:8A-B:** none; **4:8C-F:** none; **4:9-10:** IV (Tosefta-
passage cited to amplify the Mishnah-rule, but no discussion developed), VII (as
before), X.

These units take shape around exegesis of Scripture: **4:1-4** II, III, IV (Lev.
23:40: How do we know that the act of taking the lulab is done by each
individual, that the lulab must be one's own possession, that it is done even on
the Sabbath); **4:5-7:** IV re Ex. 26:15; **4:9-10:** XII-XIII (continued at XIV-XV
on a theme introduced at XIII) re Song 7:2: verse refers to making a pilgrimage
on a festival; verse refers to teachings of Torah. The extant exegeses of Lev.
23:40 include the passage at Emor cited in the translation above, with the same
view expressed at Sifré Dt. 140 (Finkelstein, p. 194, ls. 3-7. In addition, at T.
Suk. 3:1: Abba Saul cites this verse to prove that the taking of the willow
branches on the Festival of Tabernacles is a law revealed to Moses at Sinai.
Lev. R. Parashah Thirty = Pesiqta deRab Kahana 27 takes Lev. 23:39-40 as its

base verse. The main point is that the taking of the palm branch involves a great reward, because many religious duties are encompassed by that rite. XXX:VI.1 goes over the point of Sifra Emor, as cited above, but now in the name of Hiyya. The operative exegesis is the same. XXX:VIII.1 is verbatim the same as is given here at 4:1-4.

Since, with respect to exegeses of Scripture, we wish to know whether or not available treatments of a biblical verse have guided the formation of any component of our Bavli-passage, we have a fine opportunity in hand. Because Lev. R. 30 which is the same as PRK 27 deals with verses clearly important in our passage, we may rapidly review the more important treatments of the same verses in those compilations, completed earlier than Bavli's work on the same matter. We may therefore scrutinize a sizable example of the points of intersection between the Bavli's authorship and earlier an authorship's treatment of identical materials. I give the matter in my translation of PRK 27 = Lev. R. 30, which I have abbreviated so as to focus only on the question at hand. In this translation I present verses of Scripture appear in italics, since, in this document they form the counterpart of the Mishnah-passages in the Bavli.

XXVII:I

1. A. R. Abba bar Kahana commenced [discourse by citing the following verse]: *Take my instruction instead of silver, and knowledge rather than choice gold* (Prov. 8:10)."
   B. Said R. Abba bar Kahana, *"Take the instruction of the Torah instead of silver.*
   C. "Take the instruction of the Torah and not silver.
   D. *"Why do you weigh out money? [Because there is no bread]* (Is. 55:2).
   E. "'Why do you weigh out money to the sons of Esau [Rome]? [It is because] *there is no bread,* because you did not sate yourselves with the bread of the Torah.
   F. *"And [why] do you labor? Because there is no satisfaction* (Is. 55:2).
   G. *"Why do you labor* while the nations of the world enjoy plenty? *Because there is no satisfaction,* that is, because you have not sated yourselves with the bread of the Torah and with the wine of the Torah.
   H. "For it is written, *Come, eat of my bread, and drink of the wine I have mixed* (Prov. 9:5)."

2. A. R. Berekhiah and R. Hiyya, his father, in the name of R. Yose b. Nehorai: "It is written, *I shall punish all who oppress him* (Jer. 30:20), even those who collect funds for charity [and in doing so, treat people badly], except [for those who collect] the wages to be paid to teachers of Scripture and repeaters of Mishnah traditions.
   B. "For they receive [as a salary] only compensation for the loss of their time, [which they devote to teaching and learning rather than to earning a living].
   C. "But as to the wages [for carrying out] a single matter in the Torah, no creature can pay the [appropriate] fee in reward."

3. A. It has been taught on Tannaite authority: On the New Year, a person's sustenance is decreed [for the coming year],

B. except for what a person pays out [for food in celebration] of the Sabbath, festivals, the celebration of the New Month,

C. and for what children bring to the house of their master [as his tuition].

D. If he deducts [from what he should give], [in Heaven] they deduct [from his wealth], but if he adds [to what is originally decreed], [in Heaven] they add to his [resources]. [Margulies, *Vayyiqra Rabbah*, p. 688, n. to 1. 5, links this statement to Prov. 8:10.]

4. A. R. Yohanan was going up from Tiberias to Sepphoris. R. Hiyya bar Abba was supporting him. They came to a field. He said, "This field once belonged to me, but I sold it in order to acquire merit in labor in the the Torah."

B. They came to a vineyard, and he said, "This vineyard once belonged to me, but I sold it in order to acquire merit in labor in the the Torah."

C. They came to an olive grove, and he said, "This olive grove once belonged to me, but but I sold it in order to acquire merit in labor in the the Torah."

D. R. Hiyya began to cry.

E. Said R. Yohanan, "Why are you crying?"

F. He said to him, "It is because you left nothing over to support you in your old age."

G. He said to him, "Hiyya, my disciple, is what I did such a light thing in your view? I sold something which was given in a spell of six days [of creation] and in exchange I acquired something which was given in a spell of forty days [of revelation].

H. "The entire world and everything in it was created in only six days, as it is written, *For in six days the Lord made heaven and earth* (Ex. 20:11)

I. "But the Torah was given over a period of forty days and forty nights, as it was said, *And he was there with the Lord for forty days and forty nights* (Ex. 34:28). [Leviticus Rabbah adds: And it is written, *And I remained on the mountain for forty days and forty nights* (Deut. 9:9).]"

5. A. When R. Yohanan died, his generation recited concerning him [the following verse of Scripture]: *If a man should give all the wealth of his house for the love* (Song 8:7), with which R. Yohanan loved the Torah, *he would be utterly destitute* (Song 8:7).

B. When R. Abba bar Hoshaiah of Tiria died, they saw his bier flying in the air. His generation recited concerning him [the following verse of Scripture]: *If a man should give all the wealth of his house for the love* , with which the Holy One, blessed be He, loved Abba bar Hoshaiah of Tiria, *he would be utterly destitute* (Song 8:7).

C. When R. Eleazar b. R. Simeon died, his generation recited concerning him [the following verse of Scripture]: *Who is this who comes up out of the wilderness like pillars of smoke, [perfumed with myrrh and frankincense, with all the powders of the merchant?]* (Song 3:6).

D. What is the meaning of the clause, *With all the powders of the merchant?*

E. [Like a merchant who carries all sorts of desired powders,] he was a master of Scripture, a repeater of Mishnah traditions, a writer of liturgical supplications, and a poet.

6. A. Another interpretation of the verse, *Take my instruction instead of silver, [and knowledge rather than choice gold]* (Prov. 8:10): Said R. Abba bar Kahana, "On the basis of the reward paid for one act of *taking,*

you may assess the reward for [taking] the palm branch [on the festival of Tabernacles].

B.   "There was an act of taking in Egypt: *You will take a bunch of hyssop* (Ex. 12:22).

C.   "And how much was it worth? Four *manehs,* maybe five.

D.   "Yet that act of taking is what stood up for Israel [and so made Israel inherit] the spoil of Egypt, the spoil at the sea, the spoil of Sihon and Og, and the spoil of the thirty-one kings.

E.   "Now the palm branch, which costs a person such a high price, and which involves so many religious duties – how much the more so [will a great reward be forthcoming on its account]!"

F.   Therefore Moses admonished Israel, saying to them, *[On the fifteenth day of the seventh month, when you have gathered in the produce of the land, you shall keep the feast of the Lord seven days...] And you shall take on the first day [the fruit of goodly trees, branches of palm trees and boughs of leafy trees and willows of the brook; and you shall rejoice before the Lord your God seven days. You shall keep it as a feast to the Lord seven days in the year; it is a statute for ever throughout your generations; you shall keep it in the seventh month. You shall dwell in booths for seven days; all that are native in Israel shall dwell in booths, that your generations may know that I made the people of Israel dwell in booths when I brought them out of the land of Egypt: I am the Lord your God* (Leviticus 23:39-43).

1.B seems to me to employ Is. 55:2 as an intersecting-verse for the base-verse of Prov. 8:10. That, at any rate, is the force of the exegesis of 1.C-G. Then the citation of Prov. 9:5 presents a secondary expansion of what has been said about Is. 55:2, that is, 1.F-G lead us directly to H. What has happened to Lev. 23:39? In fact, 1.B-H are inserted whole because of the use of the key word, *take,* at Lev. 23:39 and Prov. 8:10. From that point, Lev. 23:39 plays no role whatsoever. It is only at No. 6 that Lev. 23:39 – with stress on the word "take" – recurs. The theme of the intervening passages is established at 1.B, namely, Torah and the value and importance of study of Torah. Nos. 2, 3, 4, and 5 all present variations on amplifications of that theme. I cannot follow Margulies in linking No. 3 to the intersecting-verse. No. 5 is attached because of No. 4, and No. 4 because of its homily on the Torah. Since No. 6 ignores all that has gone before, and since No. 6 alone alludes to 1.A, we have to regard as remarkable the insertion of the rather sizable construction, 1.B through 5.E. In some other passages we see subtle connections between the base-verse, or, at least, the theme of the base-verse, and the exegesis of the intersecting-verse, and the secondary exegetical expansions of verses introduced in connection with the intersecting one. But here I see none. Even the key word, "take," does not recur beyond the intersecting-verse. So the editorial principle accounting for the inclusion of 1.B-5.E is the occurrence of a single shared word, that alone. That seems to me uncommon in our document. As to No. 6, of course, the homily rests on the key word, "Take," and that is made explicit. But No. 6 does not rest upon the exegesis of any intersecting-verse; it is a simple exegetical homily.

6.F, of course, is secondary, a redactional filling we shall see again. I present only the concluding unit of XXVII:II because it shows us merely one more exercise on an intersecting-verse, leading back to Lev. 23:40 as the base-verse so as to make the same point.

XXVII:II

5. A. Another matter concerning the verse *You show me the path of life, in your presence there is fulness of joy, in your right hand are pleasures for evermore* (Ps. 16:11): *In your presence there is fulness (SWB') of joy* (Ps. 16:11):

B. [Leviticus Rabbah adds: Read only "seven (SB') joys."] These are the seven religious duties associated with the Festival [Tabernacles].

C. These are they: the four species that are joined in the palm branch, [the building of] the Tabernacle, [the offering of] the festal sacrifice, [the offering of] the sacrifice of rejoicing.

6. A. If there is the offering of the sacrifice of rejoicing, then why is there also the offering of the festal sacrifice? And if there is [the offering of] the festal sacrifice, then why also is there [the offering of] the sacrifice of rejoicing?

B. Said R. Abin, "The matter may be compared to two who came before a judge. Now we do not know which one of them is the victor. But it is the one who takes the palm branch in his hand who we know to be the victor.

C. "So is the case of Israel and the nations of the world. The [latter] come and draw an indictment before the Holy One, blessed be He, on the New Year, and we do not know which party is victor.

E. "But when Israel goes forth from before the Holy One, blessed be He, with their palm branches and their citrons in their hands, we know that it is Israel that are the victors."

F. Therefore Moses admonishes Israel, saying to them, *[On the fifteenth day of the seventh month, when you have gathered in the produce of the land, you shall keep the feast of the Lord seven days...] And you shall take on the first day [the fruit of goodly trees, branches of palm trees and boughs of leafy trees and willows of the brook; and you shall rejoice before the Lord your God seven days. You shall keep it as a feast to the Lord seven days in the year; it is a statute for ever throughout your generations; you shall keep it in the seventh month. You shall dwell in booths for seven days; all that are native in Israel shall dwell in booths, that your generations may know that I made the people of Israel dwell in booths when I brought them out of the land of Egypt: I am the Lord your God* (Leviticus 23:39-43).

Nos. 5-6 go over Ps. 16:11 with respect to Israel, introducing the matter of the New Year, Day of Atonement, and Festival. Then each clause suitably links to the several themes at hand. 6.F of course is tacked on.

XXVII:III

1. A. *He will regard the prayer of the destitute [and will not despise their supplication]* (Ps. 102:17):

B. Said R. Reuben, "We are unable to make sense of David's character. Sometimes he calls himself king, and sometimes he calls himself destitute.

C. "How so? When he foresaw that righteous men were going to come from him, such as Asa, Jehoshaphat, Hezekiah, and Josiah, he would call himself king as it is said, *Give the king your judgments, O God* (Ps. 72:1).

D. "When he foresaw that wicked men would come forth from him, for example, Ahaz, Manasseh, and Amon, he would call himself destitute, as it is said, *A prayer of one afflicted, when he is faint [and pours out his complaint before the Lord]* (Ps. 102:1)."

2. A. R. Alexandri interpreted the cited verse, *He will regard the prayer of the destitute [and will not despise their supplication]* (Ps. 102:17), to speak of a worker: "[Margulies, ad loc., explains: The one afflicted is the worker. The word for faint, 'TP, bears the meaning, *cloak oneself,* hence in prayer. The worker then has delayed his prayer, waiting for the overseer to leave, at which point he can stop and say his prayer. So he postpones his prayer.] [So Alexandri says], "Just as a worker sits and watches all day long for when the overseer will leave for a bit, so he is late when he says [his prayer], [so David speaks at Ps. 102:1: *Hear my prayer, O Lord; let my cry come to you*]."

B. "That [interpretation of the word 'TP] is in line with the use in the following verse: *And those that were born late belonged to Laban* (Gen. 30:42)."

C. What is the meaning of *those that were born late?*

D. R. Isaac bar Haqolah said, *"The ones that tarried."*

3. A. [Another interpretation: *He will regard the prayer of the destitute [and will not despise their supplication]* (Ps. 102:17):] Said R. Simeon b. Laqish, "As to this verse, the first half of it is not consistent with the second half, and vice versa.

B. "If it is to be, *'He will regard the prayer of the destitute* [individual],' he should then have said, 'And will not despise *his* supplication.'

C. "But if it is to be, *'He will not despise their supplication,'* then he should have said, 'He will regard the prayer of *those* who are destitute.'

D. "But [when David wrote,] *He will regard the prayer of the individual destitute,* this [referred to] the prayer of Manasseh, king of Judah.

F. "And [when David wrote,] *He will not despise their supplication,* this [referred to] his prayer and the prayer of his fathers.

G. "That is in line with the following verse of Scripture: *And he prayed to him, and he was entreated of him* (2 Chron. 33:13)."

H. What is the meaning of the phrase, *He was entreated* (Y'TR) *of him?*

I. Said R. Eleazar b. R. Simeon, "In Arabia they call a breach an *athirta* [so an opening was made for his prayer to penetrate to the Throne of God]" (Slotki, p. 385, n. 3).

J. *And he brought him back to Jerusalem, [his kingdom]* (2 Chron. 33:13).

K. How did he bring him back?

L. R. Samuel b. R. Jonah said in the name of R. Aha, "He brought him back with a wind.

M. "That is in line with the phrase [in The Prayer], *He causes the wind to blow.*"

N.   [At that moment:] *And Manasseh knew that the Lord is God* (2 Chron. 33:13). Then Manasseh said, "There is justice and there is a judge."

4 . A.   R. Isaac interpreted the verse *He will regard the prayer of the destitute [and will not despise their supplication]* (Ps. 102:17) to speak of these generations which have neither king nor prophet, neither priest nor Urim and Thummim, but who have only this prayer alone.

B.   "Said David before the Holy One, blessed be He, 'Lord of the ages, "Do not despise their prayer. *Let this be recorded for a generation to come'* (Ps. 102:19).

C.   "On the basis of that statement, [we know that] the Holy One, blessed be He, accepts penitents.

D.   *"So that a people yet unborn may praise the Lord* (Ps. 102:19).

E.   "For the Holy One, blessed be He, will create them as a new act of creation."

5 . A.   Another interpretation: *Let this be recorded for a generation to come* (Ps. 102:18):

B.   This refers to the generation of Hezekiah, [Leviticus Rabbah adds: which was tottering toward death].

C.   *So that a people yet unborn may praise the Lord* (Ps. 102:18): for the Holy One, blessed be He, created them in a new act of creation.

6 . A.   Another interpretation: *Let this be recorded for a generation to come* (Ps. 102:18):

B.   This refers to the generation of Mordecai and Esther, which was tottering toward death.

C.   *So that a people yet unborn may praise the Lord* (Ps. 102:18): for the Holy One, blessed be He, created them in a new act of creation.

7 . A.   Another interpretation: *Let this be recorded for a generation to come* (Ps. 102:18):

B.   This refers to these very generations [in our own day], which are tottering to death.

C.   *So that a people yet unborn may praise the Lord* (Ps. 102:18):

D.   For the Holy One, blessed be He, is going to create them anew, in a new act of creation.

8 . A.   What do we have to take [in order to reach that end]? Take up the palm branch and citron and praise the Holy One, blessed be He.

B.   Therefore Moses admonishes Israel, saying, *[On the fifteenth day of the seventh month, when you have gathered in the produce of the land, you shall keep the feast of the Lord seven days...] And you shall take on the first day [the fruit of goodly trees, branches of palm trees and boughs of leafy trees and willows of the brook; and you shall rejoice before the Lord your God seven days. You shall keep it as a feast to the Lord seven days in the year; it is a statute for ever throughout your generations; you shall keep it in the seventh month. You shall dwell in booths for seven days; all that are native in Israel shall dwell in booths, that your generations may know that I made the people of Israel dwell in booths when I brought them out of the land of Egypt: I am the Lord your God* (Leviticus 23:39-43).

Until the very final lines, No. 8, we have no reason at all to associate the exegesis of Ps. 102:17-18 with the theme of the Festival. On the contrary, all of the materials stand autonomous of the present "base-verse," and none of them hints at what is to come at the end. On that basis I regard the construction as complete prior to its insertion here, with a redactional hand contributing only No. 98 to validate the inclusion of an otherwise irrelevant exegetical exercise. The established pattern – the tripartite exegesis of Ps. 102:17, 18 – is worked out at Nos. 1 (supplemented by Nos. 2 and 3), then Nos. 4-7. I now bypass other exercises in the intersecting-verse/base-verse model and proceed directly to another treatment of the established theme of our base-verse.

XXVII:V

1. A. *I wash my hands in innocence and go about your altar, O Lord, [singing aloud a song of thanksgiving, and telling all your wondrous deeds]* (Ps. 26:6-7):

    B. [What I require I acquire] through purchase, not theft.

    C. [Leviticus Rabbah adds:] **For we have learned there: A stolen or dried up palm branch is invalid. And one deriving from an** *asherah* **or an apostate town is invalid** (M. Suk. 3:1A-B).

    D. *And go about your altar, O Lord* (Ps. 26:7).

    E. That is in line with what we have learned there: **Every day they circumambulate the altar one time and say, "We beseech you, O Lord, save now. We beseech you, O Lord, make us prosper now [Ps. 118:25]. R. Judah says, "I and him, save now." On that day they circumambulate the altar seven times** (M. Suk. 4:5).

2. A. *Singing aloud a song of thanksgiving* (Ps. 26:7) – this refers to the offerings.

    B. *And telling all your wondrous deeds* (Ps. 26:7):

    C. Said R. Abun, "This refers to the *Hallel* Psalms [Ps. 113-118], which contain [praise for what God has done] in the past, also [what he has done] during these generations, as well as what will apply to the days of the Messiah, to the time of Gog and Magog, and to the age to come.

    D. *"When Israel went forth from Egypt* (Ps. 114:1) refers to the past.

    E. *"Not for us, O Lord, not for us* (Ps. 115:1) refers to the present generations.

    F. *"I love for the Lord to hear* (Ps. 116:1) refers to the days of the Messiah.

    G. *"All the nations have encompassed me* (Ps. 118:10) speaks of the time of Gog and Magog.

    H. *"You are my God and I shall exalt you* (Ps. 118:28) speaks of the age to come."

No. 1 makes a point quite distinct from No. 2. "The innocence" of Ps. 26:6 refers to the fact that one must not steal the objects used to carry out the religious duty of the waving of the palm branch at Tabernacles. I assume that the allusion to Tabernacles in Ps. 26:6-7 is found in the referring to circumambulating the altar, such as is done in the rite on that day, as 1.C makes explicit. No. 2 then expands on the cited verse in a different way. To be sure, the *Hallel* Psalms are recited on Tabernacles, but they serve all other festivals as well. Only No. 1 therefore relates to the established context of Lev. 23:40. It follows that the exegeses of Ps. 26:6-7 were assembled and only then utilized – both the relevant and also the irrelevant parts – for the present purpose. Now we move on to the verse in its own terms, worked out clause by clause. We see the point of intersection with our Talmud's treatment of the same verse.

XXVII:VI

1. A. *And you will take [for yourselves*](Lev. 23:40):
   B. R. Hiyya taught, "The act of taking must be accomplished by each and every one of you."
   C. *"For yourselves"* – for every one of you. They must be yours and not stolen.

2. A. Said R. Levi, "One who takes a stolen palm branch – to what is he comparable? To a thief who sat at the cross roads and mugged passersby.
   B. "One time a legate came by, to collect the taxes for that town. [The thug] rose before him and mugged him and took everything he had. After some time the thug was caught and put in prison. The legate heard and came to him. He said to him, 'Give back what you grabbed from me, and I'll argue in your behalf before the king.'
   C. "He said to him, 'Of everything that I robbed and of everything that I took, I have nothing except for this rug that is under me, and it belongs to you.'
   D. "He said to him, 'Give it to me, and I'll argue in your behalf before the king.'
   E. "He said to him, 'Take it.'
   F. "He said to him, 'You should know that tomorrow you are going before the king for judgment, and he will ask you and say to you, "Is there anyone who can argue in your behalf," and you may say to him, "I have the legate, Mr. So-and-so, to speak in my behalf," and he will send and call me, and I shall come and argue in your behalf before him.'
   G. "The next day they set him up for judgment before the king. The king asked him, saying to him, 'Do you have anyone to argue in your behalf?'
   H. "He said to him, 'I have a legate, Mr. So-and-so, to speak in my behalf.'
   I. "The king sent for him. He said to him, 'Do you know anything to say in behalf of this man?'
   J. "He said to him, 'I do indeed have knowledge. When you sent me to collect the taxes of that town, he rose up before me and mugged me and took everything that I had. That rug that belongs to me gives testimony against him.'
   K. "Everyone began to cry out, saying, 'Woe for this one, whose defense attorney has turned into his prosecutor.'
   L. "So a person acquires a palm branch to attain merit through it. But if it was a stolen one, [the branch] cries out before the Holy One, blessed be He, 'I am stolen! I am taken by violence.'
   M. "And the ministering angels say, 'Woe for this one, whose defense attorney has turned into his prosecutor!'"

The theme of the preceding, the prohibition against using a stolen palm branch, is given two further treatments. Except in a formal way none of this pretends to relate to the specific verses of Lev. 23:40ff., nor do we find an intersecting-verse.

XXVII:VII

1. A. *[On the fifteenth day of the seventh month, when you have gathered the produce of the land, you shall keep the feast of the Lord seven days;] on the first day [shall be a solemn rest]* (Lev. 23:40).

   B. This in fact is the fifteenth day, yet you speak of the first day!

   C. R. Mana of Sheab and R. Joshua of Sikhnin in the name of R. Levi said, "The matter may be compared to the case of a town which owed arrears to the king, so the king went to collect [what was owing]. [When he had reached] ten *mils* [from the town], the great men of the town came forth and praised him. He remitted a third of their [unpaid] tax. When he came within five *mils* of the town, the middle-rank people came out and acclaimed him, so he remitted yet another third [of what was owing to him]. When he entered the town, men, women, and children, came forth and praised him. He remitted the whole [of the tax].

   D. "Said the king, 'What happened happened. From now on we shall begin keeping books [afresh].'

   E. "So on the eve of the New Year, the Israelites repent, and the Holy One, blessed be He, remits a third of their [that is, Israel's] sins. On the ten days of repentance from the New Year to the Day of Atonement outstanding individuals fast, and the Holy One, blessed be He, remits most of their [that is, Israel's] sins. On the Day of Atonement all Israel fasts, so the Holy One, blessed be He, forgives them for all their sins [Leviticus Rabbah: says to Israel, 'What happened happened. From now on we shall begin keeping books afresh].'"

2. A. Said R. Aha, *"For with you there is forgiveness* (Ps. 80:4). From the New Year forgiveness awaits you.

   B. "Why so long? *So that you may be feared* (Ps. 80:4). To put your fear into creatures.

   C. "From the Day of Atonement to the Festival, all the Israelites are kept busy with doing religious duties. This one takes up the task of building his tabernacle, that one preparing his palm branches. On the first day of the Festival, all Israel they take their palm branches and citrons in their hand and praise the Holy One, blessed be He. The Holy One, blessed be He, says to them, 'What happened happened. From now on we shall begin keeping books [afresh].'"

   D. Therefore Scripture says, *On the first day.* What is the sense of the first day? It is first in the task of reckoning sins [done in the future[, that is, from the first day of the festival.

Nos. 1 and 2 go over the same matter. It seems to me that Aha's version puts into concrete terms the basic point of Levi's. 2.D is out of place, since it ignores the antecedent materials and takes as its proof text a formula in no way important in the preceding. Once more the ultimate redactor's hand is in evidence.

XXVII:VIII

1. A. *On the first day* (Lev. 23:40):
   B. By day and not by night.
   C. *On the...day* – even on the Sabbath.
   D. *On the* first *day* – only the first day [of the Festival] overrides the restrictions [of Sabbath rest. When the Sabbath coincides with other than the first day of the Festival, one does not carry the palm branch.]

2. A. *[And you shall take...] the fruit of a goodly tree [branches of palm trees and boughs of leafy trees and willows of the brook]* (Lev. 23:40).
   B. R. Hiyya taught, "A *tree:* the taste of the wood and fruit of which is the same. This is the citron."
   C. *Goodly (HDR):* Ben Azzai said, "[Fruit] that remains [HDR] on its tree from year to year."
   D. Aqilas the proselyte translated [HDR] as, "That which dwells by water (Greek: *hudor*)."
   E. *Branches of a palm tree* (Lev. 23:40): R. Tarfon says, "[As to branch of palm tree (KPWT)], it must be bound. If it was separated, one has to bind (YKPWT) it up."
   F. *Boughs of leafy trees:* The branches of which cover over the wood. One has to say, "This is the myrtle."
   G. *Willows of the brook:* I know only that they must come from a brook. How do I know that those that come from a valley or a hill [also are valid]? Scripture says, "*And* willows of a brook."
   H. Abba Saul says, "'*And* willows of the brook' refers to the requirement that there be two, one willow for the palm branch, and a willow for the sanctuary."
   I. R. Ishmael says, "'The fruit of goodly trees' indicates one; 'branches of palm tree' also one; 'boughs of leafy trees,' three; 'willows of the brook,' two. Two [of the myrtles] may have the twigs trimmed at the top, and one may not."
   J. R. Tarfon says, "Even all three of them may be trimmed."

We have a mass of exegetical materials, linking laws of the Festival to the verses of Scripture at hand. No. 1 conducts an inquiry into law, and No. 2 provides a word-for-word exegesis of the cited verse. Let us now jump to the end of the matter and see the goal and purpose of the exegete of Lev. 23:40, as the treatment of the verse in Leviticus Rabbah and Pesiqta deRab Kahana has matters.

XXVII:X

1. A. R. Berekhiah in the name of R. Levi: "[God speaks], 'Through the merit [attained in fulfilling the commandment], *And you will take for yourself on the first day...* (Lev. 23:40), lo, I shall be revealed to you first; I shall exact punishment for you from the first one; I shall build for you first; and bring to you the first one.'"
   B. "I shall be revealed for you first, refers to the Holy One, blessed be He, as it is said, *I the Lord am first* (Is. 41:4).
   C. "I shall exact punishment for you from the first one refers to the wicked Esau, as it is written, *And the red one came forth first* (Gen. 24:24).

D. "And I shall build for you first [refers to the house of the sanctuary], concerning which it is written, *Your throne of glory, on high from the first* (Jer. 17:12).

E. "And I shall bring to you the first one, namely, the king messiah, concerning whom it is written, *The first to Zion I shall give* (Is. 41:27)."

The eschatological-salvific character of the Festival is now spelled out in specific detail. Esau, that is, Rome, will be punished, the Temple will be rebuilt, and the Messiah will come, all by virtue of the merit attained in observing the Festival. The remainder of the passage takes up elements not treated in our sample selection of the Bavli.

We once again revert to the issues we raised at the outset. Let us consider and now answer the questions just as I originally asked them.

1. *The topical program of prior writings on the subject as compared to the topical program of the Bavli on the same subject:* The Bavli does not systematically follow the response to the Mishnah characteristic of the authorship of the Tosefta, though it at a few points intersects with the program of the Tosefta. The same may be said for the Bavli's authorship's relationships to the interests and programs of the authorships of Sifra and Sifré to Deuteronomy. The Bavli's authorship obviously has its own inquiry, remote, except in episodic detail, from the interests of the authorships of Leviticus Rabbah and Pesiqta deRab Kahana when all parties address a verse important, for diverse reasons, to each authorship. I cannot imagine more striking proof of that simple fact than has been laid forth in the present chapter.

2. *The Bavli's use or neglect of the available treatments ("sources") in the prior literature:* when the Bavli does make use of available materials, it imposes its own issues upon those materials even when it reproduces those materials as they occur elsewhere. The authorship of the Bavli over all simply has not carried forward issues important in prior writings.

3. *The traits of the Bavli's canonical statement, that is, derivative and summary at the end, or essentially fresh and imputed retrospectively?* In consequence of the detailed examination of the Bavli's authorship's use of and response to available sources, we may definitively characterize the statement of the Bavl as a whole for our sample as original, fresh, autonomous of all that had gone before, while, of course, accessible to available materials where they proved relevant to the determined task at hand.

For I shall demonstrate, for the case at hand, that the dual Torah is made up not of sources transformed into a single source, e.g., in the Talmud of Babylonia, but of an essentially independent construction and system, one that stands essentially upon its own ground and takes its own position, framed in a balance and proportion of its own, and so issues its own distinctive statement. The Judaic system of the dual Torah – so we shall see – recognizes a corpus of authoritative writings, but that corpus does not form a tradition, a "tradition formed out of prior sources," books that serves as sources for their continuators and so are continuous with one another and stand in close relationship with one another, borrowing each from its predecessor, handing on each to its successor in a relationship of sources nourishing tradition.

To state the upshot in negative terms first, the dual Torah is made up not of sources transformed into a single source, e.g., in the Talmud of Babylonia, but of an essentially independent construction and system, one that stands essentially upon its own ground and takes its own position, framed in a balance and proportion of its own, and so issues its own distinctive statement. The Judaic system of the dual Torah – so we have now seen – while recognizing a corpus of authoritative writings,does not accord to that that corpus the status and authority of a tradition, that is, of a "tradition formed out of prior sources." The Bavli does not fall into the classification of traditional books, that is, of books that serve as sources for their continuators and so are continuous with one another and stand in close relationship with one another, borrowing each from its predecessor, handing on each to its successor in a relationship of sources nourishing tradition.

Let me now say matters in a positive way. So far as our authorship has made a definitive and canonical statement on the subject at hand, that systematic statement derives not from prior sources but from the interests of the authorship before us. True, the Bavli would become a tradition. But when it emerged, the Bavli constituted a remarkably fresh and independent version of the received documents and their meaning. Our sample points toward the hypothesis that in its essential independence of prior formulations of, and on, its several topics, the Bavli's system, its Judaism, came forth as anything but traditional. As between the classifications of tradition or new system, the Bavli clearly belongs in the latter. Receiving reverently the heritage of a long and honored past, studying carefully the positions taken by sages of a now-ancient time, the authorship of the Bavli has its own say and sets forth its own views, and this it does in its own original and independent way. The Bavli adds up to considerably more than the sum of its parts, and the authorship of the Bavli has accomplished not a restatement of available sources but an essentially new construction.

We now have compared the whole of the exegesis of Mishnah-tractate Sukkah accomplished by the authorship of the Yerushalmi, Talmud of the Land of Israel, with the complete exegesis of that same chapter produced by their counterparts in the Bavli. We have furthermore surveyed the relationship between the larger part of the entire Bavli tractate and the prior documentary statements, now extant, on the same subject. This two-sided inquiry permits us to frame and test a hypothesis concerning the relationship between a document universally declared to be traditional and received as canonical, namely the Bavli, and the prior sources on which that document drew, and, in consequence, to form a still larger thesis on the literary character and definition of traditionality in the

Judaism of the dual Torah. We can now give the answer to the question: is the Bavli, as represented by our sample, document received as traditional, essentially a restatement of what has gone before, or is its authorship engaged in a work that is fresh and original? If the answer is that it is a traditional document, restating a consensus formed through ages, then our conception of the literary definition of the tradition and consequent canon of Judaism will take one form. If the answer is that the Bavli's authorship makes an essentially new statement, then the issue of traditionality and, later on, of canonicity – the continuities among documents, in the language just now used – will prove to stand quite independent of the traits of the writings accepted within the canon. To this matter we turn in the closing chapter.

Chapter Six

Sources and Traditions:
The Canon and the System

I

From Connection to Continuity?

Each document in the corpus of the rabbinic writings of late antiquity bears points in common with others. In their ultimate condition, they did form a tradition, understood in that sense of tradition as a fixed and unchanging essence deriving from an indeterminate past, a truth bearing its own stigmata of authority, e.g., from God at Sinai. Each document in proportion and measure constitutes a partial statement of that complete tradition. But, as we now understand, we have first of all to know whether and how all – or at least some – of them constitute a tradition in that other sense, that is a tradition derived from and formed out of prior sources. This sense of "tradition," as I said in the preface, refers to the matter of process, specifically, an incremental and linear process that step by step transmits out of the past statements and wordings that bear authority and are subject to study, refinement, preservation and transmission. In that sense, tradition is supposed to describe a process.

The relevance of the relationships of connection and continuity has now to be made clear. The authorship of a document that stands in a relationship of connection to prior writings will make use of their materials essentially in its own way. The authorship of a document that works in essential continuity with prior writings will cite and quote and refine those received writings but will ordinarily not undertake a fundamentally original statement of its own framed in terms of its own and on a set of issues defined separately from the received writings or formulations. The Bavli proves connected with earlier documents and also with some received sayings not written down in a systematic way in prior compilations. But the connections appear episodic and haphazard, not systematic, except in respect to the Mishnah, The Bavli cannot be shown systematically and generally to continue the program and inquiry of predecessors. Therefore with the Bavli a new tradition got underway, but the Bavli does not derive from, and state, a prior tradition in the sense just now spelled out. For in few ways does the Bavli give evidence of taking its place within such a process of tradition, and we cannot appeal to the document to demonstrate that the authorship of the Bavli represented itself as traditional and its work as authoritative *on that account?* The appeal of the authorship of the Bavli is to the ineluctable verity of well-applied logic, practical reason tested and retested against the facts, whether deriving from prior authorities, or emerging from examples and decisions of leading contemporary authorities. We have now tested the hypothesis that the Bavli forms an essentially traditional document, in the sense given in the preface, and the further claim that the reason for the Bavli's traditional – and, by the way, canonical – status lies in its success in completing work begun by the predecessors of the document, for instance, the Yerushalmi. If we can demonstrate a systematic exercise of refinement, completion, summary, we may propose the hypothesis that one definitive trait of a canonical statement is its position at the end of a sustained and continuous process of thought.

True enough, the Bavli contains ample selections from available writings. The authorship of the Bavli leaves no doubt that it makes extensive use of extant materials, sayings and stories. Readers who review the sizable sample before us will see numerous indications – much like footnotes and references – of that fact. For example, the authorship of the Bavli invokes verses of Scripture. It further takes as its task the elucidation of the received code, the Mishnah. More to the point, frequent citations of materials now found in the Tosefta as well as allusions to sayings framed in Tannaite Hebrew and attributed to Tannaite authority – marked, for instance, by TN' – time and again alert us to extensive reference, by our authorship, to a prior corpus of materials. Not only so, but contemporary scholarship has closely read both brief sayings and also extended discourses in light of two or three or more versions and come to the conclusion that a later generation has taken up and made use of available materials.[1] Most strikingly of all, our authorship claims in virtually every line to come at the end of a chain of tradition, since the bulk of the generative sayings – those that form the foundation for sustained inquiry and dialectical discourse – is assigned to named authorities clearly understood to stand prior to the work of the ultimate redactors. Even if we preserve a certain reluctance to take at face value all of these attributions to prior authorities, we have to take full account of the authorship's insistence upon its own traditionality. In all of these ways, the authorship of the Bavli assuredly stands in a line of tradition, taking over and reworking received materials, restating viewpoints that originate in prior ages. And that fact makes all the more striking the fundamental autonomy of discourse

---

[1] I present a sizable sample of these prior exercises in source-criticism in the volumes edited by me, *The Formation of the Babylonian Talmud. Studies on the Achievements of Late Nineteenth and Twentieth Century Historical and Literary-Critical Research* (Leiden, 1970: E. J. Brill) and *The Modern Study of the Mishnah* (Leiden, 1973: E. J. Brill). These two volumes cover the more important contemporary figures, with special attention to David Weiss Halivni. The only figure omitted did his important work afterward, Shamma Friedman, and to a sample of his work I devoted a seminar, the papers of which were then published in William Scott Green, ed., *Law as Literature, Semeia* XX (Chico, 1984: Scholars Press).

displayed by the document at the end. So let us serve as interlocutors for the great authorship at hand and present some pointed questions.

Were we therefore to enter into conversation with the penultimate and ultimate authorship of the Bavli, the first thing we should want to know is simple: what have you made up? And what have you simply repeated out of a long-continuing heritage of formulation and transmission? And why should we believe you? The authorship then would be hard put to demonstrate in detail that its fundamental work of literary selection and ordering, its basic choices on sustained and logical discourse, its essential statement upon the topics it has selected – that anything important in their document derives from long generations past.

Should they say, "Look at the treatment of the Mishnah," we should answer, "But did you continue the Yerushalmi's program or did you make up your own?" And in the total candor we rightly impute to that remarkable authorship, the Bavli's compositors would say, "It is our own – demonstrably so."

And if we were to say, "To what completed documents have you resorted for a ready-made program?" our *soi-disant* traditionalists would direct our attention to Tosefta, their obvious (and sole) candidate. And, if they were to do so, we should open the Tosefta's treatment of, or counterpart to, a given chapter of the Mishnah and look in vain for a systematic, orderly, and encompassing discourse, dictated by the order and plan of the Tosefta, out of which our authorship has composed a sizable and sustained statement.

True, we readily recognize that the Tosefta's materials play their role. But seeing the Tosefta in its terms, noting how slight a portion of a given Tosefta chapter the Mishnah's authorship has found accessible and urgent, we should dismiss out of hand any claim that the Bavli's fundamental structure and plan encompasses systematic and orderly exposition of the Tosefta's structure and plan for a given Mishnah-chapter. The opposite is the case.[2] Tosefta makes its contribution unsystematically and episodically, where and when the authorship of the Bavli, for its reasons (not always obvious to us) has permitted the Tosefta to do so. That is hardly the mark of traditionality, subservience to a received text, such as the counterpart treatment of the Mishnah by the Bavli's authorship – a treatment that is orderly, routine, complete, and systematic – indicates.

And when, finally, we ask our authorship to state its policy in regard to Scripture and inquire whether or not a sustained and on-going tradition of

---

[2] Rabbi Yaakov Elman's study of the impact of Tosefta Pisha upon Bavli Pesahim has shown beyond all doubt the fact that there is no systematic and orderly plan of Tosefta-citation and exegesis at the foundations of the Bavli's inquiry into the matter. Quite to the contrary, reference to the Tosefta's materials on the same topic turns out to be casual, episodic, and unpredictable. The sustained research behind his oral report, at the Society of Biblical Literature meeting in Atlanta on November 24, 1986, of this matter will in due course be published in this series.

exegesis of Scripture has framed discourse, the reply will prove quite simple. "We looked for what we wanted to seek, and we found it."

That "we" then requires identification, and when we interrogate the "we" of Leviticus Rabbah = Pesiqta deRab Kahana and ask for their program, we meet one community of inquiry, which scarcely has met, though at a few points claims common descent from, the "we" of the Bavli. Distant cousins, each has pursued its own set of questions – no continuities here.

These four loci at which boundaries may have merged, and intersections turned into commonalities, therefore mark walled and sealed borders. A received heritage of sayings and stories may have joined our authorship to its teachers and their teachers – but not to that larger community of sustained learning that stands behind the entirety of the writings received as authoritative, or even a sizable proportion of those writings. The presence, in the ultimate statement of the Bavli, of sayings imputed to prior figures – back to Scripture, back to Sinai – testifies only to the workings of a canon of taste and judgment to begin with defined and accepted as definitive by those who defined it: the authorship at hand itself. The availability, to our authorship, of a systematic exegesis of the same Mishnah-chapter has not made self-evident to our authorship the work of continuation and completion of a prior approach. Quite to the contrary, we deal with an authorship of amazingly independent mind, working independently and in an essentially original way on materials on which others have handed on a quite persuasive and cogent statement. Tosefta on the one side, Scripture and a heritage of conventional reading thereof on the other – neither has defined the program of our document or determined the terms in which it would make its statement, though both, in a subordinated position and in a paltry limited measure, are given some sort of a say. The Bavli is connected to a variety of prior writings but continuous with none of them.

II

Adieu to Intertextuality

These findings, which any attentive reader will adjudge to be accurate, factual, and entirely within the limits of the sample at hand, bear consequences for the literary reading of the Bavli, among the other late antique[3] writings of the

---

[3]I have no idea of the character and condition of the medieval writings of that same on-going tradition of Judaism. I have the impression that an attitude of imitation took over the literary processes, an impression conveyed if only by indirection in my *From Tradition to Imitation: The Plan and Program of Pesiqta deRab Kahana and Pesiqta Rabbati* (Atlanta, 1987: Scholars Press for Brown Judaic Studies). But I have not studied the matter at all and do not plan to. Since current scholarship on the literary aspects of the Judaism of the dual Torah tends to ignore the documentary limits of writings and to treat as an undifferentiated *canon* the entire *corpus* at hand, ancient, medieval, and early modern, always affirming, but never proving on literary grounds, the canonicity of that corpus of writings, I am not hopeful that in the near term a clearly differentiated picture of the medieval writings out of the same on-going tradition will emerge.

Judaism of the dual Torah. As we move from the literary to the hermeneutical issues, we confront the received hermeneutic in a modern garment. The accepted approach to the reading of the Bavli, among all rabbinic writings, is to take for granted that every text requires a hearing in the interpretation of all passages in all texts. Whether an authorship comes earlier or late, what it has to say must register. The modern restatement of that received hermeneutic, guiding us in reading the documents at hand, lays the claim that the rabbinic literature forms an arena for what is called "intertextuality," and, indeed, Orthodox Jewish literary critics tell their gentile colleagues that Judaism presents the world with a particularly fine specimen of this "intertextuality."

Specifically, a broadly-held view maintains that everything we find in every document of the literary corpus of the Judaism of the dual Torah contributes to common discourse, so we may read one thing in light of all things – and vice versa. This view is expressed in various ways. One may frame this striking allegation, for example, in terms of the synoptic reading of the Gospels of Mark, Matthew, and Luke, and sees in the rabbinic writings parallel synoptic relationships. So Shaye J. D. Cohen, "Synoptic texts must always be studied synoptically, even if one text is 'later' than another."[4] A more extreme statement sees each component of each document as autonomous and available for joining with all components of all other documents. Lest the reader (reasonably) wonder whether I may have overstated matters, I point to the statement that derives from Lawrence Schiffman: "This system, composed of interlocking and re-interlocking parts possessed of an organic connection one to another, is never really divisible."[5] The language, *never really divisible,* leaves no reasonable doubt that I have stated matters just as some represent them. Schiffman, indeed, alludes not to the rabbinic literature alone, but to all writings of all Jews, here in the context of the Dead Sea scrolls: "The essential characteristic of Judaism, in each and every one of its pre-modern manifestations, is that it is all encompassing in its nature. Further, it is organic in that its components are seen as constantly combining and recombining such that no aspect can be studied without recourse to others."[6]

The phenomenon to which Cohen and Schiffman allude, finally, is given the name "intertextuality" and introduced into the discourse of contemporary literary criticism by Susan Handelman in a series of remarkably self-confident statements worth reading *in toto:*

---

[4]See his "Jacob Neusner, Mishnah, and Counter-Rabbinics," *Conservative Judaism* (1983), 37:48-63, and his teacher, Morton Smith's, *Tannaitic Parallels to the Gospels* (Philadelphia, 1951: Society of Biblical Literature Monograph Series). Compare my "The Synoptic Problem in Rabbinic Literature: The Cases of the Mishnah, Tosefta, Sifra, and Leviticus Rabbah," *Journal of Biblical Literature* (1986), 105:499-507.

[5]See his *Sectarian Law in the Dead Sea Scrolls. Courts, Testimony, and the Penal Code* (Chico, 1983: Scholars Press for Brown Judaic Studies), p. 2-3.

[6]*Ibid.,* p. 2.

...all units are so closely interwoven and simultaneously present that none can be considered in separation from any other at any given moment; it is a world of "intertextuality"...

....interpretation is not essentially separate from the text itself–an external act intruded upon it – but rather the extension of the text, the uncovering of the connective network of relations, a part of the continuous revelation of the text itself, at bottom, another aspect of the text.

Assessing these statements requires us to specify exactly what is meant by the word, intertextuality. By "intertextuality" people ordinarily mean documents that merge so that the boundaries between one and the next are obliterated. Handelman herself so states. Is she right of the rabbinic writings in hand?

On the face of it, intertextuality as a category does not apply. Indeed, the word invokes precisely the opposite of the literary facts as we have surveyed them in our document, with those vast stretches of plain type, explicit and self-aware citation of another text, the Mishnah or Scripture or Tosefta, and, otherwise, rare intersections indeed with documents of the same corpus. An intertextual corpus of texts, we are told, attains intertextuality by *obliterating* lines between one document and another. But the Bavli does not merge with the Mishnah. It always *cites* the Mishnah as a distinct statement – a document out there – and does not merely allude to it as part of an internally cogent statement – a formulation of matters in here. That is the opposite of what Handelman leads us to anticipate. This claim of Handelman's produces a characterization of the literature so far-reaching, a hermeneutics of such fundamental consequence, that we had best dwell on it with some care.

In light of the sample of Bavli we have examined, may we really describe within the canon of intertextuality the summa and climax of the rabbinic corpus, the Talmud of Babylonia? Alas, we may not. The authorship of the Bavli begins with precisely that program that Handelman denies, by stating its interpretation of the Mishnah-paragraph in words made up essentially independent of that paragraph – different in language, formulation, syntax, and substance alike. The marks of independent, post facto, autonomous interpretation are always vividly imprinted upon the Bavli's encounter with the Mishnah. For these reasons I should have thought that the Bavli testified to the opposite of intertextuality (so far as the category is supposed to have any bearing at all upon the writings at hand). The midrash-compilation we read in Chapter Four, for its part, clearly differentiates a verse of Scripture from its interpretation. Interpretation by midrash-exegetes as collected in midrash-compilations is essentially separate from the text itself and an external act intruded upon it. The Bavli never appears to be, nor is it ever by internal evidence represented as, the extension of the text, in formal terms the uncovering of the connective network of relations, as literature a part of the continuous revelation of the text itself, in its material condition as we know it "at bottom, another aspect of the text." The text we have examined – and every other document of the rabbinic corpus – exhibits precisely the opposite traits from those that Handelman imputes to the literature. True, she may claim to speak not of literary but of *intellectual* continuities. But she does not tell us what these are, and every word I have cited imputes *literary* and not merely theological qualities to the documents.

As a literary category, intertextuality therefore does not seem congruent to the literary corpus-become-canon of Judaism as it took shape in late antiquity. Still, the relevance of the category, intertextuality, as we see, derives from a broadly-held and widely circulated characterization of the writings of the Judaic sages of late antiquity. Literary critics who claim to be familiar with the writings of the ancient rabbis – as we see in the quotations above, representative of widely held opinion – propose to treat the whole as harmonious, uniform, indivisible. That literary judgment further accords with theological convictions of faithful Jews, whether Orthodox or Reform, Conservative or Israeli or Reconstructionist. That is why the received hermeneutic, long governing how the ancient texts are read, invokes all passages in the exposition of each, and each for all: intertextuality as the paramount hermeneutic, resting on theological principles. Contemporary expositions follow suit, so Handelman: "The rabbinic world is, to use a contemporary term, one of *intertextuality*. Texts echo, interact, and interpenetrate...."[7] But – to repeat in the face of such stupefying certainty about the facts – our survey of the sample of Bavli leaves no doubt as to the facts. Our texts do not intersect with other texts, let alone interpenetrate; one cites another, and that is the opposite of interpenetration, I should imagine. That characterization of the documents at hand as exemplary instances of intertextuality and occasions, therefore, for the nurture of that theory of literary connection and continuity constitutes not a literary judgment, based on intrinsic

---

[7] *The Slayers of Moses* (Albany, 1982: State University of New York Press), p. 47.

traits of the writings, but – if pertinent at all to facts – a merely theological and social judgment, resting on extrinsic and imputed ones.[8]

Viewing the documents exemplified by the Bavli from the angle of their intrinsic traits, we find no pervasive continuities, no single community of texts. That position claims too much and finds no substantiation in the data. I see not only an absence of a collectivity, but a failure even of sustained imitation of later texts by earlier ones.[9] Indeed I am struck by the independence of mind and the originality of authorships that pretend to receive and transmit, but in fact imagine and invent. True, individual texts do relate to other individual texts, either in a sustained dialectical relationship, as in the case of Mishnah and its continuator-exegeses, or in a taxonomic relationship of connection, as in the case of Sifra and Sifré to Numbers and of Genesis Rabbah and Leviticus Rabbah, or in an episodic and anecdotal relationship, as in the case of documents that

---

[8] I have pursued this matter on a much broader front in my *Canon and Connection: Intertextuality in Judaism* (Lanham, 1987: University Press of America *Studies in Judaism* series). In that book my method in particular is to construct two different ways of uncovering intrinsic connections between and among the documents and to find out whether, as a matter of fact, because of intrinsic traits of literary connection, all passages must be read in the light of all others. This exercise served the broader purpose of investigating the heuristic and hermeneutic pertinence of the concept of intertextuality, as just now defined, to a literature that, on the face of it, invites the application of that very concept. Since in that book I supply two sizable samples of the documents under discussion, the reader is able to participate in the systematic exercise at hand. The present remarks underline the results achieved in the more systematic study of the problem, because of the relevance of the claim of intertextuality in behalf of the Bavli. In that book I test the imputation of "intertextuality" simply by asking what intrinsic traits of the entirety of the corpus of Judaism in late antiquity validate an intertextualist reading of that corpus. Of interest is not the well-known fact that one text relates to another. In this book we have seen of what, for the Bavli, that relationship consists. That truism will not have surprised anyone who has ever opened a single text, since all texts cite Scripture, or any passage of the Talmud, since the Talmud cites the Mishnah. The position at hand addresses the *entirety* of the writings of the ancient rabbis, all together, all at once, everywhere and all the time. In light of the citations just now given, readers cannot imagine that I exaggerate the radical-intertextualist position on the Judaic canon: everything, everywhere, all at once. I do not impute to the proponents of the intertextualist theory of rabbinic writings positions they do not take: *"all units are so closely interwoven and simultaneously present that none can be considered in separation from any other at any given moment."* Nor do the figures cited at the outset – Cohen, Schiffman, Handelman – stand for idiosyncratic positions, since the received and paramount hermeneutic of the rabbinic literature demands precisely the reading they advocate. So we take up a genuinely orthodox and not merely Orthodox hermeneutic, today advocated by nearly everyone. But as we see in our sample, that hermeneutical claim is not only not true as a matter of literary fact (as distinct from theological conviction or social construction), it is in fact the exact opposite of the truth as a matter of literary fact. Viewed from the angle of their intrinsic traits, the documents scarcely connect at all. Intertextuality constitutes a social construction, a theological conviction, not a literary dimension of the canon at hand, not an operative category for hermeneutics. We can read these texts one by one, we do well to consult points of intersection with other texts of the same canon where relevant, but we have no reason as a matter of a literary interpretation to invoke that invitation to chaos represented by the counsel: read everything in light of everything, everywhere, all at once.

[9] The matter of imitation I take up in a separate, and very preliminary study, *From Tradition to Imitation.*

make use of sayings or stories in common. (The connection between these sayings or stories that occur in two or more documents scarcely requires analysis in the present context; what we have is simply diverse versions of given units of discourse.) But the received position, outlined by Cohen, Schiffman, and Handelman, will not find satisfaction in the modest points of intersection and overlap that we have noted in our survey of the sample of the Bavli. In fact, overall, there is no community of texts existence of which is proven by intrinsic traits.

Let me qualify this negative judgment in behalf of the interlocuters at hand. Cohen is certainly right that we must take account of diverse versions of a given saying or story as these may occur in two or more documents in sequence. But if that is *all* he means, then he has not told us something anyone doubted. Since he borrows language from Gospels' research, he clearly intends something more than the admonition that we not ignore parallel versions of a single story or saying. But claiming to say more, he produces less than meets the eye. He errs, specifically, in invoking the metaphor of the Synoptic Gospels, or of synoptic relationships among some of the Gospels and Q. The metaphor does not pertain.

Schiffman too is right that sayings and stories do recur in two or more documents. He is wrong to maintain that, on that account, documents are not divisible (as he says), and what he further may mean by "possessed of an organic connection to one another" I cannot say. The formulation, so far as it pertains to literary and redactional traits, is murky, the sense unclear. My best guess is that Schiffman, like Cohen, refers to the mere fact that we have some sayings and stories occur in more than a single document. Cohen's and Schiffman's formulation of the issue of connection leads nowhere. My sense is that, in their rather portentous framing of matters, there is less than meets the eye.[10]

With her introduction of the category, intertextuality, Handelman presents a weightier claim, but her mastery of the texts, conspicuously less than that of Cohen and Schiffman, leads to some infelicities of thought and argument. As we noted, Handelman states:

> ...interpretation is not essentially separate from the text itself–an external act intruded upon it–but rather the extension of the text, the uncovering of the connective network of relations, a part of the continuous revelation of the text itself, at bottom, another aspect of the text.

To repeat, interpretation of the Mishnah by the Bavli is – and is persistently represented as – entirely separate from the text of the Mishnah, which is quoted as language out there, not reframed into the idiom of discourse in here – and

---

[10]Still, I do not regret publishing Schiffman's book in a series edited by me. He is a scholar of merit, especially when he concentrates on matters of philological interest or legal fact. The remarks I have cited are an aside and off-handed.

operates very much as "an external act intruded upon it," not as an extension of the text. The same obviously may be said of the treatment by the authorship of the Tosefta of the Mishnah, the treatment by the authorship of Leviticus Rabbah of the book of Leviticus, and every other rabbinic text of late antique origin known to me. The "connective network of relations," in Handelman's formulation, would correspond to that dimension of "continuity" in my opening remarks in Chapter One. For it is an extrinsic, not an intrinsic, aspect of the document to which, in the nature of things, we speak when we ask about relations. People impute meanings to texts, and that too forms a dimension of interpretation. But we commit anachronism and so misinterpret a text if we find in a text of the second century issues otherwise first attested in the seventh. When we treat as indivisible the text and its later interpretation, what we describe is not the text and its author's meaning, but the community and its enduring values. These relate, but they are not one and the same thing.

When Handelman says that no document or unit of discourse can be considered on its own, she lays down a claim that she does not – and cannot – make stick. True, quite what she means is not entirely clear. If all she means is that when a unit of discourse occurs in more than a single document, we cannot consider one version in isolation from another, then she has found a remarkably portentous (not to say pretentious) way in which to express a perfectly routine fact of everyday observation. If she means more than that, I cannot say what she wishes to propose. It is that some units of discourse appear more than in one passage of a given document, e.g., the Bavli, or play a role in two or more documents altogether, e.g., Sifra, Levitricus Rabbah, Pesiqta deRab Kahana, and Bavli (as we saw in Chapter Four). If that is all Handelman has in mind, then she covers the ground stated with more felicity by Cohen.

My guess, however, is that she does mean to say we have to read everything in light of everything else. On literary grounds, she does not prove why we have to do so. On theological grounds, proof is not necessary. Indeed – indeed we do, when we propose to describe, analyze, and interpret a system whole and complete, in light of all its literature. But if we ignore the lines of structure and order that separate one text from another and that account for the sequence in which the textual canon unfolds, we invite chaos. Then how to sort things out and find the rules of order? – That is the challenge to learning, which in time to come all parties to the debate will have to undertake. But Handelman's contribution is not only to set the terms for debate. She introduces the issue of intertextuality.

Precisely what do literary critics in general mean by intertextuality, when speaking of documents other than those of Judaism? Leaving Handelman for a moment, let us measure our data against other definitions of intertextuality, besides Handelman's. Professor Thais Morgan, Arizona State University, in her article, "Is there an Intertext in this Text? Literary and Interdisciplinary

Approaches to Intertextuality" (*American Journal of Semiotics* 3 [1985])[11] provides a clear account of basic issues of intertextuality Her guidance allows us to compare our results to those among the theorists of intertextuality whom Morgan renders accessible.   In general, I find in theories of intertextuality somewhat less than meets the eye, because definitions of terms turn out to be few, applications of theory episodic and anecdotal, criteria for validation or invalidation pretty much absent. But we do gain from Morgan's excellent reprise of the subject access to one theory that comes to clear expression and proposes interesting criteria of inquiry.   Among the diverse theories at hand, the one of greatest relevance[12] is that of Genette.

As represented by Morgan, Genette defines the matter as "a relation of co-presence between two or more texts, that is to say,...the demonstrable presence of one text in another...." Obviously, Scripture appears everywhere; people quote proof-texts. But does that mean that Scripture "penetrates everything"? By the criterion of whether or not Scripture proves paramount in the Bavli, as our sample suggests, Scripture hardly "penetrates everything." It assuredly serves diverse purposes, and these alway are defined by the authorship at hand and not by an authorship of Scripture. So that does not establish a dimension of intertextuality that yields important hermeneutic, let alone heuristic, consequences. In fact, citing proof-texts from Scripture presents us with a merely formal fact, bearing no meaning at all. For it does not tell us how to interpret a text that, not knowing that banality, we did not know how to read. There are then these subcategories: quotation, which is explicit, allusion, implicit, and plagiarism, falling between the two. By that definition, of course, we correctly invoke the category of intertextuality. All components of the rabbinic canon quote from Scripture, and some of them quote from the Mishnah, or the Tosefta. Allusion is another matter; I am inclined to think allusion always bears a material mark, e.g., a brief indication of a few words to direct attention to another passage. As to plagiarism, that seems to me to address the appearance of a single story or saying in two or more documents. Then either one has borrow from the other, or both from a third authorship.

None of these observations seems to me to open any important and now-locked doors. They all pertain to our corpus of writings, but they present no astounding insights into its hermeneutics. If on that basis we are supposed, as Handelman demands, to read everything in terms of everything else, then we accept an invitation to either chaos or banality. For the fact that millions of

---

[11]Kindly called to my attention by my colleague, Robert Scholes, in Brown's Department of Semiotics, and sent to me in manuscript by Professor Morgan.

[12]Or, at any rate, the only one I could understand. The others did not seem to me pertinent to the issues at hand.   That is to state as a simple fact, theories of intertextuality do not illuminate that sizable corpus of documents that form a single canon, rich in reciprocal allusion and citation, of Judaism. My suspicion is that the fault lies with a theory not much tested against cogent data. Or, to state matters more boldly, the emperor looks naked. But, then, most emperors do.

diverse pieces of stationery in New York City all cite the New York City phone book does not bear profound consequences for the reading of mail that I receive from diverse sources in New York City. In the histories of Judaisms and of Christianities Scripture is inert and malleable, serving many purposes for many parties, determining meaning for none – except after the fact. Everyone finds in it pretty much anything he or she wants. Intertextuality meaning merely the propensity to cite a common corpus of proof-texts presents us in wonderful new garb with what is in fact entirely familiar, a not very interesting triviality. It is hardly even a fact of literature.

A further point of relevance to the relevance of "intertextuality" is Genette's notion of "metatextuality," by which he means, "the relation of 'commentary,' which unites one text to another text about which the former speaks, without necessarily citing it." This relationship presents difficulties. It is one thing to identify a text on which another depends. We may even demonstrate that fact, e.g., Tosefta contains numerous passages that without actually citing them in fact comment on Mishnah-passages. Quoting, paraphrasing, commenting – these are not mysterious matters but subject to demonstration and exposition. The task of the exegete is to sort out precisely these matters. Where we have difficulty is demonstrating that sort of inchoate metatextual-intertextuality in texts in which there is no clear paraphrase, citation, or commentary. Search as we may, we find it exceedingly difficult to specify concrete criteria to tell us where we do, and do not, deal with that sort of interpenetration of texts. How shall we know the difference between the presence of an allusion and our imputation of the presence of an allusion? Criteria, to be sure, can be defined – that is the work of sustained and rigorous scholarship. Surely these criteria will give slight satisfaction to those who concur with Handelman's wild claim that "all units are so closely interwoven and simultaneously present that none can be considered in separation from any other at any given moment." Surely she lays down a claim that demands more than the mere citation of texts, directly or palimpsestually – or even allusion. But in a moment we shall see what misled Handelman to her extreme position, which far transcends the sense of intertextuality before us.

Morgan cites the following statement: "Each literary or aesthetic text produces a palimpsest, superimposing several other texts which are never completely hidden, but always hinted it." The literary palimpsest hovers between originality and imitation, she explains. But, she judges, "The idea that the other texts can be seen transparently through the centering text is highly dubious." The evidence of the Bavli, relevant as it is, assuredly supports Morgan's position. The conception of imitation as against originality stimulates us to see things in a fresh way. If we ask which documents in our entire corpus, as represented by our sample, imitates any other, the answer is:

only one.[13]   The Bavli in important ways imitates the Yerushalmi. But its authorship does not then undertake a recapitulation of the position even of its closest friend and teacher, the position of the Yerushalmi!

To state the negative: the authorship of the Tosefta does not imitate the Mishnah; that of Leviticus Rabbah does not imitate that of the Sifra; and on and on. There are paramount and definitive points of originality in *every* document, including the Bavli. In fact, we now realize, a criterion for an adequate theory of the intrinsic connections among the documents ("locking and reinterlocking parts" indeed) of the rabbinic canon must derive from the issue of not originality but imitation. Let us ask ourselves in retrospect just where and how the diverse components of the Mishnah, Tosefta, and Bavli, which we have reviewed, actually imitate one another – and where and how they do not. When we rapidly survey our sample,[14] we see few marks of imitation, and a vast corpus of indications of total independence, one document from the other, and thus of essential originality. Our difficulty in discerning connections between and among documents underlines that simple fact. Genette through Morgan opens our eyes to a potential inquiry by asking whether text imitates text.

If I had to specify a single aesthetic tension confronting any of our authorships, it is to establish a claim of continuity while doing pretty much anything someone wanted to do. The Mishnah's authorship rejected that matter altogether, ignoring the inherited conventions of language as Scripture dictated the characteristics of Hebrew, ignoring the topical program of Scripture's legal codes for its own program (absorbing the received one to be sure), ignoring the entire structure of authority based on pseudepigraphic authorship characteristic of Scripture ("Moses" as author of Deuteronomy, for instance). No imitation here! Nor any in Tosefta. And even the Bavli at the end yielded a fundamental structure utterly original, independent of that of the Yerushalmi, as I have shown elsewhere.[15]

But the criterion of imitation as against originality does lead us toward relationship imputed extrinsically, that is, socially, specifically to the concept of the textual community. What is of special interest is Genette's judgment: "I see the relation between the text and its reader as more socialized, more openly contractual, as the result of a conscious and organized practice." That view

---

[13]The matter of imitation, of course, is much more complex. As noted earlier, I have dealt with it only casually in my *From Tradition to Imitation: The Plan and Program of Pesiqta deRab Kahana and Pesiqta Rabbati* (Atlanta, 1987: Scholars Press for Brown Judaic Studies). My sense is that it is a phenomenon for study in the context of medieval, not ancient Judaic religious writing. I do not see how any rabbinic document redacted down through the Bavli imitates any other, and, of course, none imitates Scripture or the Mishnah.

[14]The appendices of *Canon and Connection* present a much larger sample and yield the same result.

[15]*Judaism: The Classic Statement. The Evidence of the Bavli* (Chicago, 1986: University of Chicago Press), and compare *The Talmud of the Land of Israel. 35. Introduction. Taxonomy* (Chicago, 1984: University of Chicago Press).

places us squarely into the category of the textual community, a topic not relevant to our present inquiry. The appeal is to extrinsic, not intrinsic, traits of the documents – continuity not connection. But no one has ever doubted that the rabbinic corpus constitutes a socially-constructed canon – and that by definition. The perspective of intertextuality teaches lessons of literature in society, writings received and read. The more we labor to uncover the inner traits of system and order among diverse documents, the less we yield, beyond banality. For citation, allusion, reference to something else and other – these are just other forms of words, things the author uses to say whatever he or she wishes to say. Art comes from color, but also from collage, and references, allusions, citations – these form, in writing, the counterpart to the raw materials of collage.

A further statement on intertextuality derives from Handelman's exposition of Edward Said's definition of the matter.[16] I have already cited part of Handelman's use of Said's theory. Let me now go over her exposition of the two points of particular interest:

> The fourth convention, *finality,* is the assumption that each portion of the text is a discrete unit, firmly established in its place, precluding consideration of what precedes and follows it at any given moment. This convention obviously never applied to Rabbinic interpretation. There, not only is contextual reading and exegetical principle, but all units are so closely interwoven and simultaneously present that none can be considered in separation from any other at any given moment; it is a world of "intertextuality," to use a contemporary literary term.

> Said's fifth category, *finality,* is the maintenance of the unit of the text through genealogical connections, such as author-text, beginning-middle-end, text-meaning, and reader-interpretation. These distinctions are blurred in rabbinic thought: the text has a divine author, but is continuously created by its readers-interpreters.

We have labored long and hard to discover grounds for maintaining, as Handelman proposes, that "all units are so closely interwoven...that none can be considered in separation from any other at any given moment." That theory of intertextuality, however, applies only occasionally, which is to say, that theory is only partly true and therefore wholly false. It opens no doors but, as I said, by tearing down all walls it invites utter chaos: everything comes in, by whichever way.

As to "genealogical connections," here it seems to me Handelman grossly confuses quite distinct categories. Specifically, in order to provide a *literary* theory on the heuristic and hermeneutic requirements of a text (or a set of texts), she has drawn upon a *theological* conception, namely God's giving of the one whole Torah, oral and written, to Moses at Sinai. It is true that the faithful impute the authorship to God. But I do not think literary scholarship of a

---

[16]*Slayers of Moses*, pp. 77-79.

descriptive and interpretive character has to invoke that fact of faith as a fact of literature. So Handelman seems to me guilty of confusing categories to be kept apart. If we do not acknowledge as a matter of descriptive fact that "the text has a divine author" – thus One Authorship, Creator of not only this text, but, as it happens, of heaven and earth, the fish in the sea, the birds in the sky, and you and me and all – then genealogical connections have, as a matter of fact, to emerge on their own. We may find some between one document and another, but there is none among all the documents.

I have many times referred to the perfectly preserved boundaries that distinguish one text from another. What about the distinction between the author and the text? The distinctions between author and text; beginning, middle, and end; text and meaning; reader and interpretation – Handelman says – are blurred in what she calls "rabbinic thought." But the category "rabbinic thought" itself blurs distinctions among and between documents, so the blurring derives not from the data but from the category. If I knew to what court of facts and judgments she here appeals in speaking of "rabbinic thought," if I could specify how she knows what falls within, and what is excluded from, "rabbinic thought," I could propose modes of analyzing and evaluating her thesis as to that sort of genealogical connections that she wishes to evoke in showing "the unity of the text." Not a few scholars have devoted their careers to the elucidation of "rabbinic thought," and if Handelman were to tell us which one(s) she has in mind, we could more adequately understand what she here purports to tell us. So, to conclude this painful passage, our inquiry into the Bavli's relationship to its sources has sorted out a variety of possibilities.[17] None serves to validate applying to the literature at hand the conception of "intertextuality" as defined by Handelman in her reading of Said. All of the evidence before us fundamentally contradicts her description of the literature, so far as she may mean the Bavli.

If the matter has become tedious, it remains important. For, as is clear, the position outlined by Handelman is in line with Schiffman and Cohen.[18] I find a measure of pathos in Handelman's reading, because she has made every effort to master a theoretical literature in the service of a received and holy canon which, as a matter of fact, she seems to know only imperfectly and at second hand. The work derives from piety, reverence for the received canon, as the imputation of the single authorship of God suggests. Certainly the givens of her thought, like those of Cohen and Schiffman, accord more comfortably with Orthodox Judaic than with secular literary or historical canons of inquiry. But good will and faith do not substitute for the hard work of learning, including mastery of not only the

---

[17]This is in *Canon and Connection.*

[18]Not to mention James Kugel, treated in *Midrash and Literature: The Primacy of Documentary Discourse* (Atlanta, 1987: Scholars Press for Brown Judaic Studies). But Kugel does not specialize in the rabbinic writings, which he knows imperfectly (as his discussions repeatedly show), while Cohen and Schiffman have mastered the texts which they discuss. In this regard, once more, we have to distinguish the one set from the other.

texts but the scholarly debates that do, after all, circulate today. My sense is that Handelman's (to me) impressive mastery of contemporary critical thought finds no match in her (to me) rather limited knowledge of contemporary debates on the canon of Judaism in its formative age, which I doubt she has fully sorted out for herself. Joined to convictions of a profoundly theological character treated as matters of literary fact, these imbalances in learning produce propositions that prove somewhat awry. The upshot is that so far as definitions and theories of intertextuality serve at all, intrinsic traits of the canonical writings indicate that those theories form a faulty fit, proving asymmetrical to the data at hand. I should expect that other versions of the category of intertextuality will provide more substantial guidance in tracing lines of connection from one document to the next. These have offered none. So we bid a final adieu to an idea the day of which is over and done.

Cohen, Schiffman, and Handelman correctly express the consequences of theology – that is, of canon – in their incorrect (because simply wrong, inaccurate, and misrepresentative) literary judgments. This they do when they confuse theology with literary criticism, finding traits dictated by theological conviction in documents that, as a matter of fact, only occasionally exhibit the allegedly paramount traits. They therefore commit the equivalent of creationism, confusing propositions of the faith with properties of the world out there. Creationism maintains that, since Scripture says God created the world this way, not that, therefore geology must be rejected. For hermeneutics the equivalent error is to maintain that, since the system joins the texts, therefore the texts are indivisible and have to be read each in the light of all, always all together and all at once. But the correct theologoical conviction has misled the faithful into insisting that, because everything is Torah, and Torah is everywhere, therefore, in hermeneutical terms, nothing may be read in its own setting. We could not demonstrate the presence of those connections that would as a matter of fact validate theological convictions. So, as hermeneutic, they do not apply.

But when Handelman says,

> ...interpretation is not essentially separate from the text itself–an external act intruded upon it–but rather the extension of the text, the uncovering of the connective network of relations, a part of the continuous revelation of the text itself, at bottom, another aspect of the text

as a matter of theology she speaks with accuracy. But it is solely from the aspect of theology, that is, of the canon. It is therefore a social judgment, extrinsic to the traits of the texts and intruded upon them. Once canonical texts then do participate in that common discourse, each contributing its component of the single, continuous discussion.

Let me account for the enormous error of Cohen, Schiffman, and Handelman, as well, as a matter of fact, as all the faithful past and present for whom they speak:

We err when we seek to demonstrate that a system recapitulates its texts.

That is what leads us to impute to texts intrinsic traits of order, cogency, and unity. It is, further, what provokes us to postulate connection, rather than demonstrating it. The source of error flows from treating as literary facts what are, in fact, judgments of theology, that is, the reification of faith, the transformation of convictions of culture into facts of literature and – it must follow – a theory of hermeneutics. The fact is that the system not only does not recapitulate its texts, it selects and orders them, imputes to them as a whole cogency that their original authorships have not expressed in and through the parts, expresses through them its deepest logic, and – quite by the way – also dictates for them the appropriate and operative hermeneutics. The canon (so to speak) does not just happen after the fact, in the aftermath of the texts that make it up. The canon is the event that creates of documents holy texts before the fact: the canon is the fact.

The system – the final and complete statement –does not recapitulate the extant texts. The antecedent texts – when used at all – are so read as to recapitulate the system. The system comes before the texts and defines the canon.

So we bid farewell to the phantom, elusive intertextuality. We shall miss your made-up portrait of those universally shared traits, those common characteristics – topical, logical, rhetorical – that made diverse texts into one united and uniform statement, "Judaism," "the Torah." We shall think fondly of that pleasing exercise, which you made possible, of opening any Judaic – or even Jewish – book anywhere and allowing anyone, with any education or none at all, expertly to define "Judaism," "the Torah." As we move onward, toward a more complicated universe, nostalgically we shall think upon that simpler world you gave us. Now, alas, literature must be only literature. But, by way of compensation, theology may become truly theological: a rigorous and searching statement of systematic convictions, based upon the evidence of revelation knowledgeably construed, bearing intellectual weight, thoroughly examined, thoughtfully reflected upon – facts of faith not merely pronounced and forthwith proved authoritative by appeal to a labor-saving device. Ah, intertextuality – you would have been wonderful if you had worked. Adieu.

III

From Documents to Doctrines: Bavli as a New Tradition

As we come back to the unromantic world of learning, we revert to the first of the two meanings of the word tradition. That permits us to ask about the continuities that join the Bavli to the entirety of a "traditional" literature. We have found none. True, we have marked out some points of connection. Sustained work on other chapters of our tractate as well as on the rest of the thirty-seven tractates of the Bavli devoted to that number of the Mishnah's sixty-two usable tractates (excluding Abot) will call attention to a great many more crossovers from one document to the next. But the upshot will, I am confident, not vastly change.

The Bavli in relationship to its sources is simply not a traditional document, in the plain sense that most of what it says in a cogent and coherent way expresses the well-crafted statement and viewpoint of its authorship. Excluding, of course, the Mishnah, to which the Bavli devotes its sustained and systematic attention, little of what our authorship says derives cogency and force from a received statement, and most does not. But that is only beginning the question: no one (outside the circles of the believers) ever said that the Bavli's authorship has slavishly taken its message merely from the Mishnah, in which its authorship picks and chooses as much as it does in Scripture, first of all deciding to deal with thirty-nine tractates and to ignore twenty-three.

The premise of all learning of an independent order is that the Bavli's authorship has imputed to the Mishnah those meanings that that authorship, on the foundations of its own critical judgment and formidable power of logical reasoning in a dialectical movement, itself chose to impute. That reading of the Mishnah became the substance and center of tradition, that is, the ultimate statement, out of late antiquity, of the Judaism of the dual Torah. We do not know that that reading triumphed because of the persuasive power of applied reason, rationality, cogent discourse resting on acute reasoning that together comprise the hermeneutics of the Bavli. But in an ideal world, that purely intellectual achievement would have accounted for its success. In any event, the Bavli's authorship's cogent, rigorously rational reading of the received heritage has demonstrably emerged *not* from a long process of formulation and transmission of received traditions, in each generation lovingly tended, refined and polished, and handed on essentially as received. Indeed, to revert to the opening question of the preface, I should doubt that it could have, for the literary evidence we have examined hardly suggests that a system of applied reason and sustained, rigorously rational rational inquiry can coexist with a process of tradition. The thought-processes of tradition and those of system-building scarcely cohere. Where applied reason prevails, the one – tradition – feeds the other – the system – materials for sustained reconstruction.

How things are in theory I cannot say. But in fact, as we see here, the Bavli's statement has given us such tradition as the Bavli's penultimate and ultimate authorship has chosen and has worked out. This statement we now receive according to the choices dictated by that authorship's sense of order and proportion, priority and importance, and it is generated by the problematic found by that authorship to be acute and urgent and compelling. When confronting the exegesis of the Mishnah, which is its indicative trait and definitive task, the authorship of the Bavli does not continue and complete the work of antecedents. Quite to the contrary, that authorship made its statement essentially independent of its counterpart and earlier document. We revert to the decisive observation, which forms the thesis of this study.

The system comes first. In the present context, that means that the logic and principle of orderly inquiry take precedence over the preservation and repetition of received materials, however holy. The mode of thought defined, the work of applied reason and practical rationality may get underway.

To state matters in more general terms, first in place is the system that the Bavli as a whole expresses and serves in stupefying detail to define. Only then comes that selection, out of the received materials of the past, of topics and even concrete judgments, facts that serve the Bavli's authorship in the articulation of its system. Nothing out of the past can be shown to have dictated the Bavli's program, which is essentially the work of its authorship. In this context, the Mishnah forms no exception, for the work of the Bavli's authorship began with the selection of tractates to study and designation of those to ignore. I cannot think of a more innovative or decisive – reforming – judgment than one simply to bypass fully a third of what is allegedly to be "the Tradition." No one to our knowledge rejected the ignored tractates; but everyone concurred on ignoring them.[19]

So Judaism – the Judaism of the dual Torah that appeals for its ultimate encyclopaedic statement of law and theology to the Bavli – really is the making of the authorship of the Bavli, not principally the accumulation, in the Bavli, of the sifted-over detritus of prior authorships. The upshot as to theory may be stated very simply, and in a way to be tested in the study of the history of other religions as well:

The system begins exactly where and when it ends.

In the example of the Judaism of the dual Torah come to full expression in the Bavli, such tradition as the authorship at hand has received ends when the system that receives that tradition begins. So I conclude that where reason

---

[19]Many years ago Jacob Sussman, professor of Talmud at the Hebrew University, completed his dissertation on whether the authorship of the Bavli studied the orders, Agriculture and Purities, to which no Talmud-tractates are devoted. Hearsay has it that he concluded that it did not, though materials were available for the construction of an appropriate set of tractates. But to my knowledge the dissertation has not been published, so we do not have the advantage of what appears to have been ground-breaking and painstaking research. The possibilities of a Talmud Bavli to Purities were fully exploited by the brilliant work on Kelim and Ohalot by Gerson Enoch Leiner, in Sifré Tohorot (1873, repr. N.Y., 1960), I. Kelim, II. Ohalot. Leiner created the Talmud for those two tractates out of the available materials of Tosefta and scattered Tannaite sayings, as well as Amoraic discourse on those sayings found in the extant writings. He then wrote a commentary on whatever he had assembled. Abraham J. Heschel, who called Leiner's work to my attention, told me that he understood Leiner had done the same for all of the tractates of Mishnah's Division of Purities, but that, when accused of trying to write a new Talmud, Leiner had burned his manuscripts. I cannot vouch for the accuracy of the story, but Heschel spoke, so he told me, from first-hand knowledge of the matter.

reigns, its inexorable logic and order, proportion and syllogistic reasoning govern supreme and alone, revising the received materials and restating into a compelling statement, in reason's own encompassing, powerful and rigorous logic, the entirety of the prior heritage of information and thought. That restatement is the Bavli.

IV

Hermeneutics and the Judaism Beyond the Document

At stake in these findings are substantial matters, affecting hermeneutics in the context of literature, and the analysis of religion and culture in the context of society. Let us consider first of all the hermeneutical matter, which leads us to the larger cultural and religious question. But, as we see, the hermeneutical debate recapitulates the literary-critical one, since, on the hermeneutical side, what we confront is a restatement in terms of interpretation of the "intertextualist" position of Orthodox Judaism. It is the claim that there is a "Judaism out there," beyond any one document, to which in some way or other all documents attest. And that Judaism out there, prior to, encompassing all documents in here, imposes its judgment upon our reading of every sentence, every paragraph, every book. A reading of a single document therefore is improper. If, as we see, the Bavli (for instance) not only may be, but must be, read in its own terms so as to present its distinct and distinctive statement, then that hermeneutic that appeals to an ever-present and prevailing "Judaism out there" must be set aside, except, once more, for what I regard as fully legitimate theological purposes. But then it is a theological, not a hermeneutical, judgment, to be set forth and defended in its own terms and context. Let me explain.

A considerable debate concerning the Judaism supposedly implicit in, and beyond, any given document of that Judaism presently enlivens all scholarship on the literature of formative Judaism. Specifically, people wonder whether and how we may describe, beyond the evidence of what an authorship has given us in its particular piece of writing, what that authorship knew, had in mind, took for granted, and otherwise affirmed as its larger "Judaism." I precipitated matters in my *Judaism: The Evidence of the Mishnah*. Specifically, I proposed to describe the system and structure of a given document and ask what "Judaism" – way of life, world-view, address to a defined "Israel" – emerged from that document. The notion that documents are to be read one by one and not as part of a larger canonical statement – the one whole Torah of Moses, our rabbi, for example – troubled colleagues, and not without reason. For reading the literature one book at a time and describing, analyzing, and interpreting the system presented by a document that to begin with invited systemic analysis set aside received notions in three ways.

First, as is clear, the conception of the document as part of a prior and encompassing tradition now met competition.

Second, I dismissed the prevailing notion that we may describe on the basis of whatever we find in any given document a composite "Judaism" (or some qualification thereof, e.g., classical, rabbinic, Talmudic, normative, what-have-you Judaism).

Third, I treated as merely interesting the received and hitherto commanding tradition of exegesis, imputing to the ancient texts meanings not to be tampered with.

For example, I translated fully half a dozen tractates of the Bavli without referring once to Rashi's interpretation of a single passage, let alone accepting at face value his reading and sense of the whole. I dismissed as pertinent only to their own times the contributions of later authorships to the description of the Judaism attested by earlier documents. These things I did for good and substantial reason, which Western academic learning has recognized since the Renaissance: the obvious fallacy of anachronism being the compelling and first one, utter gullibility as to assertions of received writings, an obvious second. But, further, I maintain, along with nearly the whole of academic secular learning, that each document derives from a context, and to begin with is to be read in that context and interpreted, at the outset, as a statement of and to a particular setting. Constructs such as -*isms* and -*ities* come afterward (if they are admitted into discourse at all). Not only so, but in the case of ancient Judaism, a mass of confused and contradictory evidence, deriving from Jews of a broad variety of opinion, requires not harmonization but sorting out. The solution to the disharmonies – a process of theological selection, e.g., of what is normative, classical, Talmudic, rabbinic, or, perhaps, Jewish-Christian, Hellenistic-Jewish, and the like – no longer solved many problems.

From this quest for "the Judaism beyond" the documents, so familiar and so much cherished by the received scholarly and theological tradition, with no regret I took my leave. My absence was soon noticed – and vigorously protested, as is only right and proper in academic discourse. One statement of the matter derives from the British medievalist, Hyam Maccoby:

> Neusner argues that since the Mishnah has its own style and program, nothing outside it is relevant to explaining it. This is an obvious fallacy. The Mishnah, as a digest, in the main, of the legal...aspect of rabbinic Judaism, necessarily has its own style and program. But to treat it as something intended to be a comprehensive compendium of the Oral Torah is simply to beg the question. Neusner does not answer the point, put to him by E. P. Sanders and myself, that the liturgy being presupposed by the Mishnah, is surely relevant to the Mishnah's exegesis. Nor does he answer the charge that he ignores the aggadic material within the Mishnah itself, e.g., Avot; or explain why the copious aggadic material found in roughly contemporaneous works should be regarded as irrelevant. Instead he insists that he is right to carry out

the highly artificial project of deliberately closing his eyes to all aggadic material, and trying to explain the Mishnah without it.[20]

Maccoby exhibits a somewhat infirm grasp upon the nature of the inquiry before us. If one starts with the question, "What does the authorship of this book mean to say, when read by itself and not in light of other, *later* writings?" then it would be improper to import into the description of the system of the Mishnah in particular (its "Judaism" – hence "Judaism: The evidence of the Mishnah") conceptions not contained within its pages.[21] Tractate Avot, for one instance, cites a range of authorities who lived a generation beyond the closure of the (rest of the) Mishnah and so is ordinarily dated[22] to about 250, with the Mishnah dated to about 200. On that basis how one can impute to the Mishnah's system conceptions first attaining closure half a century later I do not know. To describe the Mishnah, for example, as a part of "rabbinic Judaism" is to invoke the premise that we know, more or less on its own, just what this "rabbinic Judaism" is and says.

But what we cannot show we do not know. And, as a matter of established fact, many conceptions dominant in the final statements of Rabbinic Judaism to emerge from late antiquity play no material role whatsoever in the system of the Mishnah, or, for that matter, of Tosefta and Abot. No one who has looked for the conception of "the Oral Torah" in the Mishnah or in the documents that succeeded it, for the next two hundred years, will understand why Maccoby is so certain that the category of Oral Torah, or the myth of the dual Torah, applies at all. For the mythic category of "Oral Torah" makes its appearance, so far as I can discern, only with the Yerushalmi and not in any document closed prior to that time, although a notion of a revelation over and above Scripture – not called "oral Torah" to be sure – comes to expression in Avot. Implicitly, moreover, certain sayings of the Mishnah itself, e.g., concerning rulings of the Torah and rulings of sages, may contain the notion of a secondary tradition, beyond

---

[20]Writing in the symposium, "The Mishnah: Methods of Interpretation," *Midstream* (October, 1986), p. 41. Maccoby's deplorable personal animadversions may be ignored.

[21]I stated explicitly at no fewer than six points in the book my recognition that diverse ideas floated about, and insisted that the authorship of the Mishnah can have entertained such ideas. But the statement that they made in the Mishnah did not contain them, and therefore was to be read without them. Alas, the few reviews that the book did receive contained no evidence that the reviewers understood that simple and repeated caveat. Jakob J. Petuchowski in *Religious Studies Review* for July, 1983, subjected the book to a savage attack of trivializing and with vast condescension imputed to the book precisely the opposite of its message, as, we see, does Maccoby.

[22]I take responsibility for not a single date in any writing of mine, culling them all from available encyclopaedia articles, in the notion that those articles, e.g., the splendid one by M. D. Heer in *Encyclopaedia Judaica* s.v. *Midrash*, represent the consensus of learning at this time. I do not know why Maccoby and Sanders reject the consensus on Avot, since, to my knowledge, neither of them has published a scholarly article on the dating of the document. But I believe my position accords from what is presently "common knowledge." If it does not, I should rapidly correct it.

revelation. But that tradition is not called "the oral Torah," and I was disappointed to find that even in the Yerushalmi the mythic statement of the matter, so far as I can see, is lacking. It is only in the Bavli, e.g., in the famous story of Hillel and Shammai and the convert at b. Shab. 31a, that the matter is fully explicit. Now, if Maccoby maintains that the conception circulated in the form in which we know it, e.g., in the Yerushalmi in truncated form or in the Bavli in complete form, he should supply us with the evidence for his position.[23] As I said, what we cannot show we do not know. And most secular and academic scholarship concurs that we have no historical knowledge *a priori*, though in writing Maccoby has indeed in so many words maintained that we do.

Sanders and Maccoby seem more certain of the content of the liturgy than the rest of scholarship, which tends to a certain reserve on the matter of the wording and language of prayer. Maccoby's roughly contemporaneous aggadic works cite the Mishnah as a completed document, e.g., Sifra and the two Sifrés, and so therefore are to be dated in the period beyond the closure of the Mishnah.[24] Unless we accept at face value the attribution of a saying to the person to whom a document's editorship assigns it, we know only that date of closure for the contents of a document. True, we may attempt to show that a saying derives from a period prior to the closure of a document; but we cannot take for granted that sayings belong to the age and the person in whose name they are given. These are simple truisms of all critical learning, and, once we understand and take them to heart, we find it necessary to do precisely what I

---

[23]Maccoby may not have read my *Torah: From Scroll to Symbol in Formative Judaism* (Philadelphia, 1985: Fortress Press). There I survey the materials that stand behind the statements made here.

[24]I utterly ignore Mekhilta deR. Ishmael, because of the important article by Ben Zion Wacholder on the date of the document, published in 1969 in *Hebrew Union College Annual*. I have not worked on that Mekhilta and have yet to see any scholarly discussion of Wacholder's most interesting arguments in behalf of the view that in Mekhilta deR. Ishmael we deal with what is in fact a medieval document. Not knowing how to sort out the issues, I have simply bypassed the evidence of that document at this time. Wacholder takes for granted that merely because the names of authorities that occur in the Mishnah also occur in Mekhilta deR. Ishmael, we cannot maintain that that writing derives from the period of the Mishnah. Since everyone has known for a half-century that the Zohar, attributed to Tannaite authority, in fact was made up in the high Middle Ages as a work of pseudo-imitation (there is in fact nothing imitative about it), Wacholder surely expressed a kind of consensus. But that consensus has not yet affected the reading of the documents of late antiquity, all sayings of which are assigned to those to whom they are attributed – pure and simple.

have done, which is to read each document first of all on its own and in its framework and terms.[25]

At stake are not merely literary, but also cultural and religious conceptions. So let us return to this matter of "the Judaism beyond" to explain the connection between a narrowly hermeneutical debate and the much broader issue of culture and the nature of religion. When I speak of "the Judaism beyond," I mean a conception of a very concrete character. To define by example, I invoke the definition of this "Judaism out there" operative in the mind of E. P. Sanders when Sanders describes rabbinic writings. In my debates with Sanders[26] I have complained that his categories seem to me improperly formed, since the rabbinic texts do not conform to the taxonomy Sanders utilizes. They in other words are not talking about the things Sanders wants them to discuss. That complaint is turned against me, as we see, in Maccoby's critique of my picture of how we may describe (not "explain," as Maccoby would have it) the system of the Mishnah in particular.

Commenting on this debate with Sanders, William Scott Green says, Sanders "reads rabbinic texts by peering through them for the ideas (presumbly ones Jews or rabbis believed) that lie beneath them." This runs parallel to Maccoby's criticism of my "ignoring" a variety of conceptions I do not find in the Mishnah. Both Maccoby and Sanders, in my view, wish to discuss what *they* think important – that is, presentable in terms of contemporary religious

---

[25]Maccoby further seems not to have read a variety of scholarship. He says that it is absurd to say that "the Mishnah is not much concerned with justice, or with repentance, or with the Messiah." He does not seem to realize the way in which the Messiah-theme is used in the Mishnah, by contrast to its use in other documents, as demonstrated in my *Messiah in Context. Israel's History and Destiny in Formative Judaism* (Philadelphia, 1983: Fortress Press). I am genuinely puzzled at who has said that the Mishnah is not much concerned with justice or with repentance. I look in vain for such statements on the part of any scholar, myself included. Mishnah-tractate Yoma on repentance and Mishnah-tractate Sanhedrin on the institutions of justice have not, to my knowledge, been ignored in my account of the Mishnah and its literature and system. It would appear that Maccoby reads somewhat selectively.

[26]These begin in my review of his *Paul and Palestinian Judaism,* in *History of Religion* (1978), 18:177-191. I reprinted the review in my *Ancient Judaism: Debates and Disputes* (Chico, 1984: Scholars Press for Brown Judaic Studies), where I review more than a score of modern and contemporary books in the field in which I work and also present several bibliographic essays and state of the question studies. I also reworked parts of my Sanders' review in essays on other problems. To my knowledge he has not reviewed my *Judaism: The Evidence of the Mishnah,* and if he has in print responded to my questions of method addressed to his *Paul and Palestinian Judaism,* I cannot say where he has done so. Quite to the contrary, in his *Paul, The Law, and the Jewish People* (Philadelphia, 1985: Fortress), which I review also in my *Ancient Judaism,* where he claims to reply to critics of the original book, he not only ignores my review, and also that of Anthony J. Saldarini in *Journal of Biblical Literature,* cited in my review of *Paul, The Law, and the Jewish People,* which makes the same point, but he even omits from his list of reviews of the original work Saldarini's review as well as mine. This seems to me to impede scholarly debate.

disputation[27] – and therefore to ignore what the texts themselves actually talk about, as Green says, "the materials that attracted the attention and interest of the writers."[28] In my original review I pointed out that Sanders' categories ignore what the texts actually say and impose categories the Judaic-rabbinic texts do not know. Sanders, in Green's judgment, introduces a distinct premise:

> For Sanders, the religion of Mishnah lies unspoken beneath its surface; for Neusner it is manifest in Mishnah's own language and preoccupations.[29]

Generalizing on this case, Green further comments in those more general terms that bring us into a debate on the nature of religion and culture, and that larger discourse lends importance to what, in other circumstances, looks to be a mere academic argument. Green writes as follows:

> The basic attitude of mind characteristic of the study of religion holds that religion is certainly in your soul, likely in your heart, perhaps in your mind, but never in your body. That attitude encourages us to construe religion cerebrally and individually, to think in terms of beliefs and the believer, rather than in terms of behavior and community. The lens provided by this prejudice draws our attention to the intense and obsessive belief called "faith," so religion is understood as a state of mind, the object of intellectual or emotional commitment, the result of decisions to believe or to have faith. According to this model, people have religion but they do not do their religion. Thus we tend to devalue behavior and performance, to make it epiphenomenal, and of course to emphasize thinking and reflecting, the practice of theology, as a primary activity of religious people....The famous slogan that "ritual recapitulates myth" follows this model by assigning priority to the story and to

---

[27]Maccoby makes this explicit in his contribution to the symposium cited above, "The Mishnah: Methods of Interpretation," *Midstream* (October, 1986), p. 41, "It leads to Neusner's endorsement of 19th-century German anti-Jewish scholarship...[Neusner] admires the Mishnah for the very things that the New Testament alleges against the Pharisees: for formalism, attention to petty legalistic detail, and for a structuralist patterning of reality in terms of 'holiness' rather than of morality, justice, and love of neighbor." Here Maccoby introduces the bias of Reform Judaism, with its indifference to "petty legalistic detail." But I (among millions of Jews) find intensely meaningful the holy way of life embodied, for one example, in concern for what I eat for breakfast, along with love of neighbor, and the conception that the Judaic way of life leads to a realm of holiness is hardly my invention. It is contained in the formula of the blessing, *..who has sanctified us by the commandments and commanded us to....* I can treat with respect Maccoby's wish to describe as his Judaism some other system than the received one, but the "very things" that the New Testament alleges against the Pharisees are recapitulated by the Reform critique of the way of life of the Judaism of the dual Torah, today embodied in Orthodoxy and Conservative Judaism, to which I adhere. It follows that not all of the "other side" are Orthodox, although, as to intertextuality, that seems to be the sector from which the principal advocates derive.

[28]Personal letter, January 17, 1985.

[29]William Scott Green in his Introduction, *Approaches to Ancient Judaism* (Chicago, 1980: Scholars Press for Brown Judaic Studies) II, p. xxi.

peoples' believing the story, and makes behavior simply an imitation, an aping, a mere acting out.[30]

Now as we reflect on Green's observations, we of course recognize what is at stake. It is the definition of religion, or, rather, what matters in or about religion, emerging from one reading of Protestant theology and Protestant religious experience.

For when we lay heavy emphasis on faith to the exclusion of works, on the individual rather than on society, on conscience instead of culture, and when, as in the language of Maccoby, we treat behavior and performance by groups as less important, and present as more important the matters of thinking, reflecting, theology and belief – not to mention the abstractions of "love of neighbor" and "morality," to which Reform theologians in the pattern of Maccoby adhere, we simply adopt as normative for academic scholarship convictions critical to the Lutheran wing of the Protestant Reformation. And that accounts for the absolutely accurate instinct of Maccoby in introducing into the debate the positions of the Lutheran New Testament scholars who have dominated New Testament scholarship in Germany and the USA (but not Britain or France).

Judaism and the historical, classical forms of historical Christianity, Roman Catholic and Orthodox, as well as important elements of the Protestant Reformation, however, place emphasis on religion as a matter of works and not faith alone, behavior and community as well as belief and conscience. Religion is something that people do, and they do it together. Religion is not something people merely have, as individuals. Since the entire civilization of the West, from the fourth century onward, has carried forward the convictions of Christianity, not about the individual alone but about politics and culture, we may hardly find surprising the Roman Catholic conviction that religion flourishes not alone in heart and mind, but in eternal social forms: the Church, in former times, the state as well.

V

Sources and Traditions: The Priority of the System

This long detour explains what is at stake in my representation of the Bavli as a systemic, and not as a traditional, statement and document. In the model of the Bavli I therefore claim that the canonical documents of formative Judaism constitute, each on its own, statements at the end of a sustained process of rigorous thought and logical inquiry, applied logic and practical reason. The only way to read a reasoned and systematic statement of a system is defined by the rules of general intelligibility, the laws of reasoned and syllogistic discourse about rules and principles. The way to read a traditional and sedimentary document by contrast lies through the ad hoc and episodic display of instances

---

[30]Personal letter, January 17, 1985.

and examples, layers of meaning and eccentricities of confluence, intersection, and congruence. That is why, for my part I maintain that tradition and system cannot share a single crown, and that, the formative documents of Judaism demonstrate, Judaism constitutes not a traditional but a systemic religious statement, with a hermeneutics of order, proportion, above all, reasoned context, to tell us how to read each document. We cannot read these writings in accord with two incompatible hermeneutical programs, and, for reasons amply stated, I argue in favor of the philosophical and systemic, rather than the agglutinative and traditional, hermeneutics.

At stake in the present debate therefore is the fundamental issue of hermeneutics. For claims as to the character of the literature of Judaism entail judgments on the correct hermeneutics, down to the interpretation of words and phrases. We can read everything only in light of everything else, fore and aft. That is how today nearly everyone interested in these writings claims to read them – citing the Bavli as proof for that hermeneutics. Or we can read each item first of all on its own, a document as an autonomous and cogent and utterly rational, syllogistic statement, a unit of discourse as a complete and whole composition, entire unto itself, taking account, to be sure, of how, in the larger context imposed from without, meanings change(d). That is how – and not solely on the basis of the sample we have surveyed – I maintain any writing must be read: in its own context, entirely on its own, not only in the one imposed by the audience and community that preserved it.

For whatever happens to thought, in the mind of the thinker ideas come to birth cogent, whole, complete – and on their own. Extrinsic considerations of context and circumstance play their role, but logic, cogent discourse, rhetoric – these enjoy an existence, an integrity too. If sentences bear meaning on their own, then to insist that sentences bear meaning only in line with friends, companions, partners in meaning contradicts the inner logic of syntax that, on its own, imparts sense to sentences. These are the choices: everything imputed, as against an inner integrity of logic and the syntax of syllogistic thought.[31] But there is no compromise between what I shall argue is the theologically grounded hermeneutic, taken as a given by believers represented in our own time by Cohen, Schiffman, and Handelman, and the descriptive and historical, utterly secular hermeneutic which I advocate. As between the philosophical heritage of Athens and any other hermeneutics, I maintain that "our sages of blessed memory" demonstrate the power of the philosophical reading of the one whole Torah of Moses, our rabbi. And, further, I should propose that the reason for our sages' remarkable success in persuading successive generations of Israel of

---

[31]No one can maintain that the meanings of words and phrases, the uses of syntax, bear meanings wholly integral to discrete occasions. Syntax works because it joins mind to mind, and no mind invents language. But that begs the question and may be dismissed as impertinent, since the contrary view claims far more than the social foundation of the language.

the Torah's ineluctable truth lies not in arguments from tradition, from "Sinai," so much as in appeals to the self-evidence of the well-framed argument, the well-crafted sentence of thought.

If the mythic appeal stands for religion, and the reasoned position for secularity, then I point to our sages of blessed memory, masters of the one whole Torah of Moses, our rabbi, as paragons of practical logic and secular reason. Why at the end introduce the (inflammatory) category of secularity? The reason is that the literature of Judaism, exemplified by the Bavli, commonly finds representation as wholly continuous, so that everything always testifies to the meaning of everything else, and, moreover, no book demands or sustains a reading on its own. As a theological judgment, that (religious) view enjoys self-evidence, since, after all, "Judaism" is "a religion," and it presents its doctrines and dogmas, rules and regulations. So every document contributes to that one and encompassing system, that Judaism. But a system, a religion, makes its judgments at the end, *post facto*, while the authorships at hand worked at the outset, *de novo*. They were philosophers in the deepest and richest sense of the tradition of philosophy. In that sense (but that sense alone) I classify our sages as fundamentally secular. I mean to say that a secular hermeneutics for a theological literature alone can lead us to learn how to read their writing. The upshot of such a hermeneutics can only be a profoundly reasoned, religious view of a rational and well-proportioned world: a world of rules and order and reason and rationality. That constitutes their religion: the affirmation of creation as a work of logic and order and law, to which the human mind, with its sense of logic, order, and rule, conforms, as it was created to conform.

So reading what they wrote – a problem of textual analysis and interpretation – undergoes distortion of we impose, to begin with, the after-the-fact interpretation of the audience that received the writing. We err if we confuse social and theological with literary and hermeneutical categories, and the religious system at the end constitutes a social and theological, not a literary classification. Hermeneutics begins within the text and cannot sustain definition on the basis of the (later, extrinsic) disposition of the text. Nor should we miss the gross anachronism represented by the view that the way things came out all together at the end imposes its meaning and character upon the way things started out, one by one. Reading the Mishnah, ca. 200, as the framers of the two Talmuds read it two hundred, then four hundred years later, vastly distorts the original document in its own setting and meaning – and that by definition. But the same must be said, we now see, of the Bavli: reading the Bavli as if any other authorship but the Bavli's authorship played a part in making the statement of the Bavli is simply an error.[32]   A mark of the primitive character of discourse[33] in the field at hand derives from the need to point to self-evident anachronism in the prevailing hermeneutics.

Much is at stake. For I see irreconcilable choices and that is why I paid my fond adieu to the hermeneutic of intertextuality. On the one side I identify a heuristic system, with a hermeneutic built out of theology and anachronism, yielding a chaotic and capricious, utterly atomistic reading of everything in light of everything else, all together, all at once. In such a situation no test of sense limits the free range of erudition, and erudition transforms discourse into political contest: who can make his judgment prevail against whom. Against that I offer an orderly and systematic reading of the documents, one by one, then in their second order connections, so far as they intersect, finally, as a cogent whole – thus a genuinely secular reading of documents, one by one, in connection with others, as part of a continuous whole, each in its several contexts, immediate and historical, synchronic and diachronic.

We therefore conclude by recalling and reaffirming for the Bavli the second sense of the word tradition: a fixed and unchanging essence deriving from an indeterminate past, a truth bearing its own stigmata of authority, from God at Sinai. Because of its compelling and, in terms now defined, secular demonstration of the reasoned and rational character of all of created existence, the authorship of the Bavli created what assuredly became a profoundly traditional and, again in defined terms, religious and theological document, laying forth in its authorship's terms and language the complete and authoritative statement of the Torah, oral and written, that is the world-creating statement, made by Judaism, of that reasoned and orderly world that God had by rule created and by rule now sustains, world without end until by God's will and reasoned rule, the Messiah comes – an eternity of perfect rationality.

---

[32]Critics of my translations of the Bavli into English prove the necessity of making this simple point, because they invariably fault me for translating not in accord with the medieval interpreter, Solomon Isaac (1040-1105), "Rashi." They accuse me not of ignoring Rashi, to which I plead guilty, but of not understanding Rashi. But I consistently translate the words before me, as best I can, without reference to Rashi's interpretation of them, except – for reason, not for piety – as an interesting possibility. I point to the world of biblical scholarship, which manages to translate the Hebrew Scriptures without consistently accepting the interpretation of the medieval commentators. Why should the Talmuds be treated differently? There are other approaches to the sense and meaning, other criteria, other definitions of the problem. But we cannot expect a hearing from those who know in advance that Rashi has said the last word on the matter.

[33]We note that Shaye Cohen is explicit about indifference to priority or documents. But in other writings, he takes a far more critical view.

Index

BROWN JUDAIC STUDIES SERIES

BROWN JUDAIC STUDIES SERIES

BROWN JUDAIC STUDIES SERIES

BROWN JUDAIC STUDIES SERIES